THE FOURTH POLITICAL THEORY

THE FOURTH
POLITICAL
THEORY

ALEXANDER DUGIN

ARKTOS

London 2012

ΛRKTOS

⊕ Arktos.com ❶ fb.com/Arktos ◕ ⊙ arktosmedia ✖ arktosjournal

ISBN

978-1-907166-65-5 (Paperback)
978-1-907166-56-3 (Hardback)
978-1-912975-07-5 (Ebook)
978-1-917646-03-1 (Leather-bound)

Translation
Mark Sleboda & Michael Millerman

Editing
John B. Morgan

Proofreading
Michael J. Brooks

Layout
Daniel Friberg

Cover
Tor Westman (2024)
Andreas Nilsson (2012)

TABLE OF CONTENTS

A Note from the Editor

The bulk of the text in this book was published as *Chetvertaia politicheskaia teoriia*, which was published in St. Petersburg in 2009 by Amphora. The text has been revised by the author, and additional chapters have been added to this edition from other writings by Professor Dugin which were published later, dealing with the same theme.

Unless otherwise indicated, the footnotes to the text were included by the author himself. Additional footnotes which were added by me for reference are so marked. Where sources in other languages have been cited, I have attempted to replace them with existing English-language editions. Citations to works for which I could locate no translation are retained in their original language. Web site addresses for on-line sources were verified as accurate and available during the period of March through May, 2012.

I would like to thank Alain Soral, who allowed us to use his Preface from the French edition of this book here, and also Sergio Knipe, who translated it into English. I would also like to extend my gratitude to Mark Sleboda, who spent many hours working on the translation and improving it; to Michael Millerman, who provided us with the translations for chapters 6 through 9; and to Michael J. Brooks, who proofread the manuscript. Others who volunteered their time in working on the translation were Natella Speranskaja, Zhirayr Ananyan, Nina Kouprianova, Fedor Smirnov, Valentin Cherednikov, Cyrill Lazareff, and Ivan Fedorov. I also extend my appreciation to Mark Dyal, who helped by tracking down the source of a very tricky Nietzsche quotation cited in the text.

JOHN B. MORGAN IV
Bangalore, India, May 2012

Foreword by Alain Soral:

WHY WE SHOULD READ
ALEXANDER DUGIN

When the notions of Right and Left have become politically meaningless, in the West as much as everywhere else in the world; when liberals and libertarians agree on the essentials; when the three grand political theories of the Twentieth century — capitalism, Communism and fascism — have ultimately proven incapable of governing peoples peaceably, what is left to do?

According to Alexander Dugin, a teacher of sociology and geopolitics at the renowned Lermontov University of Moscow, and one of the most influential intellectuals in Russia, only one, radical solution remains: to devise a different approach, a Fourth Political Theory.

Conceptualising and theorising it: such is the aim of the present book.

The thought of this brilliant Moscow intellectual, which transcends our Western ideological divides and media-conditioned reactions, will not fail to surprise conformists: for it suggests that in order for us to face the future in a resolute and victorious way, we should revert to traditional forms of spirituality. According to Dugin, the primary target must be Western postmodernism: we must wage war upon this thalassocratic Empire — a morbid blend of the society of the spectacle[1] and consumer culture — and its plan for ultimate world domination.

In *Fourth Political Theory*, Dugin shows that the only way to build a multipolar world, founded on authentic values, is to resolutely turn one's back on the Atlanticist West and its false values.

---

1   This refers to one of the key concepts of Guy Debord (1931-1994), a French Marxist philosopher and the founder of the Situationist International whose ideas have become influential on both the radical Left and Right. The spectacle, as described in his principal work, *The Society of the Spectacle*, is one of the means by which the capitalist establishment maintains its authority in the modern world — namely, by reducing all genuine human experiences to representational images in the mass media, thus allowing the powers-that-be to determine how individuals experience reality.-Ed.

And how can this be achieved? Only by unconditionally preserving the geopolitical sovereignty of the powers of the Eurasian continent — Russia, China, Iran and India — which safeguard the freedom of all other peoples on the planet.

A genuine manual for cultural guerrilla warfare, *Fourth Political Theory* is a book that can be seen as a complement to my own *Comprendre l'empire*[2] (which has been translated into Russian by friends of Alexander Dugin's).

Dugin in Moscow, I (and others) in Paris...while we only met for the first time in January 2011, and never consulted with one another, our ideas — no doubt formulated differently — agree on all the important points: from the need to unite the value-centred Right and the labour-centred Left to the imperative need for resistance against the Empire, from the appeal to Tradition as well as to many other concepts...

Once again, this shows that the only worthwhile international is that of the spirit, led by good men!

Alain Soral

(Translated by Sergio Knipe)

---

2   Alain Soral, *Comprendre l'empire: demain la gouvernance globale ou la révolte des nations?* (Understanding Empire: Global Government Tomorrow or the Revolt of the Nations? — Paris: Blanche, 2011).-Ed.

Introduction: To Be or Not to Be?

In today's world, politics appears to be a thing of the past, at least as we used to know it. Liberalism persistently fought against those of its political enemies which had offered alternative systems; that is, conservatism, monarchism, traditionalism, fascism, socialism, and Communism, and finally, by the end of the Twentieth century, had defeated them all. It would be logical to assume that politics would become liberal, while all of its marginalised opponents, surviving in the peripheral fringes of global society, would reconsider their strategies and formulate a new united front according to Alain de Benoist's[1] *periphery against the centre*.[2] Instead, at the beginning of the Twenty-first century, everything followed a different script.

Liberalism, which had always insisted on de-emphasising the importance of politics, made the decision to abolish politics completely after its triumph. Maybe this was to prevent the rise of political alternatives and to ensure its eternal rule, or because its political agenda had simply expired with the absence of ideological rivals, the existence of which Carl Schmitt[3] had considered indispensable for the proper construction of a political position.[4] Regardless of the rationale, liberalism did everything possible

---

1   Alain de Benoist (b. 1943) founded the Groupement de Recherches et d'Études pour la Civilisation Européenne, the first and most prominent group of what came to be termed the 'European New Right', in 1968, and continues to be its most well-known representative.-Ed.

2   In an address given in France on 12 May 1993, Benoist called for a rejection of the traditional Left/Right dichotomy, instead preferring the terms 'centre' and 'periphery'. He defined the centre as the various factions comprising the dominant ideology of the country from both ends of the spectrum, and the periphery as all those forces which reject this ideology. Thus, in his view, the far Right and far Left should naturally ally with one another, rather than joining with any groups (such as mainstream conservatives or liberals) who accept the prevailing order, and therefore compromise themselves.-Ed.

3   Carl Schmitt (1888-1985) was an important German jurist who wrote about political science, geopolitics and constitutional law. He was part of the Conservative Revolutionary movement of the Weimar era. He also briefly supported the National Socialists at the beginning of their regime, although they later turned against him. He remains highly influential in the fields of law and philosophy.-Ed.

4   Carl Schmitt wrote that the enemy is 'the shape or configuration of our own question', in *Theory of the Partisan* (New York: Telos Press, 2007), p. 85. A footnote to this

to ensure the collapse of politics. At the same time, liberalism itself has changed, passing from the level of ideas, political programmes and declarations to the level of reality, penetrating the very flesh of the social fabric, which became suffused with liberalism and, in turn, it began to seem like the natural order of things. This was presented not as a political process, but as a natural and organic one. As a consequence of such a historical transformation, all other political ideologies, passionately feuding against each other during the last century, lost their currency. Conservatism, fascism and Communism, together with their many variations, lost the battle, and triumphant liberalism mutated into a lifestyle: consumerism, individualism, and a postmodern manifestation of the fragmented and sub-political being. Politics became biopolitical,[5] moving to the individual and sub-individual level. It turns out that it was not only the defeated political ideologies that left the stage, but politics itself, and even liberalism, in its ideological forms, exited. This is why it became nearly impossible to imagine an alternative form of politics. Those who do not agree with liberalism find themselves in a difficult situation — the triumphant enemy has dissolved and disappeared; now they are left struggling against the air. How can one engage in politics, if there is no politics?

There is only one way out — to reject the classical political theories, both winners and losers, strain our imaginations, seize the reality of a new world, correctly decipher the challenges of postmodernity, and create something new — something beyond the political battles of the Nineteenth and Twentieth centuries. Such an approach is an invitation to the development of the Fourth Political Theory — beyond Communism, fascism and liberalism.

To move forward towards the development of a Fourth Political Theory, it is necessary to:

- reconsider the political history of recent centuries from new positions beyond the frameworks and clichés of the old ideologies;

---

phrase in the Telos Press edition of this work notes that its meaning is explained in Schmitt's post-war notebooks: 'Historia in nuce [history in a nutshell]. Friend and Enemy. The friend is he who affirms and confirms me. The enemy is he who challenges me (Nuremberg 1947). Who can challenge me? Basically, only myself. The enemy is he who defines me. That means in concreto: only my brother can challenge me and only my brother can be my enemy.' From Glossarium: Aufzeichnungen der Jahre 1947-1951 (Berlin: Duncker & Humblot, 1991), p. 217.-Ed.

5   Biopolitics, as defined by Michel Foucault in his book The History of Sexuality, as well as in his lectures, is the means by which a political system regulates the actual physical, biological lives of the people it governs, such as through health and medicine, sexuality and reproduction, and family life.-Ed.

- realise and become aware of the profound structure of the global society emerging before our eyes;

- correctly decipher the paradigm of postmodernity;

- learn to oppose not the political idea, programme or strategy, but the 'objective' reality of the status quo, the most social aspect of the apolitical, fractured (post-) society;

- and finally, construct an autonomous political model which offers a new way and a project for the world of deadlocks, blind alleys, and the endless recycling of the 'same old things' (post-history, according to Baudrillard).[6]

This book is dedicated to this very problem — as the beginning of the development of a Fourth Political Theory, through an overview and re-examination of the first three political theories, and to the closely-related ideologies of National Bolshevism and Eurasianism that came very close indeed to the Fourth Political Theory. This is not dogma, nor a complete system, nor a finished project. This is an invitation to political creativity, a statement of intuitions and conjectures, an analysis of new conditions, and an attempt to reconsider the past.

The Fourth Political Theory is not the work of a single author, but is rather a trend comprising a wide spectrum of ideas, researches, analyses, prognoses, and projects. Anyone thinking in this vein can contribute his own ideas. As such, more and more intellectuals, philosophers, historians, scientists, scholars, and thinkers will respond to this call.

It is significant that the book, *Against Liberalism*,[7] by the renowned French intellectual Alain de Benoist, which has also been published in Russian by Amphora, has a subtitle: *Towards the Fourth Political Theory*. Undoubtedly, many things can be said on this theme by representatives of both the old Left and the old Right and, most likely, even by liberals themselves, who are conceptualising qualitative changes to their own political platform, even while politics is disappearing.

---

6   Jean Baudrillard (1929-2007) was a French philosopher and cultural theorist who is regarded as one of the most important postmodernist thinkers. In several of his works, such as The Illusion of the End, he posited that civilisation is entering a period in which the notion of history itself, and of historical progress as described by Marx, no longer has any meaning. Therefore, history is ending, not because any sort of goal has been reached, but because history has become irrelevant.-Ed.

7   In Russian, *Protiv liberalizma: K chetvertoi politicheskoi teorii*. This is a collection of essays that was put together by Dugin, in consultation with Alain de Benoist, for the Russian readership. There is no corresponding title in French or English.-Ed.

For my own country, Russia, the Fourth Political Theory, among other things, has an immense practical significance. The majority of Russian people suffer their integration into global society as a loss of their own identity. The Russian population had almost entirely rejected the liberal ideology in the 1990s. But it is also apparent that a return to the illiberal political ideologies of the Twentieth century, such as Communism or fascism, is unlikely, as these ideologies have already failed and proven themselves unequal to the challenge of opposing liberalism, to say nothing of the moral costs of totalitarianism.

Therefore, in order to fill this political and ideological vacuum, Russia needs a new political idea. For Russia, liberalism does not fit, but Communism and fascism are equally unacceptable. Consequently, we need a Fourth Political Theory. And if, for some readers, this is a question of freedom of choice and the realisation of a political will, which can always be viewed from a positive or negative position, then for Russia, it is a matter of life or death — 'to be or not to be', in terms of Hamlet's eternal question.

If Russia chooses 'to be', then it will automatically bring about the creation of a Fourth Political Theory. Otherwise, for Russia there remains only the choice 'not to be', which will mean to quietly leave the historical and world stage, dissolving into a global order which is not created or governed by us.

1

THE BIRTH OF THE CONCEPT

The End of the Twentieth Century
— the End of Modernity

The Twentieth century has ended, but it is only now that we are truly beginning to realise and to understand this fact. The Twentieth century was *the* century of ideology. If, in the previous centuries, religion, dynasties, estates, classes, and nation-states played an enormous role in the lives of peoples and societies, then, in the Twentieth century, politics had shifted into a purely *ideological* realm, having redrawn the map of ethnicities, civilisations, and the world in a new way. On the one hand, political ideologies represented early and deeply rooted civilisational tendencies. On the other hand, they were completely innovative.

All political ideologies, having reached the peak of their dominion and influence in the Twentieth century, were the product of the new, modern era, embodying its spirit, albeit in different ways and under different symbols. Today, we are rapidly leaving this era. Thus everyone speaks, more and more frequently, of the 'crisis of ideology', or even the 'end of ideology'.[1] For instance, the existence of a state ideology is explicitly denied in the Constitution of the Russian Federation. It is time to address this issue more closely.

The Three Main Ideologies and their
Fate in the Twentieth Century

The three main ideologies of the Twentieth century were:

1) *liberalism* (Left and Right)

---

1   Daniel Bell, *The End of Ideology* (Cambridge: Harvard University Press, 1960).

15

2) *Communism* (including both Marxism and socialism, along with social democracy)

3) *fascism* (including National Socialism and other varieties of the Third Way[2] — Franco's National Syndicalism, Perón's 'Justicialism', Salazar's regime, etc.).

They fought among themselves to the death, creating, in essence, the entire dramatic and bloody political history of the Twentieth century. It is logical to number these ideologies (or political theories) based in part on their significance, as well as in the order of their occurrence, as was done above.

The first political theory is *liberalism*. It arose first, as early as the Eighteenth century, and turned out to be the most stable and successful ideology, having ultimately prevailed over all its rivals. As a result of this victory, it proved, among other factors, the justification of its claim to the entire legacy of the Enlightenment. Today, it is obvious that it was liberalism that was the best fit for modernity. However, this legacy was disputed earlier, dramatically, actively, and, at times, convincingly, by another political theory — Communism.

It is reasonable to call *Communism,* much like socialism in all its varieties, the second political theory. It appeared later than liberalism as a critical response to the emergence of the bourgeois-capitalist system, which was the ideological expression of liberalism.

And, finally, fascism is the third political theory. As a contender for its own understanding of modernity's spirit, many researchers, particularly Hannah Arendt,[3] in particular, reasonably consider totalitarianism one of the political forms of modernity. Fascism, however, turned toward the ideas and symbols of traditional society. In some cases, this gave rise to eclecticism, in others — to the desire of conservatives to lead their own revolution instead of resisting another's, and leading their society in

---

2   The Third Way is a term used for a wide variety of political and economic ideologies that have attempted to to transcend the dichotomy between liberal democracy and socialism.-Ed.

3   Hannah Arendt (1906-1975) was a German-Jewish political theorist who studied with Martin Heidegger. She fled the Nazis and lived for most of the remainder of her life in the United States, becoming one of the most influential political philosophers of the Twentieth century. Here Dugin is referring to her book, *The Origins of Totalitarianism* (New York: Harcourt, Brace & Co., 1951).-Ed.

the opposite direction, such as Arthur Moeller van den Bruck,[4] Dmitry Merezhkovsky,[5] and so on.

Fascism emerged later than the other major political theories and vanished before them. The alliance of the first political theory with the second political theory, as well as Hitler's suicidal geopolitical miscalculations, caused it to expire prematurely. The third political theory was a victim of 'homicide', or perhaps 'suicide', not living long enough to see old age and natural decay, in contrast to the ideology of the Soviet Union. Therefore, this bloody vampiric ghost tinged with an aura of 'absolute evil' is attractive to the decadent tastes of postmodernity, and is still used as a bogeyman to frighten humanity.

With its disappearance, fascism cleared the field for the battle between the first and second political theories. This battle took the form of the Cold War and gave birth to the strategic geometry of the bipolar world which lasted for nearly half a century. By 1991, the first political theory, liberalism, had defeated the second political theory, socialism. This marked the global decline of Communism.

As a result, by the end of the Twentieth century, liberal theory is the only one remaining of the three political theories of modernity that is capable of mobilising the vast masses throughout the entire world. Yet, now that it is left on its own, everyone speaks in unison about 'the end of ideology'. Why?

The End of Liberalism and the Arrival of Postliberalism

It turns out that the triumph of liberalism, the first political theory, coincided with its end. This only seems to be a paradox.

---

4   Arthur Moeller van den Bruck (1876-1925) was one of the principal authors of the German Conservative Revolution. He is best known for his 1923 book, *Das Dritte Reich* (translated as *Germany's Third Empire*). A follower of Nietzsche, he advocated the idea of a third German empire to replace the Weimar Republic which would embody a synthesis of socialism and nationalism and provide for the needs of all citizens, but within a hierarchical framework based on traditional values. Despite Hitler's appropriation of his book's title, he rejected National Socialism for its anti-intellectual nature in a note he left just prior to his suicide.-Ed.

5   Dmitri Merezhkovsky (1865-1941) was a Russian novelist with a strong mystical bent associated with Symbolism and the Silver Age of Russian literature. Many of his books are available in English, including *Death of the Gods, Resurrection of the Gods,* and *The Romance of Leonardo da Vinci.* He fled Russia after the Revolution of 1917 and became a virulent anti-Communist, supporting Mussolini and Hitler.-Ed.

Liberalism had been an ideology from the start. It was not as dogmatic as Marxism, but was no less philosophical, graceful, and refined. It ideologically opposed Marxism and fascism, not only undertaking a technological war for survival, but also defending its right to monopolise its own image of the future. While the other competing ideologies were in existence, liberalism continued and grew stronger precisely as an ideology, in other words as a set of ideas, viewpoints, and projects that are typical for a historical subject. Each of the three political theories had its own subject.

The subject of Communism was class. Fascism's subject was the state, in Italian Fascism under Mussolini, or race in Hitler's National Socialism. In liberalism, the subject was represented by the *individual*, freed from all forms of *collective identity* and any 'membership' (*l'appartenance*).

While the ideological struggle had formal opponents, entire nations and societies, at least theoretically, were able to select their subject of choice — that of class, racism or statism, or individualism. The victory of liberalism resolved this question: the individual became the normative subject within the framework of all mankind.

This is when the phenomenon of globalisation entered the stage, the model of a post-industrial society makes itself known, and the postmodern era begins. From now on, the individual subject is no longer the result of choice, but is a kind of mandatory given. Man is freed from his 'membership' in a community and from any collective identity, and the ideology of 'human rights' becomes widely accepted, at least in theory, and is practically compulsory.[6]

Humanity under liberalism, comprised entirely of individuals, is naturally drawn toward universality and seeks to become global and unified. Thus, the projects of 'world government' or globalism are born.

A new level of technological development makes it possible to achieve independence from the class structuralisation of industrial societies, in other words, post-industrialism.

The values of rationalism, scientism, and positivism are recognised as 'veiled forms of repressive, totalitarian policies', or the grand narrative, and are criticised. At the same time, this is accompanied by the glorification of total freedom and the independence of the individual from any kind of limits, including reason, morality, identity (social, ethnic, or even gender), discipline, and so on. This is the condition of postmodernity.

---

6   See Alain de Benoist, *Beyond Human Rights: Defending Freedoms* (London: Arktos, 2011).-Ed.

At this stage, liberalism ceases to be the first political theory and becomes the only post-political practice. Fukuyama's 'end of history'[7] arrives, economics in the form of the global capitalist market, replaces politics, and states and nations are dissolved in the melting pot of world globalisation.

Having triumphed, liberalism disappears and turns into a different entity — into postliberalism. It no longer has political dimensions, nor does it represent free choice, but instead becomes a kind of historically deterministic 'destiny'. This is the source of the thesis about post-industrial society: 'economics as destiny'.

Thus, the beginning of the Twenty-first century coincides with the end of ideology — that is, all three of them. Each met a different end: the third political theory was destroyed in its 'youth', the second died of decrepit old age, and the first was reborn as something else — as postliberalism and the 'global market society'. In any case, the form which all three political theories took in the Twentieth century is no longer useful, effective, or relevant. They lack the ability to explain contemporary reality or to help us understand current events, and are incapable of responding to the new global challenges.

The need for the Fourth Political Theory stems from this assessment.

The Fourth Political Theory as Resistance to the Status Quo

The Fourth Political Theory will not simply be handed to us without any effort. It may or may not emerge. The prerequisite for its appearance is dissent. That is, dissent against postliberalism as a universal practice, against globalisation, against postmodernity, against the 'end of history', against the status quo, and against the inertia of the processes of civilisation at the dawn of the Twenty-first century.

The status quo and this inertia do not presuppose any political theories whatsoever. A global world can only be ruled by the laws of economics and the universal morality of 'human rights'. All political decisions are

---

7   Francis Fukuyama (b. 1952) is an American political philosopher who is best known for his 1992 book, *The End of History and the Last Man*, which postulated that with the triumph of liberal democracy at the end of the Cold War, humanity had attained the perfect form of government and that the remnants of other ideologies would soon pass away. It was viewed by many as the credo of America's political and economic dominance of the world during the 1990s. Although widely associated with American neoconservatism at that time, he has distanced himself from the movement in recent years.-Ed.

replaced by technical ones. Machinery and technology substitute for all else. The French philosopher, Alain de Benoist, terms this *la gouvernance*, or 'micromanagement'. Managers and technocrats take the place of the politician who makes historical decisions, optimising the logistics of management. Masses of people are equated to a mass of identical objects. For this reason, postliberal reality, or, rather, virtuality increasingly displacing reality from itself, leads straight to the complete abolition of politics.

Some may argue that the liberals lie to us when they speak of the 'end of ideology' (this was my debate with the philosopher, Alexander Zinoviev);[8] 'in reality', they remain believers in their ideology and simply deny all others the right to exist. This is not exactly true. When liberalism transforms from being an ideological arrangement to the only content of our extant social and technological existence, then it is no longer an 'ideology', but an existential fact, an objective order of things. It also causes any attempt to challenge its supremacy as being not only difficult, but also foolish. In the postmodern era, liberalism moves from the sphere of the subject to the sphere of the object. Potentially, this will lead to the complete replacement of reality by virtuality.

The Fourth Political Theory is conceived as an alternative to postliberalism, but not as one ideological arrangement in relation to another. Instead, it is as an incorporeal idea opposed to corporeal matter; as a possibility entering into conflict with the actuality, as that which is yet to come into being attacking that which is already in existence.

At the same time, the Fourth Political Theory cannot be the continuation of either the second political theory or the third. The end of fascism, much like the end of Communism, was not just an accidental misunderstanding, but the expression of a rather lucid historical logic. They challenged the spirit of modernity (fascism did so almost openly, Communism more covertly: see the review of the Soviet period as a

---

8   Alexander Zinoviev (1922-2006) was a Russian logician who served in the Red Army with distinction during the Second World War. During the Brezhnev era, he became one of the Soviet Union's most noted logicians, but he also gained notoriety for expressing mild dissent against the regime. After he wrote several works of fiction that were critical of the Soviet Union in the 1970s, he was stripped of his honours and allowed to emigrate to West Germany in 1978, and continued to write critiques of the Soviets until the mid-1980s. With the rise of Gorbachev and *perestroika*, however, he began to defend Communism, and viewed the post-Soviet regime of Boris Yeltsin as part of a Western conspiracy to destroy Russia. He returned to Russia in 1999, becoming an outspoken critic of globalization.-Ed.

special, 'eschatological' version of the traditional society by Mikhail S. Agursky[9] or Sergei Kara-Murza)[10] and lost.[11]

This means that the struggle with the postmodern metamorphosis of liberalism into the form of postmodernity and globalisation should be qualitatively different; it must be based on new principles and propose new strategies.

Nevertheless, the starting point of this ideology is precisely the rejection of the very essence of postmodernity. This starting point is possible — but neither guaranteed, nor ordained by fate — because it arises from man's free will and his spirit, rather than an impersonal historical process.

However, this essence (much like the rationale behind modernity itself — imperceptible earlier, but later realising its essence so fully that it exhausted its internal resources and switched to the mode of ironically recycling its earlier stages) is something completely new, previously unknown, and only surmised intuitively and fragmentarily during the earlier stages of ideological history and the ideological struggle.

The Fourth Political Theory is a 'crusade' against:

- postmodernity,

- the post-industrial society,

- liberal thought realised in practice,

- and globalisation, as well as its its logistical and technological bases.

If the third political theory criticised capitalism from the Right, and the second from the Left, then the new stage no longer features this political topography: it is impossible to determine where the Right and the Left are located in relation to postliberalism. There are only two positions:

9   Mikhail S. Agursky, *Ideologiia natsional-bolshevizma* (Moscow: Algoritm, 2003) [The Ideology of National Bolshevism]. (See also his earlier book: Mikhail Agursky, *The Third Rome: National Bolshevism in the USSR* [Boulder: Westview Press, 1987].-Ed.)

10 Sergei Kara-Murza, *Sovetskaia tsivilizatsiia: ot nachala do nashikh dnei* (Moscow: Algoritm, 2008) [The Soviet Civilization: From the Beginning until Today].

11 English speakers may have an easier time accessing somewhat related works on the Soviet Union, modernity, and traditionalism, such as David L. Hoffman, *Stalinist Values: The Cultural Norms of Soviet Modernity, 1917-1941* (Ithaca: Cornell University Press, 2003); and David Brandenberger, *National Bolshevism: Stalinist Mass Culture and the Formation of the Modern Russian National Identity, 1931-1956* (Cambridge: Harvard University Press, 2002).

compliance (the centre) and dissent (the periphery). Both positions are global.

The Fourth Political Theory is the amalgamation of a common project and arises from a common impulse to everything that was discarded, toppled, and humiliated during the course of constructing 'the society of the spectacle' (constructing postmodernity). 'The stone that the builders rejected has become the cornerstone'.[12] The philosopher Alexander Sekatsky rightly pointed out the significance of 'marginalia' in the formation of a new philosophical age, suggesting the term 'metaphysics of debris' as a metaphor.

The Battle for Postmodernity

The Fourth Political Theory deals with the new reincarnation of an old enemy. It challenges liberalism, much like the second and third political theories of the past, but it does so under new conditions. The principal novelty of these conditions lies in the fact that of all the three great political ideologies, only liberalism secured the right to the legacy behind the spirit of modernity and obtained the right to create the 'end of history' based on its own premises.

Theoretically, the end of history could have been different: a 'planetary Reich', if the Nazis had won, or 'global Communism', had the Communists been right. However, the 'end of history' has turned out to be, precisely, liberal. The philosopher Alexandre Kojève[13] was one of the first to predict this; his ideas were later restated by Francis Fukuyama.[14] But since this is the case, then any appeals to modernity and its assumptions, to which the representatives of the second (to a greater extent) and third political theories appealed in varying degrees, lose their relevance. They lost the battle for modernity as the liberals triumphed. For this reason, the issue of modernity, and, incidentally, of modernisation, may be removed from the agenda. Now the battle for post-modernity begins.

It is here that new prospects open up for the Fourth Political Theory. The kind of postmodernity which is currently being realised in practice, postliberal postmodernity, cancels out the strict logic of modernity itself — after the goal had been achieved, the steps taken to reach it lose their meaning. The pressure of the ideological shell becomes less rigid.

---

12 *Mark* 12:10.

13 Alexandre Kojève, *Introduction to the Reading of Hegel: Lectures on the Phenomenology of the Spirit* (New York: Basic Books, 1969).

14 Francis Fukuyama, *The End of History and the Last Man* (New York: Free Press, 1992).

The dictatorship of ideas is replaced by the dictatorship of things, login passwords, and bar codes. New holes are appearing in the fabric of post-modern reality.

As the third and second political theories, conceived as an eschatological version of traditionalism, once tried to 'saddle modernity' in their struggle with liberalism, the first political theory, today there is a chance of accomplishing something analogous with postmodernity, using these 'new holes', in particular.

Liberalism developed flawless weapons aimed at achieving its straight-forward alternatives, which was the basis for its victory. But it is this very victory that holds the greatest risk to liberalism. We need only to ascertain the location of these new, vulnerable spots in the global system and decipher its login passwords in order to hack into its system. At the very least, we must try to do so. The events of 11 September 2001 in New York demonstrated that this is technologically possible. The Internet society can be useful, even for those who staunchly oppose it. In any case, first and foremost, we must understand postmodernity and our new situation no less profoundly than Marx understood the structure of industrial capitalism.

The Fourth Political Theory must draw its 'dark inspiration' from post-modernity, from the liquidation of the program of the Enlightenment, and the arrival of the society of the simulacra, interpreting this as an incentive for battle rather than as a destiny.

Rethinking the Past and Those Who Lost

The second and third political theories are unacceptable as starting points for resisting liberalism, particularly because of the way in which they understood themselves, what they appealed to, and how they operated. They positioned themselves as contenders for the expression of the soul of modernity and failed in that endeavour. Yet, nothing stops us from rethinking the very fact of their failure as something positive, and recasting their vices as virtues. Since the logic of the history of the New Era brought us to postmodernity, then it also contained the secret essence of the New Era which was only revealed to us in the end.

The second and third political theories recognised themselves as contenders for the expression of modernity's spirit. And these claims came crashing down. Everything related to these unfulfilled intentions in the previous ideologies is uninteresting for the creators of the Fourth Political Theory. However, we should attribute the very fact that they lost to one of their advantages rather than their disadvantages. By losing, they proved that they did not belong to the spirit of modernity, which, in turn, led to the postliberal matrix. Herein lie their advantages. Moreover, this means that the representatives of the second and third political theories, either consciously or unconsciously, stood on the side of Tradition, although without drawing the necessary conclusions from this, or even not recognising it at all.

The second and third political theories must be reconsidered, selecting in them that which must be discarded and that which has value in itself. As complete ideologies, trying to manifest themselves in a literal sense, they are entirely useless, either theoretically or practically. However, certain marginal elements which advocated ideas that were generally not implemented, and which remained on the periphery or in the shadows (let us recall the 'metaphysics of debris' once again), may, unexpectedly, turn out to be extremely valuable and saturated with meaning and intuition.

Yet, in any case, it is necessary to rethink the second and third political theories in a new way, and only after we reject our trust in those ideological structures on which their 'orthodoxy' rested. Their orthodoxy is their most uninteresting and worthless aspect. Cross-reading them would be far more productive: 'Marx through a positive view of the Right' or 'Evola[15] through a positive view of the Left'. This fascinating 'National Bolshevik'[16] undertaking, in the spirit of Nikolai V. Ustrialov[17] or Ernst

---

15 Julius Evola (1898-1974) was the most important Italian member of the traditionalist school, which is to say that he opposed modernity in favour of an approach to life consistent with the teachings of the ancient sacred texts.-Ed.

16 The National Bolshevik Party emerged in Russia in 1992, shortly after the collapse of the Soviet Union, seeking to continue the legacy of the original National Bolsheviks from the 1920s. It was originally led by Eduard Limonov and Dugin, although Dugin soon left the party to found his own, the National Bolshevik Front, and later abandoned National Bolshevism altogether to form the Eurasia Movement in 2001. The original NBP has been repeatedly banned by the Russian government, although its members continue to agitate. Several other groups continue to use the National Bolshevik name, both in Russia and abroad. National Bolshevik ideology, which emerged after the First World War as an attempt to synthesise Communism and nationalism, was originally formulated by some participants in Germany's Conservative Revolution, such as Ernst Jünger and Ernst Niekisch. National Bolshevism was also present among some members of the anti-Soviet White movement and even among some Soviet Communists in the days of the Russian Civil War, although Lenin and Stalin both opposed it. Regardless, elements of the ideology re-emerged in Stalin's brand of nationalism, which began to appear in the 1930s.-Ed.

17 Nikolai Ustrialov (1890-1937) was a professor and Slavophile who fled the Soviet Union following the Russian Revolution and joined the anti-Soviet White movement. Originally opposed to Communism, he later sought a fusion of elements of Soviet Communism with Russian nationalism. He returned to the Soviet Union in 1935, believing that National Bolshevik ideas were becoming more acceptable, but was charged with espionage and executed in 1937, during the Great Purge.-Ed.

Niekisch,[18] is not sufficient by itself. After all, a mechanical addition of the second political theory to the third will not, by itself, lead us anywhere. Only in retrospect can we delineate their commonalities, which were staunchly opposed to liberalism. This methodological exercise is useful as a warm-up before commencing a full-fledged elaboration of the Fourth Political Theory.

A truly significant and decisive reading of the second and third political theories is only possible on the basis of an already established Fourth Political Theory. Postmodernity and its conditions (the globalist world, *gouvernance*[19] or 'micromanagement', the market society, the universalism of human rights, 'the real domination of capital', and so on) represent the main object of the Fourth Political Theory. However, they are radically negated as values in themselves.

The Return of Tradition and Theology

Tradition (religion, hierarchy, and family) and its values were overthrown at the dawn of modernity. Actually, all three political theories were conceived as artificial ideological constructions by people who comprehended, in various ways, 'the death of God' (Friedrich Nietzsche), the 'disenchantment of the world' (Max Weber),[20] and the 'end of the sacred'. This was the core of the New Era of modernity: man came to replace God, philosophy and science replaced religion, and the rational, forceful, and technological constructs took the place of revelation.

However, if modernism is exhausted in postmodernity, then at the same time, the period of direct 'theomachy'[21] comes to an end along with it. Postmodern people are not inimical towards religion, but rather, indifferent. Moreover, certain aspects of religion, as a rule, such as Satanism, and the 'demonic texture' of postmodernist philosophers are quite appeal-

---

18 Ernst Niekisch (1889-1967) was a German politician who was initially a Communist, but by the 1920s sought to merge Communism with nationalism. He published a journal, *Widerstand* (Resistance), and applied the term National Bolshevik to himself and his followers. He rejected National Socialism as insufficiently socialist, and was imprisoned by them in 1937, and became blind. Upon his release in 1945, he supported the Soviet Union and moved to East Germany, but became disillusioned by the Soviets' treatment of workers and returned to the West in 1953.-Ed.

19 French: 'the art of governing'.-Ed.

20 Max Weber (1864-1920) was a German who is considered one of the founders of sociology. His principal work is *The Protestant Ethic and the Spirit of Capitalism*.-Ed.

21 From Greek, where it was applied to the Olympian pantheon, it means a battle among the gods.-Ed.

ing to many postmodern individuals. In any case, the era of persecuting Tradition is over, although, following the logic of postliberalism, this will likely lead to the creation of a new global pseudo-religion, based on scraps of disparate syncretic cults, rampant chaotic ecumenism, and 'tolerance'.[22] While this turn of events is, in some ways, even more terrifying than direct and uncomplicated dogmatic atheism and materialism, the decrease in the persecution of faith may offer an opportunity, if the representatives of the Fourth Political Theory act consistently and uncompromisingly in defending the ideals and the values of Tradition.[23]

It is now safe to institute a political program that was once outlawed by modernity. It no longer appears as foolish and doomed for failure as before, because everything in postmodernity looks foolish and doomed for failure, including its most 'glamorous' aspects. It is not by chance that the heroes of postmodernity are 'freaks' and 'monsters', 'transvestites' and 'degenerates' — this is the law of style. Against the backdrop of the world's clowns, nothing and no one could look 'too archaic', not even the people of Tradition who ignore the imperatives of modern life. The fairness of this assertion is not only proven by the significant achievements of Islamic fundamentalism, but also by the growing influence of extremely archaic Protestant sects (Dispensationalists,[24] Mormons, and so on) on American foreign policy. George W. Bush went to war in Iraq because, in his own words, 'God told me to invade Iraq'![25] This is quite in keeping with his Protestant Methodist teachers.

---

22 For a traditionalist take on this idea, see René Guénon, *Theosophy: History of a Pseudo-Religion* (Hillsdale, New York: Sophia Perennis, 2001), *The Spiritist Fallacy* (Hillsdale: Sophia Perennis, 2003), and *The Reign of Quantity and the Signs of the Times* (Hillsdale: Sophia Perennis, 2004); and Charles Upton, *The System of Antichrist: Truth and Falsehood in Postmodernism and the New Age* (Hillsdale: Sophia Perennis, 2005).-Ed.

23 Dugin uses the term Tradition in the same sense as René Guénon, Julius Evola and Frithjof Schuon; namely, as a set of transcendental metaphysical principles which lies at the heart of all authentic religions, and which remains the same even when there are differences in the exoteric practices and doctrines.-Ed.

24 Dispensationalism originated as a Nineteenth-century evangelical movement which holds that Christ will physically return to the world to rule for a thousand years prior to the end of the world, fulfilling God's promises to Israel by allowing the Jews to return to the Holy Land, but that prior to this event there will be a rapture in which true believers are transported to Heaven, leaving only unbelievers to suffer the catastrophes that will occur before Christ's return. In present-day America, dispensationalism is most evident in evangelical movement such as the Baptists and the Pentecostals, and has led to the rise of Christian Zionism in American politics.-Ed.

25 According to several news agencies and witnesses, President Bush, in a meeting with Palestinian leaders in Egypt in June 2003, told those in attendance that God had

Thus, the Fourth Political Theory may easily turn toward everything that preceded modernity in order to draw its inspiration. The acknowledgement of 'God's death' ceases to be the mandatory imperative for those who want to stay relevant. The people of postmodernity are already so resigned to this event that they can no longer understand it — 'Who died exactly?' But, in the same way, the developers of the Fourth Political Theory can forget about this 'event': 'We believe in God, but ignore those who talk about His death, much like we ignore the words of madmen'.

This marks the return of theology, and becomes an essential element of the Fourth Political Theory. When it returns, postmodernity (globalisation, postliberalism, and the post-industrial society) is easily recognized as 'the kingdom of the Antichrist' (or its counterparts in other religions — 'Dajjal' for Muslims, 'Erev Rav' for the Jews, and 'Kali Yuga' for Hindus, and so forth). This is not simply a metaphor capable of mobilising the masses, but a religious fact — the fact of the Apocalypse.

Myths and Archaism in the Fourth Political Theory

If atheism, in the New Era, ceases to be something mandatory for the Fourth Political Theory, then the theology of monotheistic religions, which at one time displaced other sacred cultures, will not be the ultimate truth, either (or rather, may or may not be). Theoretically, nothing limits the possibilities for an in-depth readdressing of the ancient archaic values, which can take their place in the new ideological construction upon being adequately recognised and understood. Eliminating the need to adjust theology to the rationalism of modernity, the adherents of the Fourth Political Theory are free to ignore those theological and dogmatic elements in monotheistic societies which were influenced by rationalism, especially in their later stages. The latter led to the appearance of deism upon the ruins of Christian European culture,[26] followed by atheism and materialism, during the phased development of the program of the modern age.

---

ordered him to invade Afghanistan and Iraq. The White House denied the reports.-Ed.

26 Deism, a product of the Enlightenment, arose in the Seventeenth and Eighteenth centuries, holding that the existence of God can be deduced rationally, regardless of the teachings of the Church, and that while God created the universe, he never intervenes in it, thus eliminating the possibility of divine revelation or miracles.-Ed.

Not only the highest supra-mental symbols of faith can be taken on board once again as a new shield, but so can those irrational aspects of cults, rites, and legends that have perplexed theologians in earlier ages. If we reject the idea of progress that is inherent in modernity (which as we have seen, has ended), then all that is ancient gains value and credibility for us simply by virtue of the fact that it is ancient. 'Ancient' means good, and the more ancient — the better.

Of all creations, Paradise is the most ancient one. The carriers of the Fourth Political Theory must strive toward rediscovering it in the near future.

Heidegger and the 'Event' (*Ereignis*)

Finally, we can identify the most profound — ontological! — foundation for the Fourth Political Theory. Here, we should pay attention not only to theologies and mythologies, but also to the reflective philosophical experience of one particular thinker who had made a unique attempt of constructing a fundamental ontology — the most all-encompassing, paradoxical, profound, and penetrating study of Being. I am talking about Martin Heidegger.

A brief description of Heidegger's concept is as follows: at the dawn of philosophical thought, people (more specifically, Europeans, and even more specifically, the Greeks), raised the question of Being as the focal point of their thinking. But, by making it their primary subject, they risked getting confused by the nuances of the complicated relationship between Being and thought, between pure Being (*Seyn*) and its expression in existence — *a* being (*Seiende*), between the human experience of being-in-the-world (*Dasein* — being-there) and being-in-itself (*Sein*). This failure had already occurred in the teachings of Heraclitus[27] about the *phusis*[28] and the *logos*.[29] Next, it is obvious that in Parmenides'[30] work, and, finally, in Plato, who placed ideas between man and existence, and who defined truth as that which corresponded to them — the referential theory of knowledge — reached its culmination in failure. This gave birth to alienation, eventually leading to 'calculating thinking' (*das rechnende Denken*) and then to the development of technology. Little by little, man

---

27 Heraclitus (c. 535-475 BCE) was a pre-Socratic Greek philosopher.-Ed.

28 Greek: 'nature', or more precisely, 'that which exists'.-Ed.

29 Greek: 'idea. The Greeks believed that there is a *logos* which orders the entire universe.-Ed.

30 Parmenides was a pre-Socratic Greek philosopher of the Fifth century BCE.-Ed.

lost sight of pure Being and pursued the path of nihilism. The essence of technology (based on the relationship between technology and the world) expresses this ever-increasing nihilism. In the New Era, this tendency reaches its pinnacle — technical development (*Ge-stell*)[31] ultimately displaces Being and crowns 'nothingness'. Heidegger bitterly hated liberalism, considering it an expression of 'the source of the calculative thinking' which lies at the heart of 'Western nihilism'.

Postmodernity, which Heidegger did not live to see in its full manifestation, is, in every sense, the ultimate oblivion of Being; it is that 'midnight', when nothingness (nihilism) begins to seep from all the cracks.[32] Yet his philosophy was not hopelessly pessimistic. He believed that nothingness itself is the flip side of pure Being, which — in such a paradoxical way! — reminds mankind of its existence. If we correctly decipher the logic behind the unfurling of Being, then thinking mankind can save itself with lightning speed at the very moment of its greatest risk. 'But where the danger lies, there also grows that which saves', Heidegger quotes from Friedrich Hölderlin's poetry.[33]

Heidegger used a special term, *Ereignis* — the 'event', to describe this sudden return of Being. It takes place exactly at midnight of the world's night — at the darkest moment in history. Heidegger himself constantly vacillated as to whether this point had been reached, or 'not quite yet'. The eternal 'not yet'...

Heidegger's philosophy may prove to be the central axis threading everything around itself — ranging from the reconceived second and third political theories to the return of theology and mythology.

Thus, at the heart of the Fourth Political Theory, as its magnetic centre, lies the trajectory of the approaching *Ereignis* (the 'Event'), which will embody the triumphant return of Being, at the exact moment when mankind forgets about it, once and for all, to the point that the last traces of it disappear.

---

31 *Ge-stell*, which can be translated literally as 'framing', was used by Heidegger to describe technology as the mode of human existence in the modern world.-Ed.

32 In Friedrich Hölderlin's poem 'Bread and Wine', the night is used to symbolically represent our age, when the ancient gods of Greece and Christ have left the world and it is only the poets who attempt to keep their memory alive until their return. Martin Heidegger discusses this poem at length in his famous essay 'Why Poets?', in Martin Heidegger, *Off the Beaten Track* (Cambridge: Cambridge University Press, 2002).-Ed.

33 Martin Heidegger, *Off the Beaten Track*, p. 222.

The Fourth Political Theory and Russia

Today, many people intuitively understand that Russia has no place in the 'brave new world' of globalisation, postmodernity, and postliberalism. First, the world state and the world government are gradually abolishing all nation-states in general. Even more important is the fact that the entirety of Russian history is a dialectical argument with the West and against Western culture, the struggle for upholding our own (often only intuitively grasped) *Russian* truth, our own messianic idea, and our own version of the 'end of history', no matter how it is expressed — through Muscovite Orthodoxy, Peter's secular empire, or the global Communist revolution. The brightest Russian minds clearly saw that the West was moving towards the abyss. Now, looking at where neoliberal economics and postmodern culture has led the world, we can be certain that this intuition, pushing generations of Russian people to search for alternatives, was completely justified.

The current global economic crisis is just the beginning. The worst is yet to come. The inertia of postliberal politics is such that a change of course is impossible: to save the West, unrestrained 'emancipated technology' (Oswald Spengler)[34] will search for more efficient, but a purely technical, technological means. This is the new phase in the onset of *Ge-stell*, spreading the nihilistic stain of the global market over the entire planet. Moving from crisis to crisis and from one bubble to the next, the globalist economy and the structures of post-industrial society only make mankind's night blacker and blacker. It is so black, in fact, that we gradually forget that it is night-time. 'What is light?' people ask themselves, never having seen it. For example, at the time of the eruption of the 2008 financial crisis, thousands of Americans held a demonstration, asking for the government for yet another economic bubble. Could they be any more blunt?

It is clear that Russia needs to follow a different path, its own. Yet herein lies the question and the paradox. Evading the logic of postmodernity in only one country will not be that simple. The Soviet model tried, and collapsed. After that point, the ideological situation changed irreversibly, as did the strategic balance of power. In order for Russia to

---

34 Oswald Spengler (1880-1936) was a German philosopher who is regarded as one of the principal Conservative Revolutionary figures of the Weimar period in Germany. His most important work was his two-volume 1922/23 book, *The Decline of the West*, in which he theorised that all civilisations go through an inevitable cycle of ages of rise and decline in power, with the present age of the West currently entering its declining period.-Ed.

save herself and others, creating some sort of a technological miracle or a deceptive strategy is insufficient. World history has its own logic. And the 'end of ideology' is not a random failure, but the beginning of a new stage — and apparently, the last one.

In this situation, Russia's future completely relies on our efforts to develop the Fourth Political Theory. We will not go far, and will only delay the inevitable, by attempting to sort those options that globalization offers to us on a local basis, and by trying to correct the status quo in a superficial manner. Postmodernity's challenge is tremendously significant: it is rooted in the logic of Being's oblivion and in mankind's departure from its existential (ontological) and spiritual (theological) roots. Responding to it with hat-tossing innovation or public-relations surrogates is impossible. Therefore, we must refer to the philosophical foundations of history and make a metaphysical effort in order to solve the current problems — the global economic crisis, countering the unipolar world, as well as the preservation and strengthening of sovereignty, and so on.

It is difficult to say how the process of developing this theory will turn out. One thing is clear: it cannot be an individual effort or one that is restricted to a small group of people. The effort must be shared, and collective. In this matter, the representatives of other cultures and peoples, both in Europe and Asia, can truly help us, since they sense the eschatological tension of the present moment just as acutely, and are looking for the way out of the global dead-end just as desperately.

However, it is possible to state in advance that the Russian version of the Fourth Political Theory, based on the rejection of the status quo in its practical and theoretical dimensions, will focus on the 'Russian *Ereignis*'. This will be that very 'Event', unique and extraordinary, for which many generations of Russian people have lived and waited, from the birth of our nation to the coming arrival of the End of Days.

2

DASEIN AS AN ACTOR

Stages and Problems in the Development of the Fourth Political Theory

Being a supporter of cyclical development, and an opponent of Francis Bacon and his theory of knowledge,[1] I would still like to suggest that we develop and modify approaches to specific topics and areas of thought in an ongoing manner. We have repeatedly clarified the notion of 'conservatism'. We conducted a series of conferences and scientific symposia on the Fourth Political Theory. Let us believe that these efforts, the results of which have been published in magazines,[2] anthologies, monographs, and Websites,[3] were not carried out in vain, and that the reader is more or less familiar with them. Therefore, I propose to move on.

I will demonstrate, with concrete examples, what has been done to promote the discussion of the Fourth Political Theory and, consequently, the observable results of the activities conducted by the Centre of Conservative Research at the Faculty of Sociology of Moscow State University and the St. Petersburg Conservative Club at the Faculty of Philosophy of St. Petersburg State University. This includes two books that were recently published in St. Petersburg, by the wonderful St. Petersburg

---

1   Francis Bacon (1561-1626) was an English philosopher who is credited with developing the notion of empiricism and the scientific method, which hold that knowledge can only emerge from sensory perception, and that theories can only be proven through observations of the world which can be repeated.-Ed.

2   Issue #1 of the journal *Russkoe Vremia* (Russian Time), published in 2009, was completely dedicated to the subject of conservatism. See also A. G. Dugin, 'The Fourth Political Theory', *Profile* 48 (603), 22 December 2008.

3   For English-language online resources, see, among many others, International Eurasian Movement (http://evrazia.info/index.php?newlang=english), Global Revolutionary Alliance (granews.info), The Green Star (americanfront.info), and Open Revolt! (openrevolt.info).-Ed.

publishing house Amphora: Alain de Benoist's *Against Liberalism: Towards the Fourth Political Theory* and my own *The Fourth Political Theory*.[4] The book by the philosopher Alain de Benoist, who spoke at St. Petersburg State University during the 'Philosophy Days' there, is a compendium of his views on philosophy and political science pertaining to the major issues of our time: globalisation, the economic and social crisis, the process of European integration, new political and social trends, the relationship between Europe and Russia, humanism, and so forth. All these problems are addressed from a critical standpoint toward the liberal ideology which dominates the world (the first, and the most stable, political theory). Lacking competition after the collapse of Communism, it has become the primary target for criticism by those who are acutely aware of the negative impact of the status quo in politics, the social sphere, economics, culture, ideology, and so on, and who are searching for an alternative. The old alternatives to liberalism — Communism and fascism — were overcome by history and discarded, each in its own way, and have demonstrated their ineffectiveness and incompetence. Therefore, the search for an alternative to liberalism must look somewhere else. The area to be searched is designated as the domain of the Fourth Political Theory. Such an approach corresponds exactly to the stated theme: 'Conservatism: The Future or an Alternative?' If we think about an alternative and correlate it with the existing blueprint for the future, then we should clearly understand what that alternative is going to replace. The answer is simple: liberalism as the dominant global discourse. Therefore, the only significant alternative should logically be directed against liberalism, hence the title of Alain de Benoist's book. Nevertheless, the question remains: does conservatism fit this role? In part, we heard the answer in Benoist's speech, in which he criticised the liberal theory of progress. This philosophical approach proposes that conservatism is the most logical candidate for an alternative to liberalism, either as a relativising worldview or as one which rejects progress altogether. What remains, then, is to specify the kind of conservatism in question: it is obvious that liberal conservatism[5] cannot be considered an alternative to liberalism, being its variant. Thus, by the process of elimination, we can make a proposition: we must look for an alternative to liberalism in non-liberal versions of conservatism. All this is

4   Alexander Dugin, *Chetvertaia politicheskaia teoriia* (St. Petersburg: Amphora, 2009) — on the Web: http://konservatizm.org/konservatizm/amfora/031209153016.xhtml.

5   Prof. Dugin means conservative ideologies within the domain of free market liberalism, such as the Republican Party in the United States and the Conservative Party in the United Kingdom.-Ed.

logical, since Benoist himself is known as a philosopher with conservative views (he is sometimes referred to as one of the pioneers of the European 'New Right'), but the particular kind of conservatism he has in mind is obvious from his newly published book.

There is another aspect worth mentioning in regard to the title of Benoist's book. Many readers will remember another ideological manifesto directed against liberalism called *After Liberalism* by Immanuel Wallerstein.[6] Despite the similarity in their titles and the object of criticism, there is a significant difference. Wallerstein criticises liberalism from the point of view of the Left — from the neo-Marxist position. And, like any Marxist, he sees liberalism (bourgeois democracy and capitalism) as a phase of historical development, which is progressive in comparison with the preceding phases of development (such as feudalism or slavery), but is inferior to what must come after it — socialism, Communism, and so forth. We are talking about criticism 'from the Left' and, in some ways, from the standpoint of the future (which is expressed in Wallerstein's book title — *After Liberalism*). This is a typical feature of Marxism. For Benoist, neither the superiority of liberalism over earlier types of societies, nor the advantages of a Communist future, are obvious. Therefore, despite the similarity of titles, there is a fundamental difference between the authors' initial positions: with Wallerstein, we are dealing with criticism 'from the Left'; with Benoist, with criticism 'from the Right'. Another difference involves the relationship to liberalism. According to Wallerstein, the end of liberalism is a foregone conclusion according to the very logic of socio-political and socioeconomic history, and so he easily spoke of an 'after'. For Benoist, the question remains: one must fight against liberalism, yet in this morally and historically justified struggle, there are no guaranteed results. It is important to fight against liberalism here and now; it is important to identify its vulnerabilities; it is important to forge an alternative worldview — but the future is in our hands, and it is open rather than predetermined. Wallerstein, in varying degrees, views things mechanically, like any Marxist, whereas Benoist is an organicist and holist, like any (real) conservative.

The last item that I would like to point out in regard to the ideas of Alain de Benoist and their relevance is his understanding of Carl Schmitt's concept of the 'Fourth *Nomos* of the Earth'[7] — that is, the relationship

---

6 Immanuel Maurice Wallerstein, *After Liberalism* (New York: New Press, 1995).

7 Carl Schmitt, *The Nomos of the Earth in the International Law of the Jus Publicum Europaeum* (New York: Telos Press, 2003).

between political science and 'political theology' with geopolitics and the new model of the political organisation of space.

For my part, in the book *Fourth Political Theory*,[8] I reviewed the three primary political theories of the past — liberalism, Marxism (socialism) and fascism (including National Socialism), summed up their overall balance, and attempted to identify the horizons for the development of the Fourth Political Theory beyond all three ideologies. This, of course, is extremely far from any dogmatism or proposal for a complete answer to the stated problem. Nevertheless, these are rather specific steps toward the preparation for tackling this issue. Without repeating what was said in my book and the book by Alain de Benoist, I will try to make a number of remarks about the development of this subject.

What the Fourth Political Theory is, in terms of what it opposes, is now clear. It is neither fascism, nor Communism, nor liberalism. In principle, this kind of negation is rather significant. It embodies our determination to go beyond the usual ideological and political paradigms and to make an effort to overcome the inertia of the clichés within political thinking. This alone is a highly stimulating invitation for a free spirit and a critical mind. I do not really understand why certain people, when confronted with the concept of the Fourth Political Theory, do not immediately rush to open a bottle of champagne, and do not start dancing and rejoicing, celebrating the discovery of new possibilities. After all, this is a kind of a philosophical New Year — an exciting leap into the unknown. The 'Old Year' witnessed the struggle of the three political ideologies — one of which was so bloody that it claimed millions of lives. All the criticism of liberalism was either fascist or Communist. These critical approaches have been left behind, but the oldest of these ideologies — liberalism — is still here. Liberalism is the remnant of the 'Old Year'; it is *residuo*,[9] an uncertain past that was not properly sent to oblivion. It has already passed, but does not want to leave permanently in any way. In short, it is a chimera, 'the dragon that swallowed the Sun',[10] or 'the evil spirits that kidnapped the Snow Maiden' before the New Year.[11] In a sense, liberalism embodies everything that was

---

8   This particular chapter was not included in the original Russian edition of *Fourth Political Theory*.-Ed.

9   Latin: 'residual'.-Ed.

10 According to ancient Chinese and Persian legends, solar eclipses were caused by a dragon eating the Sun.-Ed.

11 In Russian fairy tales, Snegurochka, or the Snow Maiden, is the granddaughter of Ded Moroz, the Russian equivalent of Santa Claus or Father Christmas. After the celebration of Christmas was abolished in the Soviet Union, the giving of presents and so forth moved to New Year's Day, and this remains a Russian tradition to this

in the past. The Fourth Political Theory is the name for a breakthrough and a new beginning.

Underscoring the relevance of this criticism, and especially highlighting the fact that this is a radical rejection of all three political theories (liberalism, Communism, and fascism) and their variants, I suggest we meditate on the positive aspects of the Fourth Political Theory. The fact that we have identified what we oppose is, in itself, a significant achievement, and requires a thorough understanding. The very idea of putting an end to fascism, Communism, and liberalism is an extremely liberating thing. The Fourth Political Theory proclaims, 'Say "no" to fascism, "no" to Communism, and "no" to liberalism!' 'Liberalism will not work!' It 'will not pass!' (*¡No pasarán!*),[12] much like fascism once failed (*no ha pasado*).[13] The Berlin Wall, too, collapsed; only dust remains from the only visible barrier put up by Communists to separate themselves from the liberal capitalists. The Communists 'did not pass', either. What remains is not for liberals to pass — and they will not pass! But in order for them not to pass, the fragments of the Berlin Wall are insufficient for us, as the Wall itself was insufficient. The Wall existed, but they still passed. Even less helpful are the dark shadows of the Third Reich, its *nezalezhnye*,[14] inspiring only the brutal punk youth and the perverted dreams of sadomasochists.

Consequently, we suggest moving beyond the nihilistic phase of the Fourth Political Theory toward something constructive. Once the three political theories as a systematised whole have been discarded, we can try to look at them from a different perspective. They are being rejected precisely as complete ideological systems, each on the basis of separate arguments. Like any system, they consist of elements that do not belong to them. The three political ideologies own their unique philosophical systems, groups, explanatory methodologies, and represent a whole which is a structure derived from their 'hermeneutic circle' and their fundamental beliefs. They are what they are as a *whole*. Dismembered into components, they lose their significance and become meaningless. Liberalism, Marxism (socialist or Communist), and fascism (including National Socialism) are

---

day. In modern versions of the old fairy tales, the Snow Maiden is sometimes captured by evil spirits, such as the witch Baba Yaga, before New Year's Day, and has to be rescued by Ded Moroz.-Ed.

12 *¡No pasarán!* was adopted as a battle cry by the Communist forces in the Spanish Civil War, in their fight against Franco's nationalist army. When Franco captured Madrid in 1939, he responded with '*Hemos pasado*' (we have passed).-Ed.

13 Spanish: 'has not passed'.-Ed.

14 Russian: 'independent corpses'. Russians use this term to refer to Nazi sympathisers among the West Ukrainians.-Ed.

not components of overarching liberal, Marxist, or fascist ideologies. It is not that they are completely neutral, but outside of their strict ideological context, one can find or discover a different, or new, meaning for them. The positive aspects of the development of the Fourth Political Theory are based on this principle. A revision of the three political ideologies, and an analysis of each in unconventional ways, can give certain clues to the substantive content of our own theory.

In each of the three ideologies there is a clearly defined historical subject.

In liberal ideology, the historical subject is the individual. The individual is conceived as a unit that is rational and endowed with a will (morality). The individual is both a given and the goal of liberalism. It is a given, but one that is often unaware of its identity as an individual. All forms of collective identity — ethnic, national, religious, caste, and so on — impede an individual's awareness of his individuality. Liberalism encourages the individual to become himself, that is, to be free of all those social identities and dependencies that constrain and define the individual from outside. This is the meaning of liberalism (in English, liberty; in Latin, *libertas*): the call to become 'liberated' (Latin: *liber*) from all things external to oneself. Moreover, liberal theorists (in particular, John Stuart Mill)[15] underscored the fact that we are talking about a 'freedom *from*',[16] about the release from ties, identifications, and restrictions that are an imposition upon the individual's will. As for what the purpose of this freedom is, liberals remain silent. To assert some kind of a normative goal is, in their eyes, to restrict the individual and his freedom. Therefore, they strictly separate a 'freedom *from*', which they regard as a moral imperative of social development, from the 'freedom *for*' — the normativisation of how, why, and for what purpose this freedom should be used. The latter remains at the discretion of the historical subject — in other words, the individual.

The historical subject of the second political theory is class. The class structure of society and the conflict between the exploiter and the exploited classes are the core of the Communists' dramatic vision of history. History is class struggle. Politics is its expression. The proletariat is a dialectic historical subject, which is called to set itself free from the domination of the bourgeoisie and to build a society on new foundations.

15 John Stuart Mill (1806-1873) was an English philosopher of utilitarianism and one of the most important theorists of liberalism. In his book *On Liberty*, he advanced the idea that the individual, and not the state, should be the basis of society, and that citizens should be able to exercise complete moral and economic freedom, except in cases where their actions may harm other members of the state.-Ed.

16 John Stuart Mill, *On Liberty and Other Writings* (Cambridge: Cambridge University Press, 1989).

A single individual is conceived here as a part of a class-based whole, and acquires social existence only in the process of raising class consciousness.

And, finally, the subject of the third political theory is either the State (as in Italian Fascism) or race (as in German National Socialism). In fascism, everything is based upon a Right-wing version of Hegelianism, since Hegel himself considered the Prussian state to be the peak of historical development in which the subjective spirit was perfected. Giovanni Gentile,[17] a proponent of Hegelianism, applied this concept to Fascist Italy.[18] In German National Socialism, the historical subject is the 'Aryan race',[19] which, according to racists, 'carries out the eternal struggle against the subhuman races'. The appalling consequences of this ideology are too well known to dwell upon them. However, it was this original definition of a historical subject that was at the heart of the Nazis' criminal practices.

The definition of a historical subject is the fundamental basis for political ideology in general, and defines its structure. Therefore, in this matter, the Fourth Political Theory may act in the most radical way by rejecting all of these constructions as candidates for a historical subject. The historical subject is neither an individual, nor class, nor the state, nor race. This is the anthropological and the historical axiom of the Fourth Political Theory.

We assumed that it is clear to us who, or what, cannot be the historical subject. But then who, or what, can?

We cleared a space and correctly posed the question. We specified the problem of clarifying the historical subject in the Fourth Political Theory. Now there is a gaping void, which is extremely interesting and significant.

Heading into the depths of this void, we propose four hypotheses, which are not mutually exclusive, and which can be examined both collectively and individually.

The first hypothesis suggests abandoning all types of contenders for the role of a historical subject from classical political theory, assuming that the subject of the Fourth Political Theory is some type of compound — not the individual, class, state, race, or nation on their own, but

---

17 Giovanni Gentile (1875-1944) was an Italian philosopher who developed what he termed 'Actual Idealism', in that he believed that Idealist philosophy was only relevant in terms of how it could be applied to life itself, as opposed to mere speculation. He also held to the corporative idea that an individual's life only attained meaning in relation to the state. He was a staunch Fascist from 1922 until his murder at the hands of anti-Fascist partisans in the Saló Republic, was a member of the Fascist Grand Council, and was regarded as the official philosopher of Italian Fascism.-Ed.

18 A. James Gregor, *Giovanni Gentile: Philosopher of Fascism* (New Brunswick, New Jersey: Transaction Publishers, 2001).

19 Alfred Rosenberg, *The Myth of the Twentieth Century: An Evaluation of the Spiritual-Intellectual Confrontations of Our Age* (Torrance, California: Noontide Press, 1982).

instead, a certain combination thereof. This is the hypothesis of a compound subject.

The second hypothesis is to approach the problem from the standpoint of phenomenology. Let us place all that we know about the historical subject outside the framework of classical ideologies, carry out the Husserlian[20] method of *epoché*,[21] and try to empirically define that 'lifeworld'[22] which will open up before us — the lifeworld of the political, one free from metaphysics or theology.[23] Is it possible to consider political history without a subject? History as such? After all, theoretically, there were historical periods when politics existed, but when there was no subject in the philosophical, Cartesian sense. Of course, in hindsight, even this 'pre-subject' in political history was reinterpreted in accordance with various ideologies. But, if we no longer trust ideologies, such as the three political theories, then their historic reconstruction is not an axiom for us. If we consider political history in the style of the 'Annales school' (Fernand Braudel's method),[24] then we have the chance to discover a rather polyphonic picture, expanding our understanding of the subject. In the spirit of Peter Berger,[25] we can open up the prospect of 'desecularisation' (throughout history, religious organisations frequently

---

20 Edmund Husserl (1859-1938) was a widely influential Austrian Jewish philosopher, and one of the teachers of Martin Heidegger. He founded the phenomenological school of philosophy in 1900, primarily through his book, *Logical Investigations* (London: Routledge, 1970), and elaborated further on his theories in 1913 in *Ideas* (London: Allen & Unwin, 1931).-Ed.

21 *Epoché*, or 'suspension', to the ancient Greeks, was the act of suspending all one's judgments about the way in which the world exists. Husserl expanded upon this concept, believing that the only way to study consciousness was to distinguish between consciousness and the objects in the world that it is perceiving. In doing this, Husserl believed it was possible to arrive at the essence of things.-Ed.

22 This was Husserl's term for the world of objects that lies beyond human perception.-Ed.

23 Carl Schmitt, *Political Theology: Four Chapters on the Concept of Sovereignty* (Cambridge, Massachusetts: MIT Press, 1985).

24 The Annales School, a school of historiography, was founded in 1929, but was taken in a new direction when the historian Fernand Braudel (1902-1985) began to assume the leadership of the group in the 1950s. Braudel believed that historiography was too focused on short-term events, such as crises, and specific events, while not enough attention was paid to the long-term development of history and those elements which remain consistent through long periods of time. Continuities, the school held, were much more important than sudden changes. They also rejected the Marxist view of historical materialism.-Ed.

25 Peter L. Berger (ed.), *The Desecularization of the World: Resurgent Religion and World Politics* (Grand Rapids, Michigan: W. B. Eerdmans, 1999).

act as political subjects) or, together with Carl Schmitt,[26] we can rethink the influence of Tradition on a political decision (in the spirit of Schmitt's doctrine of 'decisionism').[27] Discarding the dogma of progress will reveal a wide range of political actors, operating up until and beyond the New Age, which fits into the conservative approach. But we are free to continue our open search for what may replace the historical subject in the future — perhaps in the exotic hypotheses of Deleuze and Guattari about the rhizome,[28] a 'body without organs', 'micropolitics', and so on, or on the horizon of proto-history with Baudrillard and Derrida[29] (text, deconstruction, *différance*,[30] etc.). They offer us new — and this time, not entirely conservative — capabilities. Therefore, it is not worthwhile to reject them in advance, simply on the basis of their authors' sympathies toward Marxism and their Leftist affiliation.

The third hypothesis is about forcing the phenomenological method and rushing several steps ahead: we may propose to consider Heidegger's *Dasein*[31] as the subject of the Fourth Political Theory. *Dasein* is described in Heidegger's philosophy at length through its existential structure, which makes it possible to build a complex, holistic model based on it, the

---

26 Carl Schmitt, *Dictatorship* (Oxford: Blackwell Publishers, 2010).

27 According to Schmitt, the validity of a particular moral or legal precept has nothing to do with its specific nature, but only depends on the authority from which it was issued.

28 The rhizome concept according to Deleuze and Guattari: '1 and 2: Principles of connection and heterogeneity: any point of a rhizome can be connected to anything other, and must be... 3. Principle of multiplicity: only when the multiple is effectively treated as a substantive, "multiplicity" that it ceases to have any relation to the One as subject or object, natural or spiritual reality, image and world... 4. Principle of asignifying rupture: against the oversignifying breaks separating structures or cutting across a single structure. A rhizome may be broken, but it will start up again on one of its old lines, or on new lines... 5 and 6: Principle of cartography and decalcomania: a rhizome is not amenable to any structural or generative model. It is a stranger to any idea of genetic axis or deep structure... The rhizome is altogether different, *a map and not a tracing*'. From Gilles Deleuze and Félix Guattari, *A Thousand Plateaus: Capitalism and Schizophrenia* (London: Continuum, 2004), pp. 8-13.

29 Jacques Derrida (1930-2004) was a French philosopher who is widely regarded as the most important of the postmodernist philosophers. His work has had an enormous impact on philosophy and literary theory since the 1970s. His work led to the technique of 'deconstruction', by which it is held that no text or idea can be reduced to a single meaning, but rather that every text can be interpreted in many different, and contradictory, ways, thus denying that an authoritative meaning can be claimed for any text.–Ed.

30 *Différance* is a term coined by Derrida. Its meaning is complex, but essentially it refers to Derrida's contention that words are defined more by the way in which they distinguish a type of object from other objects, more than in terms of what they represent.-Ed.

31 Martin Heidegger, *On Time and Being* (Chicago: University of Chicago Press, 2002).

development of which will lead to, for instance, a new understanding of politics. Many researchers have lost sight of the fact that Heidegger, especially, in his middle period between 1936 and 1945, developed a complete history of philosophy centred around *Dasein,* which, it has become apparent in retrospect, can form the basis of a full-fledged and well-developed political philosophy.

Thus, accepting the *Dasein* hypothesis immediately gives us a broad map in order to navigate the construction of history necessary for political theory. If the subject is *Dasein,* then the Fourth Political Theory would constitute a fundamental ontological structure that is developed on the basis of existential anthropology. We can map out the direction to describe this type of an approach:

- *Dasein* and the state;

- *Dasein* and social stratification;

- *Dasein* and power (the will to power);

- Being and politics;

- The horizons of political temporality;

- Existential spatiality and the phenomenology of boundaries;

- The Prince and nothing;

- Parliament, the choice, and 'Being-towards-death';

- Citizenship and the role of the guardians of Being;

- Referendum and intentionality;

- The authentic and the inauthentic in jurisprudence;

- Existential philosophy of jurisprudence;

- Revolution and the flight of the gods;

- Urbanisation and the house of Being.

Naturally, this is merely a cursory outline of the areas of interest for the new political science.

The fourth hypothesis appeals to the concept of the 'imagination' (*l'imaginaire*). This topic is covered in detail in the works of Gilbert Durand,[32] the basic ideas of which I discuss in my new work *Sociology*

---

32 Gilbert Durand, *The Anthropological Structures of the Imaginary* (Brisbane: Boombana Publications, 1999).

of the Imagination.[33] Imagination, as a structure, precedes the individual, the collective, class, culture, and race (if race exists as a sociological phenomenon, which is uncertain), as well as the state. According to Durand, who developed the ideas of Carl Gustav Jung and Gaston Bachelard,[34] the imagination forms the content of human existence based on the internal, original, and independent structures that are embedded in it. The interpretation of political processes in history *a posteriori*[35] is of no difficulty for the 'sociology of the imagination', and it produces impressive results. If we interpret the imagination as an autonomous actor in the political sphere, including its ability to project, and grant it a sort of a 'legal status', then we end up with an extraordinarily fascinating and totally undeveloped trajectory. Even though the students of 1968[36] demanded 'freedom for the imagination', in that moment they were unlikely to recognise the imagination as a contender for special political subjectivity. They remained trapped in the individual — as part of liberalism, even if 'of the Left' — and class (for example, Marxism, although strictly reconsidered on the basis of psychoanalysis).

In the search for the subject of the Fourth Political Theory, we must boldly enter into a new 'hermeneutic circle'. The Fourth Political Theory is the whole, which, naturally, has not yet been sufficiently described and defined. It is comprised of the ideas of its subject, which has been suggested in a preliminary fashion. But, moving constantly between the uncertainty of the whole and the uncertainty of its parts and back again, we gradually begin to clarify more precisely what is at stake. This process, starting from the standpoint of dismissing that which came before it (the rejection of the old hermeneutic circles: liberalism and the individual, Marxism and class, fascism/Nazism and the state/race), will lead to the development of a more constructive idea sooner or later. Its structure will be further clarified when its hermeneutics comes up against explicitly absurd contradictions which cannot be resolved, or else stops corresponding to the real world. That is, after starting from a certain point, the development of the

---

33 Alexander Dugin, *Sotsiologiia voobrazheniia: Vvedenie v strukturnuiu sotsiologiiu* (Sociology of the Imagination: Introduction to Structural Sociology — Moscow, 2010).

34 Gaston Bachelard (1884-1962) was a French philosopher who applied psychology and epistemology to the philosophy of science. He was influential upon the postmodernists.-Ed.

35 Latin: 'from the observed facts'.-Ed.

36 The year 1968 marked a series of influential Left-wing protests by students and others throughout the world, the most notable being in Paris, where the students were joined in a strike by the majority of the French workforce. Although these strikes failed in their stated objectives, in France and elsewhere it marked the moment when the traditional social orders began to be forced to give way to more liberal attitudes.-Ed.

Fourth Political Theory will begin to develop scientific and rational characteristics, which, for the time being, are barely discernible behind the power of its groundbreaking intuitions and its revolutionary, herculean task of overcoming the old ideologies.

The entire hermeneutic circle of the Fourth Political Theory should be included in the 'Fourth *Nomos* of the Earth'.[37] This inclusion will specify its content in even more detail and, in particular, will reveal the colossal epistemological potential of geopolitics. The latter, in addition to its purely practical and applied objectives, can be viewed as a broad invitation to think spatially in a postmodern scenario, when historical thinking, which dominated the modern era, is becoming irrelevant. On numerous occasions, I have written about the philosophical and the sociological potential of geopolitics in my works.[38] Spatiality is one of the most important existential components of *Dasein*, so the appeal to the Fourth *Nomos* of the Earth can be tied to the third subject hypothesis of the Fourth Political Theory.

Now we can approach the problem of creating the Fourth Political Theory from another direction and examine the contenders for inclusion in this theory from the three classical models.

However, before determining which aspects of the three old ideologies can be borrowed from them, having neutralised them and taken them out of context, ripping them out of their own 'hermeneutic circle', it is important to briefly mention which aspects must be firmly discarded.

If we begin with fascism and National Socialism, then here we must definitively reject all forms of racism. Racism is what caused the collapse of National Socialism in the historical, geopolitical, and theoretical sense. This was not only a historical, but also a philosophical collapse. Racism is based on the belief in the innate objective superiority of one human race over another. It was racism, and not some other aspect of National Socialism, that brought about such consequences, leading to immeasurable suffering on both sides, as well as the collapse of Germany and the Axis powers, not to mention the destruction of the entire ideological project of the Third Way. The criminal practice of wiping out entire ethnic groups (Jews, gypsies, and Slavs) based on race was precisely rooted in

---

37 Carl Schmitt argued that, with the extension of Europe throughout the world via colonialism, a global social order had been established, which, for the first time, led to the creation of an international system of law, particularly in regard to military conflicts. However, Schmitt believed that this order is now on the decline, and that the birth of a new global order was possibly imminent.-Ed.

38 Alexander Dugin, *Myslit' prostranstvom: Osnovy geopolitiki* (Thinking Spatially: The Origins of Geopolitics — Moscow, 2000). New edition: *Sotsiologiia prostranstva, Sotsiologiia voobrazheniia: Vvedenie v strukturnuiu sotsiologiiu* (Sociology of Space, Sociology of the Imagination: Introduction to Structural Sociology — Moscow, 2010).

their racial theory — this is what angers and shocks us about Nazism to this day. In addition, Hitler's anti-Semitism, and the doctrine that Slavs are 'subhuman' and must be colonised, is what led Germany to go to war against the Soviet Union, which cost us millions of lives. It is also true that this resulted in the Germans themselves losing their political freedom and the right to participate in political history for a long time, if not forever. Today they are left only with their economy and, in the best case scenario, with a concern for ecology. The supporters of the Third Way were left in the position of ideological outcasts on the margins of society. It was racism — in theory and in practice — that criminalised all other aspects of National Socialism and fascism, causing these worldviews to become the object of curses and vilification.

Hitler's racism, however, is only one form of racism — this type of racism is the most obvious, straightforward, and biological, and therefore the most repulsive. There are other forms of racism — cultural (asserting that there are high and low cultures), civilisational (dividing people into those civilised and those insufficiently civilised), technological (viewing technological development as the main criterion for the value of a society), social (stating, in the spirit of the Protestant doctrine of predestination, that the rich are the best and the greatest as compared to the poor), economic (in which all humanity is ranked according to the degree of material well-being), and evolutionary (for which it is axiomatic that human society is the result of biological development, in which the basic processes of the evolution of species — survival of the fittest, natural selection, and so on — continue today). European and American societies are fundamentally afflicted with these types of racism, unable to eradicate them from itself despite intensive efforts. Being fully aware of how revolting this phenomenon is, people in the West tend to make racism a taboo. However, all this turns into a witch hunt — new pariahs accused of 'fascism' are its victims, often for no apparent reason. Thus, this very political correctness and its norms are transformed into a totalitarian discipline of political, purely racist exclusions. In this manner, the institutionalised French Left-liberal anti-racism has gradually become the distribution centre of 'racial hatred'. Even Africans suffer from being accused of 'fascism'. Such was the case of the unrestrained defamatory campaign against a well-known black comedian, Dieudonné M'bala M'bala, who dared to mock certain hideous features of the contemporary French establishment in his routines, including anti-racism (Ras-le-Front, SOS-Racisme, etcetera). And then what? African comedian M'bala M'bala was categorised as 'brown', that is, accused of 'fascism' and 'racism'.

The newest types of racism are glamour, fashion, and the latest trends in information technology. Its norms are set by models, designers, the socialites of political parties, and those who insist on owning only the latest models of mobile phones or laptop computers. Conformity or non-conformity with the glamour code is located at the very base of the mass strategies for social segregation and cultural apartheid. Today, this is not associated directly with the economic factor, but is gradually gaining independent sociological features: this is the ghost of the glamour dictatorship — the new generation of racism.

The very ideology of progress is racist in its structure. The assertion that the present is better and more fulfilling than the past, and continual assurances that the future will be even better than the present, are discriminations against the past and the present, as well as the humiliation of all those who lived in the past, an insult to the honour and dignity of our ancestors and those of others, and a violation of the rights of the dead. In many cultures, the dead play an important sociological role. They are considered to still be alive in a certain sense, present in this world, and participating in its life. This is true of all ancient cultures and civilisations. Billions of inhabitants on this Earth believe in this concept to this day. In Chinese civilisation, which was built upon the cult of the dead and upon their reverence alongside the living, being dead is regarded as a high social status, in some ways superior to the status of the living. The ideology of progress represents the moral genocide of past generations — in other words, *real* racism. Equally questionable is the idea of modernisation, when it is taken as a self-evident virtue. It is easy to detect the obvious signs of racism in it.

Undoubtedly racist is the idea of unipolar globalisation. It is based on the idea that the history and values of Western, and especially American, society are equivalent to universal laws, and artificially tries to construct a global society based on what are actually local and historically specific values — democracy, the market, parliamentarianism, capitalism, individualism, human rights, and unlimited technological development. These values are local ones, emerging from the particular development of a single culture, and globalisation is trying to impose them onto all of humanity as something that is universal and taken for granted. This attempt implicitly argues that the values of all other peoples and cultures are imperfect, underdeveloped, and should be subject to modernisation and standardisation in imitation of the Western model.

Globalisation is thus nothing more than a globally deployed model of Western European, or, rather, Anglo-Saxon ethnocentrism, which is the purest manifestation of racist ideology.

As one of its essential features, the Fourth Political Theory rejects all forms and varieties of racism and all forms of the normative hierarchisation of societies based on ethnic, religious, social, technological, economic, or cultural grounds. Societies can be compared, but we cannot state that any one of them is objectively better than the others. Such an assessment is always subjective, and any attempt to raise a subjective assessment to the status of a theory is racism. This type of an attempt is unscientific and inhumane. The differences between societies in any sense can, in no shape or form, imply the superiority of one over the other. This is a central axiom of the Fourth Political Theory. Furthermore, if anti-racism directly opposes the ideology of National Socialism (in other words, the third political theory), then it also indirectly attacks Communism, with its class hatred, as well as liberalism, with its progressivism as well as its inherent forms of economic, technological, and cultural racism. Instead of a unipolar world, the Fourth Political Theory insists upon a multipolar world, and instead of universalism, on pluriversalism, which Alain de Benoist brilliantly pointed out in his book.[39]

Clearly highlighting the main trajectory for the rejection of all forms and varieties of racism, including the biological theories inherent in National Socialism, we can identify what the Fourth Political Theory may borrow from it. Strongly rejecting any suggestion of racism, we, in fact, destroy the 'hermeneutic circle' of National Socialist ideology and neutralise its content, undermining its integrity and key foundations. Without racism, National Socialism is no longer National Socialism, either theoretically or practically, and becomes harmless and decontaminated. We can now proceed without fear to analyse it objectively in search of those ideas within it that could be integrated into the Fourth Political Theory.

We note a positive attitude toward the *ethnos*,[40] an ethnocentrism directed toward that type of existence which is formed within the structure of the *ethnos* itself, and which remains intact throughout a variety of stages, including the highly differentiated types of societies which a people may develop in the course of their history. This topic has found deep resonance in certain philosophical directions of the Conservative Revolution[41] (for instance, Carl Schmitt and his theory of 'the rights of peoples', in

---

39   Alain de Benoist, *Protiv liberalizma*.

40   Greek: 'nation', in the sense of a community of people who all share a common heritage.-Ed.

41   The Conservative Revolution is a term first coined by Hugo von Hoffmansthal, which has come to designate a loose confederation of anti-liberal German thinkers who wrote during the Weimar Republic. There was a great diversity of views within the ranks of the Conservative Revolutionaries, but in general they opposed both

Adam Müller,[42] Arthur Moeller van den Bruck, and so on) or the German school of ethnic sociology (Wilhelm Mühlmann,[43] Richard Thurnwald,[44] and others). *Ethnos* is the greatest value of the Fourth Political Theory as a cultural phenomenon; as a community of language, religious belief, daily life, and the sharing of resources and goals; as an organic entity written into an 'accommodating landscape' (Lev Gumilev);[45] as a refined system for constructing models for married life; as an always-unique means of establishing a relationship with the outside world; as the matrix of the 'lifeworld' (Edmund Husserl); and as the source of all the 'language-games' (Ludwig Wittgenstein).[46] Of course, ethnicity was not the focal point either in National Socialism, or in Fascism. Yet, liberalism as an ideology, calling for the liberation from all forms of collective identity in general, is entirely incompatible with the *ethnos* and ethnocentrism, and is an expression of a systemic theoretical and technological ethnocide.

Marxist ideology did not pay much attention to the *ethnos* either, believing that the *ethnos* is overcome in a class-based society, and that no trace of it remains in a bourgeois and, even more so, a proletarian society. Based on the latter, the principle of 'proletarian internationalism' becomes absolute. The only place where the *ethnos* received any kind of attention is in dissident, Third Way currents which were rather marginal in relation to the political mainstream, even though Nazi orthodoxy blocked the organic development of the ethno-sociological subject area with its racist dogma.

---

democratic capitalism and Communism in favour of a synthesis of aristocratic traditions and spiritual values with socialism.-Ed.

42 Adam Müller (1779-1829) was a German economist who opposed Adam Smith's liberal theories, calling for a return of the importance of ethics and religion in economic and social life.-Ed.

43 Wilhelm Mühlmann (1904-1988) was a German sociologist and anthropologist who worked on ethnological projects for the National Socialist regime, but was rehabilitated after the war. In his writings, he taught that an ethnic group cannot be defined by blood relationship, but only by its cultural traditions and ethnographic characteristics.-Ed.

44 Richard Thurnwald (1869-1954) was an Austrian ethnologist who is credited with founding the school of ethnosociology.-Ed.

45 Lev Gumilev (1912-1992) was a Soviet anthropologist who attempted to explain ethnic differences through geological factors, especially in his book *Ethnogenesis and the Biosphere* (Moscow: Progress Publishers, 1990). He has been very influential on modern Eurasianism. To provide an example of this concept, Gumilev held that the steppe was the 'accommodating landscape' for the Mongols, and thus they were unable to live outside of it and did not wish to give up their nomadic lifestyle.-Ed.

46 'Language-games', according to Wittgenstein, are forms of language that are offshoots of language as it normally exists, such as the language of children, which is simpler than language proper.-Ed.

Whatever the case may be, the *ethnos* and ethnocentrism (Wilhelm Mühlmann) have every reason to be considered as candidates for the becoming the subject of the Fourth Political Theory. At the same time, we must again and again pay attention to the fact that we view the *ethnos* in the plural, without trying to establish any kind of a hierarchical system: ethnicities are different, but each of them is, in itself, universal; ethnicities live and develop, but this life and this development do not fit into one specific paradigm; they are open and always distinct; ethnicities mix and separate, but neither one nor the other is good or evil *per se* — ethnicities themselves generate the criteria by which others are judged, each time in a different way. We can draw many conclusions based on this point. In particular, we can relativise the very notion of 'politics', which comes from the normative values of the city, the *polis*,[47] and, consequently, of the urban model of self-organisation within the community (or the society). As a general paradigm, we can review what Richard Thurnwald called *Dorfstaat* — a 'village-state'.[48] The village-state is an alternative view of politics from the perspective of the *ethnos* naturally living in balance with its environment. This view is not reflective of the city (projecting its struc-ture onto the rest of the country), but is that of the village or the province. It comes from the standpoint of those regions that have been peripheral in classical politics, but which are the centre of the Fourth Political Theory. However, this is only one example of all the possibilities that open up if we accept the *ethnos* as the historical subject. Yet, even this shows the pos-sibilities inherent in transforming even the most basic political concepts, and how drastic the revision of an established dogma can be.

Now let us discuss what could be taken from Communism, the sec-ond political theory. First, however, let us decide on what should be dis-carded in order to demolish its 'hermeneutic circle'. First and foremost, the Communist theories regarding historical materialism and the notion of unidirectional progress are inapplicable to our purposes. We have pre-viously talked about the racist element, which is embedded in the idea of progress. It looks particularly revolting within historical materialism, which not only prioritises the future ahead of the past, brutally violating the 'rights of the ancestors', but also equates the living 'human society' (Richard Thurnwald) with a mechanical system operating independently of humanity, according to laws that are monotonic and uniform for all. Materialist reductionism and economic determinism comprise the most

---

47 Greek: 'city-state'.-Ed.

48 Richard Thurnwald, *Die menschliche Gesellschaft in ihren ethno-soziologischen Grundlagen*, vol. 1 (Berlin: W. de Gruyter, 1931).

repulsive aspect of Marxism. In practice, it was expressed through the destruction of the spiritual and religious heritage of those societies in which Marxism came to dominate. An arrogant contempt for the past, a vulgar materialist interpretation of spiritual culture, a focus exclusively upon economic factors, a positive attitude toward the process of creating a social differential through the 'dictatorship of the proletariat', and the idea of class as the only historical subject — the Fourth Political Theory rejects all these aspects of Marxism. However, without these components, Marxism (and, more generally, socialism) ceases to be itself, and, consequently, it is rendered harmless as a full-fledged ideology, breaking into separate components that do not represent a single whole.

Marxism is relevant in terms of its description of liberalism, in identifying the contradictions of capitalism, in its criticism of the bourgeois system, and in revealing the truth behind the bourgeois-democratic policies of exploitation and enslavement which are presented as 'development' and 'liberation'. Marxism's critical potential is highly useful and applicable. It may well be included in the arsenal of the Fourth Political Theory. But, if so, Marxism will not appear as an ideology that provides answers to a full range of emerging issues — answers that are rational and axiomatic in their foundation — but as an expressive myth or a witty sociological method. The Marxism which we can accept is mythic, sociological Marxism.

As a myth, Marxism tells us the story of the original state of paradise ('primitive Communism'), which was gradually lost ('the initial division of labour and the stratification of the primitive society'). Then the contradictions grew, moving toward the point when, at the end of this world, they were reincarnated, in their most paradigmatically pure form, as the confrontation between Labour and Capital. Capital — the bourgeoisie and liberal democracy — personified global evil, exploitation, alienation, lies, and violence. Labour embodied a great dream and an ancient memory of the 'common good', and its acquisition (the 'surplus value') by an evil minority gave birth to all the problems of modern life. Labour (the proletariat) must recognise the paradoxes inherent in this state of affairs and rise up against their masters in order to build a new society — a new paradise on Earth: Communism. Only this will not be the naturally occurring primitive Communism, but an artificial, scientific kind, in which the differential, accumulated over centuries and millennia of alienation, will serve the 'commune', the 'community'. In this way, the dream will become a reality.

This myth fits neatly into the structure of eschatological consciousness, which occupies a significant place in mythologies of all tribes and peoples, not to mention the highly differentiated religions. That alone speaks in its favour in order for us to treat it with the utmost consideration.

On the other hand, as sociology, Marxism is tremendously useful in revealing those mechanisms of alienation and mystification that liberalism uses to justify its dominion, and as proof of its 'correctness'. Being a myth itself, in its polemical, activist form, Marxism serves as an excellent tool to expose the bourgeois 'great stories' in order to overthrow the credibility of liberal pathos. And in this capacity — 'against liberalism' — it can be used effectively under the new conditions: after all, we continue to exist under capitalism, and hence, Marxist criticism of it, and the struggle against it, remain on the agenda, even if the old forms of this struggle have become irrelevant.

Marxism is often correct when it describes its enemy, especially the bourgeoisie. However, its own attempts to understand itself lead to failure. The first and the most prominent contradiction is Marx's unfulfilled prediction about the type of societies that are the most prone to socialist revolutions. He was confident that this would take place in the greatly industrialised countries of Western Europe, which had a high level of manufacturing and contained a large proportion of urban proletariat. Such revolutions were considered impossible in agrarian countries, as well as those countries with an 'Asiatic' mode of production, due to their supposed backwardness. In the Twentieth century, everything occurred exactly to the contrary. Socialist revolutions and socialist societies developed in agrarian countries which had a traditional, rural population, while nothing similar occurred in any of the highly developed nations of Europe and America. However, even in those countries where socialism was victorious, Marxist dogma did not allow for a rethinking of its basic logical assumptions, such as to reconsider the role of pre-industrial factors, or to honestly evaluate the real power of myth. In its Western and Soviet versions, Marxism's self-reflection turned out to be questionable and inaccurate. While justifiably criticising liberalism, Marxism was seriously mistaken about itself, which, at some point, doomed its own fate. It eventually collapsed even in those places where it had triumphed. And, in those areas where Marx had expected it to win, capitalism prevailed; the proletariat dissolved into the middle class, and disappeared inside the consumer society, contrary to expectations and predictions. In the end, European revolutionary Communists turned into petty-bourgeois clowns, entertaining the bored and jaded democratic public.

If Marxism itself was unable to look at itself from the proper standpoint, then nothing prevents us from doing so in the context of the Fourth

Political Theory. Alain de Benoist has a classic book entitled *Vu de Droite*[49] (A View from the Right), in which he suggested the rereading of various political writers (both from the Right and the Left) from the point of view of the 'New Right'. This book led to the inception of the 'New Right' movement in Europe. It contains not only a critique of those ideas which served as dogma for the 'Old Right', but also a 'revolutionary' and well-meant reading of such authors as the Communist Antonio Gramsci,[50] examined from the point of view of the Right. It is precisely this reading of Marx — 'from the Right', from the standpoint of myths, and from archaic and holistic sociology — that would be particularly fitting at the present time.

Finally, what can we take from liberalism? And here, as always, we must begin with those aspects that must not be borrowed. Perhaps, in this case, everything is described clearly and in a fairly detailed manner in Alain de Benoist's work *Against Liberalism: Toward the Fourth Political Theory*, to which I keep constantly and consciously referring in my explanation. Liberalism is the main enemy of the Fourth Political Theory, which is being constructed specifically to be in total opposition to it. Yet, even here, as was the case with the other political theories, there is something important and something secondary. Liberalism as a whole rests on the individual as its most basic component. It is these individuals, collectively but in isolation from one another, that are taken as the whole. It is, perhaps, for this reason that the 'hermeneutic circle' of liberalism turned out to be the most durable: it has the smallest orbit and rotates around its subject — the individual. In order to shatter this circle, we must strike the individual, abolish him, and cast him into the periphery of political considerations. Liberalism is well aware of this danger, and therefore undertakes one battle after another with all other ideologies and theories — social, philosophical, and political — that encroach on the individual, inscribing his identity into a more general context. The neuroses and fears located at the pathogenic core of liberal philosophy are clearly seen in *The Open Society and its Enemies*,[51] a classic of neo-liberalism by Karl Popper. He compared

49 Alain de Benoist, *Vu de droite: Anthologie critique des idées contemporaines* (Paris: Copernic, 1977).

50 Antonio Gramsci (1891-1937) was an Italian Communist who was imprisoned by the Fascists. He developed the theory of cultural hegemony, which (in brief) holds that a political group cannot maintain power without first persuading the members of a society that the ideas it propagates are the normal state of affairs, thus giving itself legitimacy. Therefore, control over the cultural apparatus of a society is a prerequisite for holding power, rather than being something which follows a revolution. This idea has been highly influential on the European New Right.-Ed.

51 Karl Popper, *The Open Society and Its Enemies*, 2 vols. (London: Routledge & Kegan Paul, 1945).

fascism and Communism based precisely on the fact that both ideologies integrate the individual into a supra-individual community, into a whole, into a totality, which Popper immediately qualified as 'totalitarianism'. Having undermined the individual as the constitutive figure of the entire political and social system, we can put an end to liberalism. Of course, this is not that easy to achieve. Nevertheless, it is now obvious that the weakest (and the strongest) aspect of the first political theory comes from its direct appeal to the *individual,* pleading that he remain himself, by himself in his own autonomous individuality, uniqueness, particularity, and partiality. In any case, the Fourth Political Theory can interpret Popper's phobias in its favour. (This led him and his followers to anecdotal conclusions; quite telling are his feeble-minded criticisms of Hegel in the spirit of a 'smear campaign', and the accusations of fascism directed toward Plato and Aristotle!) Understanding what the enemy fears the most, we propose the theory that every human identity is acceptable and justified, except for that of the individual. Man is anything but an individual. We must look carefully at a liberal, when he reads or hears an axiom of this kind. I think this will be an impressive spectacle — all his 'tolerance' will instantly evaporate. 'Human rights' will be distributed to anyone, just not the one who dares to utter something along these lines. This, however, I described in more detail in my essay *Maximal Humanism*[52] as well as in my book, *The Philosophy of Politics*.[53]

Liberalism must be defeated and destroyed, and the individual must be thrown off his pedestal. Yet, is there anything that we could take away from liberalism — from this liberalism that is hypothetically defeated and has lost its axis?

Yes, there is. It is the idea of freedom. And not just the idea of 'freedom for' — that same substantive freedom rejected by Mill in his liberal program, which concentrated on the 'freedom from'. We must say 'yes' to freedom in all its meanings and in all its perspectives. The Fourth Political Theory should be a theory of absolute freedom, but not as in Marxism, in which it coincides with absolute necessity (this correlation denies freedom its very core). No, freedom can be of any kind, free of any correlation or lack thereof, facing any direction and any goal. Freedom is the greatest value of the Fourth Political Theory, since it coincides with its centre and its dynamic, energetic core.

The difference is that this freedom is conceived as human freedom, not as freedom for the individual — as the freedom given by ethnocentrism

---

52 Alexander Dugin, *Maksimal'nyi gumanizm* (Moscow: Russkaia vesch', 2001).

53 Alexander Dugin, *Filosofiia politiki* (Moscow, 2004).

and the freedom of *Dasein*, the freedom of culture and the freedom of society, and the freedom for any form of subjectivity except for that of an individual. Moving in the opposite direction, European thought long ago came to a different conclusion: 'man (as an individual) is a prison without walls'[54] (Jean-Paul Sartre); that is to say, the freedom of an individual is a prison. In order to attain true freedom, we must go beyond the limits of the individual. In this sense, the Fourth Political Theory is a theory of liberation, of going beyond the prison walls into the outside world, which begins where the jurisdiction of individual identity ends.

Freedom is always fraught with chaos, but is also open to opportunities. Placed into the narrow framework of individuality, the amount of freedom becomes microscopic, and, ultimately, fictitious. The individual is granted freedom because the uses to which he can put it are extremely limited — it will remain contained within the tiny scope of his individuality and that over which he has direct control. This is the flip side of liberalism: at its core, it is totalitarian and intolerant of differences, and most especially opposed to the realisation of a great will. It is only prepared to tolerate small people; it protects not so much the rights of man, but, rather, the rights of a small man. This 'small man' can be allowed to do anything, but in spite of all his desire, he will be unable to do anything. Yet, beyond the small man, on the other side of 'minimal humanism',[55] one can just glimpse the closest horizon of genuine freedom. However, it is also there that great risk and serious dangers emerge. Having left the limits of individuality, man can be crushed by the elements of life and by dangerous chaos. He may want to establish order. And this is entirely within his right — the right of a great man (*homo maximus*) — a real man of 'Being and time' (Martin Heidegger). And, like any order, this possible order, the coming order may be embodied in individual forms. Nonetheless, this is not individuality, but individuation; not empty rotations around that which has been received from the liberal authorities and which is meaningless, but the actual execution of tasks, as well as the taming of the restless and exciting horizons of the will.

The bearer of freedom in this case will be *Dasein*. The previous ideologies, each in its own way, alienated *Dasein* from its meaning, restricted it, and imprisoned it in one way or another, making it inauthentic. Each of these ideologies put a cheerless doll, *das Man*,[56] in the place of *Dasein*. The freedom of *Dasein* lies in implementing the opportunity to be authen-

---

54 Jean-Paul Sartre, *The Age of Reason* (New York: Alfred A. Knopf, 1947).

55 Alexander Dugin, *Maksimal'nyi gumanizm.*

56 Martin Heidegger, *On Time and Being.*

tic: that is, in the realisation of *Sein*[57] more so than of *da*.[58] 'There-Being'
consists of 'there' and of 'Being'. In order to understand where this 'there'
is located, we should point it out and make a basic, foundational gesture.
Yet, in order for 'Being' to flow into 'there' like a fountain, we must place
all of this together — place this entire hermeneutic circle into the domain
of complete freedom. Therefore, the Fourth Political Theory is, at the same
time, a fundamental ontological theory which contains the awareness of
the truth of Being at its core.

Without freedom, we cannot force anyone to exist. Even if we build
the optimal society, and even if we force everyone to act appropriately
and to operate within the framework of the correct paradigm, we could
never guarantee such an outcome. This results from a man's freedom to
choose Being. Of course, most often, man gravitates toward the 'inauthentic' existence of *Dasein*, trying to dodge the issue, to succumb to gossip
(*Gerede*) and to self-mockery. Liberated *Dasein* may not choose the path
to Being, may hide in shelter, and may, once again, clutter the world with
its hallucinations and fears, and its concerns and intentions. Choosing
Dasein may corrupt the Fourth Political Theory itself, turning it into a
self-parody. This is a risk, but Being is a risk, too. The only question is
who risks what. You risk everything, or everything and everyone puts you
at risk. Yet, only that which increases freedom will make the choice of
authentic Being a reality — only then will the stakes be truly great, when
the danger is infinite.

Unlike other political theories, the Fourth Political Theory does not
want to lie, soothe, or seduce. It summons us to live dangerously, to think
riskily, to liberate and to release all those things that cannot be driven back
inside. The Fourth Political Theory trusts the fate of Being, and entrusts
fate to Being.

Any strictly constructed ideology is always a simulacrum and always
inauthentic, that is to say, it always is the lack of freedom. Therefore, the
Fourth Political Theory should not hurry in order to become a set of basic
axioms. Perhaps, it is more important to leave some things unsaid, to be
discovered in expectations and insinuations, in allegations and premoni-
tions. The Fourth Political Theory should be completely open.

---

57 German: 'being'.-Ed.
58 German: 'there'.-Ed.

3

THE CRITIQUE OF MONOTONIC PROCESSES

The idea of modernisation is based on the idea of progress. When we use the term 'modernisation', we certainly mean progress, linear accumulation, and a certain continuous process. When we speak of 'modernisation', we presuppose development, growth, and evolution. This is the same semantic system. Thus, when we speak of the 'unconditionally positive achievements of modernisation', we agree with a very important basic paradigm — we agree with the idea that 'human society is developing, progressing, evolving, growing, and getting better and better'. That is to say, we share a particular vision of historical optimism.

This historical optimism pertains to the three classical political ideologies (liberalism, Communism, and fascism). It is rooted in the scientific, societal, political, and social worldview in the humanities and natural sciences of the Eighteenth and Nineteenth centuries, when the idea of progress, development, and growth was taken as an axiom that could not be doubted. In other words, this entire set of axioms, as well as the whole historiography and predictive analytics of the Nineteenth century in the humanities and the natural sciences, was built on the idea of progress. We can easily trace the development of this subject — the idea of progress — in the three political ideologies.

Let us turn to the classical liberalism of the sociologist Herbert Spencer.[1] He claimed that the development of human society is the next stage of the evolution of the animal species, and that there is a connection, and a continuity, between the animal world and social development.[2]

---

1   Herbert Spencer (1820-1903) was a theorist of evolution who was a contemporary of Darwin. It was he who coined the phrase 'survival of the fittest' in his 1864 book, *Principles of Biology*, to describe Darwin's idea of natural selection. Darwin himself later adopted Spencer's term. Spencer also applied Darwin's theories to the social realm, something Darwin never did.-Ed.

2   Herbert Spencer, *Essays, Scientific, Political, and Speculative*, 3 vols. (New York: D. Appleton, 1891).

And, therefore, all the laws of the animal world leading to development, improvement, and evolution in the animal world, within Darwin's framework, can be projected onto society. This is the basis of the famous theory, 'Social Darwinism', of which Spencer was a classic representative. If, according to Darwin, the driving force behind the evolution of the animal kingdom is the struggle for survival and natural selection, then the same process must take place in society, argued Spencer. And, the more perfect this struggle is for survival (inter-species, intra-species, the struggle of the strong against the weak, the competition for resources, pleasure), the more perfect our society becomes. The question is how to aid this process of selection. According to Spencer, this is the central theme of the liberal model, and is the meaning of social progress. Therefore, if we are liberals, in one way or the other, we inherited this 'zoological' approach to social development based on the struggle against and the destruction of the weak by the strong.

However, Spencer's theory contains one important point. He argued that there are two phases of social development. The first phase occurs when the struggle for survival is conducted crudely, by force; this is characteristic of the ancient world. The second occurs when the struggle is carried out more subtly through economic means. Once the bourgeois revolution takes place, the struggle for survival does not stop. According to Spencer, it acquires new, more advanced, and more efficient forms; it relocates into the sphere of the market. Here, the strongest survive — that is, the richest. Instead of the most powerful feudal lord, a hero, a strong person, or a leader, who simply seizes all that is up for grabs around his community, taking away all that belongs to other nations and races and sharing it with the ruling ethnicity or caste, now comes the capitalist, who brings the same aggressive animal principle to the market, the corporation, and the trading company. The transition from the order of power to the order of money, according to Spencer, does not mean the humanisation of the process, but only underscores greater effectiveness. That is to say, the struggle in the market sphere between the strong (meaning rich) and the weak (meaning poor) becomes more efficient and leads to higher levels of development until super-rich, super-strong, and super-developed countries appear. Progress, according to Spencer, and, more broadly speaking, according to liberalism, is always the growth of economic power, since this continues to refine the struggle for survival of the animal species, the warfare methods of strong nations, and the castes within the framework of pre-capitalist states. Thus, an animalistic form of aggression is embedded in the liberal idea of progress, which is regarded as the main trajectory of social development. With more economic freedom, there is greater power for takeovers, attacks, mergers and acquisitions. Liberal discourse, meaning the analysis of the liberal ideologist, is a completely *animal* discourse. In such a system, the 'more advanced' law or the more advanced, 'more modern' methods of production do not mean that they are more humane; what it means is that they allow more opportunities for the strong to more effectively realise their power, while the weak can only admit defeat, or, if they have any strength left, fight on. In this manner, the modern idea of economic growth, as we see in liberals such as Alan Greenspan and Ben Bernanke, has its foundation and origins in the idea of the struggle between species, that is, the feral destruction of the weak by the strong, or the validation of the strong at the expense of the weak. Only instead of the conflict between predators and herbivores, we have the golden billion,[3] and in that golden billion, their own 'kings of beasts' (the New York Stock Exchange and the World Bank bankers, who devour all that is up for grabs and, at the same time, turn the forests of the world into 'social infrastructures'.

Therefore, when we speak of 'modernisation' in the liberal vein, of necessity we mean the enhancement of the social, political, cultural, spiritual, and informational scenario within which the absolute aggression of the strong against the weak can be implemented.

American liberal Ayn Rand[4] (Greenspan[5] was one of her greatest admirers) created an entire philosophy (called 'Objectivism')[6] based on the following blunt idea: if one is rich, then he is good. She reached the limits of Weber's[7] idea about the origin of capitalism in the Protestant ethic and said that he who is 'rich' is always and necessarily the 'good' — almost a saint, while the 'poor' man is evil, lazy, bad, and corrupt — a 'sinner'.

---

3   'Golden billion' is a term used in Russia to describe the belief that a relatively small percentage of the world's population, located in the wealthiest nations of the West, consume the largest percentage of the world's resources.-Ed.

4   Ayn Rand (1905-1982) was a Russian-American novelist and philosopher who promoted an extreme form of individualist capitalism which she termed Objectivism.-Ed.

5   Alan Greenspan (b. 1926) was the Chairman of the United States Federal Reserve from 1987 until 2006. Beginning in the 1960s, Greenspan became part of Rand's inner circle and was one of the most prominent Objectivists. While initially quite popular, many of his policies have come under criticism. Many claim that he assisted trends which led to the 2008 subprime mortgage crisis in the United States, which in turn precipitated the global financial crisis.-Ed.

6   Ayn Rand, *Capitalism: The Unknown Ideal* (New York: New American Library, 1966).-Ed.

7   Max Weber (1864-1920) was a German who is considered one of the founders of sociology. His principal work is *The Protestant Ethic and the Spirit of Capitalism.*-Ed.

Being poor, according to Ayn Rand, is to be a sinful villain, whereas to be rich is to be a saint. She proposed to establish the 'conspiracy' of the rich (meaning the strong, bright, sacred, and powerful capitalists) against any kind of labour movement, the peasants, and against all those who stand for social justice, or those who are simply poor. Such a crusade of the rich against the poor is the basis of the Objectivist ideology. People like Greenspan and the current head of the United States Federal Reserve, Bernanke, are 'Objectivists' — that is, those who interpret modernisation, progress, economic growth, and development in the liberal vein.

If we understand modernisation like liberal democrats, then that means that we are invited to join in this terrible struggle for survival at its greatest intensity, and to become just like them, trying to grab a place at the trough of globalisation. Globalisation, in this case, is the new battle-field in the struggle for survival, the struggle of the rich against the poor.

Naturally, the ideologically philosophic and moral premise of this version of modernisation is entirely alien to the Russian people in terms of our history and our culture. We reject this type of modernisation unconditionally, and those who might try to impose it upon us will pay dearly for doing so.

In Communism, the idea of unidirectional progress is also present. Marx argued that changes in social structures, which lead to the improvement and development of societies and economies, will sooner or later result in the Communist proletarian revolution, redistributing the accumulated wealth as a result of the development of alienating technologies. The expropriation of the expropriators will occur. Nevertheless, while this has not happened, Marxists say, let everything be as it may in the development of capitalism. Marx also saw history positively, as advancement, and viewed it as a tale of growth and improvement, from the minus to the plus, from the simple to the complex.

It is telling that the lion's share of *The Communist Manifesto*[8] by Marx and Engels is devoted to criticising specifically those anti-bourgeois political philosophies that differed from Marxism; first and foremost, those that are feudal, reactionary, and nationalistic. By doing so, Marx and Engels strove to emphasise that their 'Communism' was directed against the bourgeoisie in a manner different from the criticism by the Right-wing anti-capitalists. In reality, compared to all the other 'reactionary' and 'conservative' projects, Marxists stand on the side of the bourgeoisie and seek to bring its victory closer, since it translates into the narrative of historical progress

---

8   Karl Marx and Friedrich Engels, *The Communist Manifesto: A Modern Edition* (New York: Verso, 1998).

and the logic of modernisation. For this reason, Marxism rejects conservatism in all of its forms. The contradictions between the Communists and
the capitalists acquire a particularly acute character as the triumph of capitalism becomes irreversible and complete. It is here that the Communists
enter history as the vanguard of the proletariat and push historical progress further along — toward socialism and Communism.

Once again, we see Darwinism in Marxism, including the full accept-
ance of evolutionary ideas and its belief in the miraculous power of scientific progress and technological improvement.

We lived through this kind of 'modernisation' in the Twentieth
century — paid for it more than in full; the people clearly do not have
the slightest desire to repeat such experiments. Therefore, this version
of modernisation will not work — and moreover, no one speaks out in
favour of it.

Oddly enough, fascism, too, is an evolutionary movement. We may
remember Friedrich Nietzsche, who spoke of the 'blond beast' and of
the 'will to power' that drives history. Nietzsche was an evolutionist and
believed that, based on the logic of the development of species, man will
be replaced by the 'Superman', much like how man first came to replace
the ape. He wrote, 'What is the ape to a human? A laughing stock or a
painful embarrassment. And that is precisely what the human shall be to
the overman: a laughing stock or a painful embarrasment.'[9] The National
Socialists adapted a racial interpretation of this idea: that the white race
is 'more developed' than the black, yellow, or any other kind, and on this
basis, has the 'right' to rule the world. Here, we encounter the same pro-
gressivist outlook, along with the idea of development and improvement,
all of which leads to the assumption of racial superiority on the grounds
that the white nations own sophisticated instruments of industrial production, while other ethnic groups do not.

Today, we reject and criticise fascism for its racial component, but we
forget that this ideology is also built on the ideas of progress and evolution, just like the other two political theories of modernity. If we were to
visualise the essence of Nazi ideology and the role of progress and evolution in it, then the connection between racism and evolution would
become obvious to us. This connection — in a concealed form — can be
seen in liberalism and even in Communism. Even if not biological, we see
cultural, technological, and economic racism in the ideology of the free
market and in the dictatorship of the proletariat.

---

9   Friedrich Nietzsche, *Thus Spoke Zarathustra* (Cambridge: Cambridge University
    Press, 2006), p. 6.

In one way or another, all three ideologies originate from the same trend: the idea of growth, development, progress, evolution, and of the constant, cumulative improvement of society. They all view the world and the entire historical process as linear growth. They differ in their interpretation of this process, and they attribute different meanings to it, but they all accept the irreversibility of history and its progressive character.

Thus, modernisation is a concept that sends us back directly to the three classical political ideologies. Furthermore, we can see the common ground that unites the three ideologies through the idea of progress and in their positive evaluation of the concept of 'modernisation'. Nowadays, all three of these ideologies are being gradually discarded. This is strongly evident in regard to fascism and Communism, but is somewhat less obvious with regard to liberalism, but even liberalism is gradually ceasing to satisfy the majority of the world's population and, simultaneously, is turning into something other than what it was during the 'classical' era of modernity. Consequently, it is about time that we pose the question of searching for the Fourth Political Theory[10] beyond the first three. Additionally, the radical rejection of the three classical theories reflects our attitude toward what is common to them all — that is, our attitude toward modernisation, progress, evolution, development, and growth.

The American scientist Gregory Bateson,[11] a theorist of ethno-sociology, cybernetics, and ecology, as well as a psychoanalyst and a linguist, described the monotonic process in his book *Mind and Nature*.[12] The monotonic process is the idea of constant growth, constant accumulation, development, steady progress, all accompanied by the increase of only one specific indicator. In mathematics, this is associated with the ideas of the monotonic value; in other words, the ever-increasing value — hence, monotonic functions. Monotonic processes are the type that always proceed in only one direction: for example, all their indicators consistently increase without cyclical fluctuations and oscillations. Studying the monotonic process at three levels — at the level of biology (life), at the level of mechanics (steam engines, internal combustion engines), and at the level of social phenomena, Bateson concluded that when this process occurs in nature, it immediately destroys the species; if we are talking about an artificial device, it breaks down; if we mean a society, the

---

10 Alexander Dugin, *Chetvertaia politicheskaia teoriia*; Alain de Benoist, *Protiv liberalizma: K chetvertoi politicheskoi teorii*.

11 Gregory Bateson (1904-1980) was an English anthropologist and cyberneticist whose work ranged over a wide variety of fields. In his later years, he attempted to create a 'meta-science' of epistemology.-Ed.

12 Gregory Bateson, *Mind and Nature: A Necessary Unity* (New York: Dutton, 1979).

society deteriorates and disappears. The monotonic process, in biology, is incompatible with life — it is an anti-biological phenomenon. Monotonic processes are completely absent from nature. All the processes which accumulate only one particular thing, or emphasise only one particular trait, result in death. Monotonic processes do not exist in any biological species, from cells to the most complex organisms. As soon as this kind of a monotonic process begins, deviants, giants, dwarfs, and other freaks of nature appear. They are disabled, incompatible with life, cannot produce offspring, and life itself casts them out.

Solving the problem of monotonic processes was one of the most important problems in the development of steam engines. It turns out that the most important design element in steam engines is the centrifugal governor. When a steam engine reaches cruising speed, it is necessary to regulate the intake of fuel, otherwise the monotonic process initiates, everything begins to resonate, and the speed of the engine can increase indefinitely, causing it to explode. It was precisely this solution of avoiding the monotonic process in mechanics that was the principal theoretical, mathematical, physical, and engineering problem during the early stage of industrialisation. It turns out that the monotonic process is not only incompatible with life, but also with the proper functioning of a mechanical device. The task of designing a device must avoid the monotonic process, that is, it must prevent one-dimensional progress, evolution, development, and the placement of growth into a closed cycle.

By analysing sociology, Bateson showed that there are no monotonic processes in real societies. Monotonic processes, such as population growth, in most cases led to wars, which then reduced the population. In our society today we see an unprecedented level of technological progress along with unbelievable moral degradation.

If we look at all this evidence without the evolutionary bias, then we will realise that monotonic processes exist only in people's minds; in other words, they are purely ideological models. Bateson demonstrated that they do not exist in biological, mechanical, or social reality.

Marcel Mauss,[13] a well-known French sociologist, criticised the monotonic process as well. In the book he co-authored, *Sacrifice: Its Nature and Functions*[14] and especially in his essay, *The Gift*,[15] he showed that traditional

---

13 Marcel Mauss (1872-1950) was a sociologist whose work also had a significant impact on anthropology, particularly Claude Lévi-Strauss.-Ed.

14 Henri Hubert and Marcel Mauss, *Sacrifice: Its Nature and Function* (Chicago: Chicago University Press, 1964).

15 Marcel Mauss, *The Gift: Forms and Functions of Exchange in Archaic Societies* (New York: Norton, 1967).

societies paid great attention to the ritual destruction, or sacrifice, of sur-plus goods. The surplus was seen as excessive, *likho*,[16] and usurious. *Likho* personifies evil, usury is the interest charged on borrowed capital, and excess is that which is obtained beyond one's needs. For instance, surplus crops were seen as disastrous in traditional society. The ancient world-view was based on the belief that an increase in one area translates into a decrease in another. Therefore, a surplus had to be destroyed as soon as possible. For this purpose, the community either organised a feast, con-suming all the additional food until they choked, or else gave it to the gods in the form of a sacrifice, gave it out to the needy, or destroyed it. This is the origin of a special ritual, the potlatch,[17] which brings about the deliberate gifting or destruction of excess personal property.

Marcel Mauss proved that the belief in the destructiveness of monot-onic processes lies at the foundations of human sociality. The society remains strong only through the rejection of the monotonic process, and by turning growth into a cycle.

Émile Durkheim, Pitirim Sorokin, and Georges Gurvitch, the greatest sociologists of the Twentieth century, in essence the classicists of socio-logical thought, argued that social progress does not exist, in contrast to the Nineteenth-century sociologists, such as Auguste Comte or Herbert Spencer. Progress is not an objective social phenomenon, but rather, an artificial concept, a kind of scientifically formulated myth. When we study societies, we can only speak of the different types thereof. There is no gen-eral criterion to determine which is more developed, and which is less so. Lucien Lévy-Brühl[18] attempted to prove that savages think pre-logi-cally, while modern humans use logic.[19] However, Claude Lévi-Strauss[20] demonstrated[21] that savages think in the same way that we do, only their

---

16 In ancient Russian mythology, the *likho* was a creature which embodied calamities and misfortune. The word itself is the equivalent of 'evil', and is etymologically related to *lishnii*, that is, 'excessive'. Dugin also uses the original meaning of the term *likhva*, an archaic word which signifies 'usury', and is also linked to *likho*.-Ed.

17 The potlatch is a custom practiced by various Native American tribes in North America, in spite of efforts by the Canadian and American governments to ban it during the Nineteenth and early Twentieth centuries.-Ed.

18 Lucien Lévy-Brühl (1857-1939) was a French philosopher who posited that there were two basic mentalities in humanity: 'primitive' and 'Western', with an evolution-ary chain between them.-Ed.

19 Lucien Lévy-Brühl, *Pervobytnoe myshlenie: Psikhologiia myshleniia* (Moscow: MGU, 1980).

20 Claude Lévi-Strauss (1908-2009) was the most influential anthropologist of the Twentieth century.-Ed.

21 Claude Lévi-Strauss, *The Savage Mind* (Chicago: Chicago University Press, 1966).

taxonomy is built differently, so they do not have 'less' logic than we do; perhaps even more so, and they think in a more refined manner.

As for the phases of social development, the greatest American cultural anthropologist, Franz Boas,[22] and his followers, as well as Claude Levi-Strauss and his school, proved that we cannot look at modern humans as being evolved from 'archaic' and 'primitive' tribes within the framework of anthropology. Primitives and primitive societies are simply different people and different societies. Modern humans are one group, and archaic humans another. But, they are people, too, no worse than we are. They are not an underdeveloped version of us. They have different children, who do not know myths and fairy tales, since they are not taught them, in contrast to our children. The adults are also different; their adults do know the myths, whereas ours do not believe in them. *Our* adults, our sober and practical society, are more similar to *their* children. The adults in primitive tribes are capable of telling mythological stories, sincerely believe in them, and know that they embody the feats of their ancestors and their spirits in their own lives, making no distinction between them. In contrast, the children of primitive societies are characterised by cynicism, pragmatism, scepticism, and the desire to attribute everything to material causes. This does not mean that modern societies have grown from the state of primitivism and superseded it; it is just that we have configured our society differently, neither better or worse, and built it upon other foundations and other values.

With regard to cultural studies and philosophy, Nikolai Danilevsky,[23] Oswald Spengler, Carl Schmitt, Ernst Jünger,[24] Martin Heidegger, and Arnold Toynbee[25] showed that all the processes in the history of philoso-

---

22 Franz Boas (1858-1942) was an American anthropologist who laid the groundwork for modern anthropology.-Ed.

23 Nikolai Danilevsky (1822-1885) was a Russian philosopher who proposed a cyclical cycle in the life of civilisatons, similar to the idea developed later by Spengler.

24 Ernst Jünger (1895-1998) was one of the most prominent of the German Conservative Revolutionaries, but that was only one phase in a long and varied career. He volunteered for and fought in the German Army throughout the First World War, and was awarded the highest decoration, the Pour le Mérite, for his service. After the war, he wrote many books and novels, was active in German politics, experimented with psychedelic drugs, and travelled the world. He remained ambivalent about National Socialism at first, but never joined the Party, and he had turned against the Nazis by the late 1930s. He rejoined the Wehrmacht at the outbreak of war, however, and remained in Paris as a captain, where he spent more time with Picasso and Cocteau than enforcing the occupation. His objections to the Nazis were influential upon the members of the Stauffenberg plot to assassinate Hitler in July 1944, which led to his dismissal from the Wehrmacht. After the war, Jünger's political views gradually moved toward a sort of aristocratic anarchism.-Ed.

25 Arnold J. Toynbee (1889-1975) was a British historian who wrote a 12-volume study of the cycles of civilisations, *A Study of History*, between 1934 and 1961.-Ed.

phy and the history of culture are a cyclical phenomenon. The Russian historian Lev Gumilev also suggested this in his version of cyclical history, which he explained in his famous theory of passionarity.[26] They all acknowledge that there is development, but that there is also decline. Those who place bets on there being *only* growth and development act against all norms of history, against all sociological laws, and against the logic of life. Such unidirectional modernisation, such growth, such development, and such progress do not exist.

Piotr Sztompka, a contemporary Polish sociologist, stated[27] that, in terms of how progress was viewed, the there was a change in the humanities. In the Nineteenth century, everyone believed that progress existed, and that it was the principal axiom and a scientific criterion. But, if we examine the paradigms of the Twentieth century in the humanities and the natural sciences, then we will see that almost everyone rejected them; no one is guided by it any longer. Nowadays, the paradigm of progress is considered almost antiscientific. It is incompatible with the criteria of contemporary science, just as it is incompatible with the criteria of humanism and tolerance. Any idea of progress is, in itself, a veiled or direct racism, asserting that 'our' culture, for instance, the 'White culture' or American culture, is of higher value than 'your' culture, such as the culture of Africans, Muslims, Iraqis, or Afghans. As soon as we say that the American or the Russian culture is better than that of the Chukchi[28] or the inhabitants of the Northern Caucasus, we act like racists. And this is incompatible with both science and with a basic respect toward different ethnicities.

Twentieth-century science uses cyclicality as a scientific criterion, or, according to Sztompka, we have moved from the paradigm of evolution, modernisation, and development to the paradigm of crisis and catastrophes. This means that all processes — in nature, society, and technology — must be conceived as relative, reversible, and cyclical. This is the most important point.

In terms of its methodological base, the Fourth Political Theory must be rooted in the fundamental rejection of the monotonic process. That is to say, the Fourth Political Theory must assert that the monotonic process is unscientific, inadequate, amoral, and untrue as its future axiom

---

26 Gumilev saw passionarity as the level of vitality in a given ethnic group or civilisation, a type of energy which would gradually increase until reaching its peak, at which time the group would make its greatest achievements, followed by a slow ebb. He saw European civilisation as being at its low point, and Arab civilisation as being very high in passionarity.-Ed.

27 Piotr Sztompka, *The Sociology of Social Change* (Oxford: Blackwell, 1994).

28 The Chukchi people inhabit the Chukchi Peninsula near the Bering Sea.-Ed.

(without specifying how the monotonic process must be rejected). And, everything that appeals to the monotonic process and its variations, such as development, evolution, and modernisation, should, at the very least, be understood in terms of the cyclical mode. Instead of the ideas of the monotonic process, progress, and modernisation, we must endorse other slogans directed toward life, repetition, the preservation of that which is of value and changing that which should be changed.

Instead of always looking for modernisation and growth, we should instead orient ourselves in the direction of balance, adaptability, and harmony. Instead of desiring to move upward and forward, we must adapt to that which exists, to understand where we are, and to harmonise socio-political processes.

And, most important, instead of growth, progress, and development, there is *life*. After all, there has been no proof offered yet to show that life is linked to growth. This was the myth of the Nineteenth century. Life, in contrast, is connected to the eternal return. In the end, even Nietzsche incorporated his idea of the will to power into the concept of eternal return.[29] The very logic of life to which Nietzsche was dedicated told him that if there is growth in life, the Apollonian[30] movement toward the *logos*, then the balance of the nocturnal Dionysian world exists as well. And Apollo is not just opposed to Dionysus; they *complement* each other. Half of the cycle constitutes modernisation, while the other half—decline; when one half faces up, the other half faces down. There is no life without death. Being-towards-death, careful attention to death, to the flip side of the sphere of Being, as Heidegger wrote, is not a struggle with life, but, rather, its glorification and its foundation.

We must put an end to antiquated political ideologies and theories. If we have truly rejected Marxism and fascism, then what remains is to reject liberalism. Liberalism is an equally outdated, cruel, misanthropic ideology like the two previous ones. The term 'liberalism' should be equated with the terms fascism and Communism. Liberalism is responsible for no fewer historic crimes than fascism (Auschwitz) and Communism

---

29 'What if some day or night a demon were to steal into your loneliest loneliness and say to you: "This life as you now live it and have lived it you will have to live once again and innumerable times again; and there will be nothing new in it, but every pain and every joy and every thought and sigh and everything unspeakably small or great in your life must return to you, all in the same succession and sequence..."' From Friedrich Nietzsche, *The Gay Science* (Cambridge: Cambridge University Press, 2001), p. 194. This is one of Nietzsche's central ideas.-Ed.

30 In Nietzsche's understanding of the term, the Apollonian is that which is related to reason and dreams. The Dionysian is related to intoxication and ecstasy.-Ed.

(the GULag):[31] it is responsible for slavery, the destruction of the Native Americans in the United States, for Hiroshima and Nagasaki, for the aggression in Serbia, Iraq, and Afghanistan, for the devastation and the economic exploitation of millions of people on the planet, and for the ignoble and cynical lies which whitewash this history.

But, most important, we must reject the base upon which these three ideologies stand: the monotonic process in all its forms, that is, evolution, growth, modernisation, progress, development, and all that which seemed scientific in the Nineteenth century but was exposed as unscientific in the Twentieth century.

We must also abandon the philosophy of development and propose the following slogan: life is more important than growth. Instead of the ideology of development, we must place our bets on the ideology of conservatism and conservation. However, we not only require conservatism in our daily lives, but also philosophical conservatism. We need the philosophy of conservatism. Looking toward the future of the Russian political system, if it is going to be based on monotonic processes, then it is doomed to failure. No stability will ever come from a new round of unidirectional growth derived from energy prices, real estate, stocks, and so on, nor from the growth of global economy as a whole. If this illusion persists, then it may become fatal for our country.

Today, we find ourselves in a transitional state. We know roughly what we are moving away *from*, but do not know what we are moving *toward*. If we head toward that which directly or indirectly implies the belief in any monotonic process, then we will reach a dead end.

The Fourth Political Theory must take a step toward the formulation of a coherent critique of the monotonic process. It must develop an alternative model of a conservative future, a conservative tomorrow, based on the principles of vitality, roots, constants, and eternity.

After all, as Arthur Moeller van den Bruck once said, 'Conservatism has eternity on its side.'[32]

---

31 The GULag was an acronym for the massive system of forced labour camps that existed in the Soviet Union, in which conditions were extremely harsh and many did not survive. They reached their peak under Stalin, when by 1953 over two million Soviet citizens were interned in GULags. The GULags were shut down by 1960.-Ed.

32 Arthur Moeller van den Bruck, *Germany's Third Empire* (London: Arktos, 2012).

4

THE REVERSIBILITY OF TIME

Three political theories have been produced from the ideology of modernity. They were all based on the topography of progress. Progress implicates the irreversibility of time, a forward-moving and predetermined evolutionary process. Progress is both an orthogenetic and a monotonic process. Inevitably, all three are based on Hegel's philosophy. After Hegel, the meaning of history became understood in terms of the Absolute Spirit[1] becoming estranged from itself, assuming a form as the dialectic process of history, eventually becoming a type of enlightened monarchy.

Marx accepted this topography, and after Alexandre Kojève and Francis Fukuyama, liberal thinkers have accepted it as well. In the framework of National Socialism, Hegelianism was externalised in the concept of a Final Reich, with the Third Reich as the third kingdom of Joachim of Fiore,[2] and in the concept of Social Darwinism, where the theory of natural selection has been adapted to apply to society and races. Social Darwinism is also inherent in Spencer's liberalism. Each of these three ideologies of modernity is based on the premises of the irreversibility of time and of unidirectional history. They implicitly acknowledge the totalising imperative of modernisation. Modernisation can be liberal, Communist, or fascist. An example of the effectiveness of fascist modernisation would be the success, however brutal, of Hitler's industrial modernisation of Germany in the 1930s.

---

1   In his *Philosophy of History*, Hegel postulates that there is a spirit behind civilisations which manifests itself through the dialectical process of history. He once referred to Napoleon as the 'world spirit on horseback'.-Ed.

2   Joachim of Fiore (1135-1202) was an Italian priest who was the founder of the monastic order of San Giovanni. He developed a theory that history was structured according to the Christian Trinity, consisting of the Age of the Father, the Age of the Son and the Age of the Holy Spirit, which he believed would begin in 1260. In this Age, he taught, humanity would be able to commune directly with God, rendering the structure of the Church obsolete. His ideas were condemned by the Church and are still considered heretical today.-Ed.

The Fourth Political Theory is an unmodern theory. As Bruno Latour[3] has said, 'We have never been contemporary'. The theoretical axioms of modernity are harmless because they cannot be realised in reality. In practice, they are permanently and very spectacularly self-negating. The Fourth Political Theory completely discards the idea of the irreversibility of history. This idea was interesting in a theoretical sense, as substantiated by Georges Dumézil,[4] with his anti-euhemerism,[5] and Gilbert Durand.[6] I have written previously about sociology and the morphology of time in my books *Post-philosophy*, *Sociology of the Imagination*, and *Sociology of Russian Society*. Time is a social phenomenon; its structures do not depend upon their objectives, but upon the domination of social paradigms, because the object is assigned by society itself. In modern society, time is seen as irreversible, progressive and unidirectional. But this is not necessarily true inside societies that do not accept modernity. In some societies, which lack a strict, modern conception of time, cyclic and even regressive conceptions of time exist. Therefore, political history is considered in the context of the topography of plural conceptions of time for the Fourth Political Theory. There are as many conceptions of time as there are societies.

The Fourth Political Theory does not just discard progress and modernisation, however. This theory contemplates progress and modernisation relative to, and intimately connected with, current historical, social

---

3   Bruno Latour (b. 1947) is a French anthropologist who has applied anthropology and sociology to the study of science. Dugin is referring to his book *We Have Never Been Modern* (Cambridge: Harvard University Press, 1993). In it, he argues that ancient peoples made no distinction between society and the natural world, unlike in the modern world.-Ed.

4   Georges Dumézil (1898-1986) was a French philologist best known as a pioneer in mythography. He also studied the nature of sovereignty in ancient Indo-European civilisations, which led him to postulate the Trifunctional Hypothesis: namely, that Indo-European culture had developed along a tripartite structure of warriors, priests and farmers. He believed that this was the origin of both the Hindu caste system and the feudal system in Medieval Europe.-Ed.

5   Euhemerism is named after the Fourth-century BCE Greek mythographer Euhemerus, who claimed that the Greek gods had their origin in the oral transmission of tales that were originally about great human beings, but which over time became elevated to the status of gods. Those who follow euhemerism likewise believe that myths and tales from the sacred traditions have their origin in actual historical events, albeit elaborated upon. Dumézil instead saw them as symbolic representations of sociopolitical realities.-Ed.

6   Gilbert Durand (b. 1921) is a French professor of philosophy who specialises in symbolic anthropology and the imagination. He is a member of the Eranos group and worked with C. G. Jung, Gaston Bachelard and Henry Corbin. He has theorised that there is a correspondence between physiology and the structure of society.-Ed.

and political semantic *occasions*, as in occasionalist theory.[7] Progress and modernisation are real, but relative, not absolute. What is meant are specified stages, but not the absolute trend of history. This is why the Fourth Political Theory suggests an alternative version of political history based on systematised occasionalism. Carl Schmitt was very close to this in his work. Fernand Braudel and the École des Annales have also been inspired by this in their writing. In the discussion of the political transformation of society, we place them in their specific semantic context: history, religion, philosophy, economics, and culture, with its ethnic and ethnic-sociological specifics considered. This demands a new classification of social and political transformation. We acknowledge these transformations, but we do not place them onto a broad-based scale that could be the common 'destiny' for all societies. This gives us political pluralism.

The Fourth Political Theory uses a societally-dependent conception of reversible time. In the context of modernity, turning back from some point in history to a previous one is impossible. But it is possible in the context of Fourth Political Theory. Berdyaev's idea of the 'New Middle Ages'[8] is quite applicable. Societies can be variously built and transformed. The experience of the 1990s is quite demonstrative of this: people in the Soviet Union were sure that socialism would proceed from capitalism, not vice versa. But in the 1990s they saw the opposite: capitalism following socialism. It is quite possible that Russia could yet see feudalism, or even a slave-owning society, or perhaps a Communist or primordial society emerge after that. Those who laugh at this are the captives of the modern and its hypnosis. Having acknowledged the reversibility of political and historical time, we have arrived at a new pluralist point-of-view for political science, and we have reached the advanced perspective necessary for ideological construction.

The Fourth Political Theory constructs, and reconstructs, society behind modern axioms. That is why the elements of the different political forms can be used in the Fourth Political Theory without any connection

---

7   Occasionalist theory, was originally quite prominent in Islam, and was later transmitted to Christian theology and was also taken up by Descartes and his followers. In it, all events are said to have their ultimate cause in God, since matter is incapable of causing them. The theory also maintains that God is rational and that the events he causes therefore have a logical sequence.-Ed.

8   Nikolai Berdyaev (1874-1948) was an influential Russian millenarian mystic and political philosopher. He was originally a Communist, but refused to support the Russian Revolution of 1917 due to his objection to the Communists' authoritarianism and atheism. He was expelled from the Soviet Union in 1922 and lived the rest of his life in Paris. In his book *The End of Our Time* (1924), he prophesied the imminent end of liberalism and humanism, and the return of what he termed a New Middle Ages, which would include a return to civlisations based upon religion and mysticism.-Ed.

to the time scale. There are no stages and epochs, but only pre-concepts and concepts. In this context, theological constructions, antiquity, caste and other aspects of traditional society are only some of the possible variants; along with socialism, Keynesian theory,[9] free markets, parliamentary democracy, or 'nationalism'. They are simply forms, but they would not be related to an implied topography of 'objective historical time'. There is no such thing! If time is 'historical', it is cannot 'objective'. *Dasein* says the same. *Dasein* is the subject of the Fourth Political Theory. *Dasein* can be recovered by the refinement of the existential truth derived from the ontological superstructure of society. *Dasein* is something that institutionalizes time. Durand institutionalises time by *Traiectum*[10] in his topography. Traiectum/*Dasein* is not a function of time, but time is a function of Traiectum/*Dasein*. This is why time is something that is institutionalised by politics in the context of the Fourth Political Theory. Time is a political category. *Political time is a pre-concept of a political form.*

The Fourth Political Theory has opened a unique perspective: if we comprehend the principle of the reversibility of time, we are not only able to compose the project of a future society, but we will also be able to compose a whole range of projects of different future societies — thus we would be able to suggest some non-linear strategies for a new institutionalisation of the world.

The Fourth Political Theory is not an invitation to a return to traditional society; i.e., it is not conservatism in the conventional sense. There are many characteristics of our chronological past which are pleasant, and many which are not. Similarly, the forms of traditional society can also be distinguished from each other. Finally, the ethnic and sociological matrixes, and the contexts of different contemporary societies, are also different from each other. Therefore, the Fourth Political Theory should not impose anything on anyone. Adherents of the Fourth Political Theory should act step by step: if we simply argue the reversibility of time and *Dasein* as the subjects of our theory, that would be the first and primary step. We would thus free ourselves to develop the pre-concepts. We can define several pre-concepts with regards to the reversibility of time and *Dasein*/Traiectum, and therefore we can define several political concepts of time. And each of them can be plugged into the current political project, according to the principles of the Fourth Political Theory.

---

9   John Maynard Keynes (1883-1946) was a British economist whose ideas regarding the the possibilities of the free market and business cycles have been extraordinarily influential.-Ed.

10 Traiectum was the Roman name for what is today the city of Utrecht in the Netherlands, so named because it was a place where it was possible to cross the Rhine.-Ed.

5

GLOBAL TRANSITION AND ITS ENEMIES

The World Order Questioned

The New World Order (NWO) as a concept was popularised at a concrete historical moment — namely, when the Cold War ended in the late 1980s and genuine global cooperation between the United States and Soviet Union was considered not only possible, but very probable. The basis of the NWO was presumably a product of convergence theory, predicting the synthesis of the Soviet socialist and Western capitalist political forms and close cooperation of the Soviet Union and USA in the case of regional issues — for example, in the first Gulf War at the beginning of 1991. However, as the Soviet Union collapsed soon after this, the project of a NWO was naturally set aside and forgotten.

After 1991, the New World Order was considered to be something under formation before our very eyes — a unipolar world led by the open global hegemony of the USA. It is well-described in Fukuyama's utopian work, *The End of History and the Last Man*. This world order ignored all other poles of power except the USA and its allies, including Western Europe and Japan. It was conceived as a universalisation of free market economics, political democracy, and the ideology of human rights, all of which were assumed to be part of a global system that would be accepted by all countries in the world.

Skeptics, however, thought that this was rather illusionary and that the differences between countries and peoples would reappear in other forms, for example, in Samuel Huntington's infamous 'clash of civilisations' thesis, or in ethnic or religious conflicts. Some experts, in particular John Mearsheimer,[1]

---

1   John Mearsheimer (b. 1947) is an American political scientist. He is perhaps best-known for having co-authored the book *The Israel Lobby and U.S. Foreign Policy* with Stephen Walt in 2007, which detailed the influence of special interest groups that support Israeli policies on the US government.-Ed.

regarded unipolarity not as a 'proper' world order but, rather, as 'unipolar momentum'.

In any case, what is questioned in all these projects is the existing order of nation-states and national sovereignty. The Westphalian system[2] no longer corresponds to the current global balance of powers. New actors of trans-national and sub-national scale are affirming their growing importance, and it is evident that the world is in need of a new paradigm in international relations.

Therefore, the contemporary world as we have it today cannot be regarded as a properly-realised NWO. There is no definitive world order of any kind. What we have instead is the transition from the world order we knew in the Twentieth century to some other paradigm whose features are yet to be fully defined. Will the future really be global? Or will regionalist tendencies dominate? Will there be one unique world order? Or will there instead be various local or regional orders? Or, perhaps, will we have to deal with global chaos? It is not yet clear. The transition is not accomplished. We are living in the middle of it.

If the global elite, and first of all the American political and economic elite, has a clear vision of the future, which is rather doubtful, circumstances may and can prevent its realisation in practice. If, however, the global elite lack a consensual project, the issue becomes much more complicated.

So only the fact of transition to some new paradigm is certain. The paradigm as such is, to the contrary, quite uncertain.

World Order from the American Point-of-View

The position of the United States during this shift is absolutely assured but its long-term future is under question. The US is now undergoing a test of its global imperial rule and has to deal with many challenges, some of them quite new and original. This could proceed in three different ways:

1) Creation of an American Empire *stricto sensu*[3] with a consolidated and technically and socially developed central area, or imperial core, with the periphery kept divided and fragmented in a state

2   The Thirty Years' War ended with the Peace of Westphalia in 1648, in which the nations of Europe recognised each others' territorial integrity. Some historians consider it to have been the first step in the development of the modern-day system of international relations.-Ed.

3   Latin: 'in a strict sense'.-Ed.

of permanent unrest, bordering chaos. The neoconservatives, it would seem, are in favour of such a pattern.

2) Creation of a multilateral unipolarity where the USA would cooperate with other friendly powers (Canada, Europe, Australia, Japan, Israel, Arab allies, and possibly other countries) in solving regional problems and putting pressure on 'rogue states' (such as Iran, Venezuela, Belarus, or North Korea), or preventing other powers from achieving regional independence and hegemony (China, Russia, etc.). It would seem that the Democrats and President Obama are inclined to this vision.

3) Promotion of accelerated globalisation with the creation of a world government and swift de-sovereignisation of nation-states in favour of the creation of a 'United States' of the world ruled by the global elite on legal terms (for example, the CFR project represented by the strategy of George Soros and his foundations).[4] The Colour Revolutions[5] are viewed here as the most effective weapon of destabilising and finally destroying states).

The US often seems to be simultaneously promoting all three strategies at the same time, as part of a multi-vector foreign policy. These three strategic directions of the USA create the global context in international relations, the USA being the key actor on a global scale. Beyond the evident differences between these three images of the future, they have some essential points in common. In any case, the USA is interested in affirming its strategic, economic and political domination; in strengthening its control of other global actors and in weakening them; in the gradual or

---

4   The Council on Foreign Relations (CFR) is a privately-owned political think tank in the United States, which has its origins in the peace process at the end of the First World War. The CFR, it itself claims, seeks to influence global politics in a direction that provides peaceful conflict resolutions and multilateralism.George Soros (b. 1930) is an American billionaire who uses his wealth to promote liberal causes around the world. He funded many dissident groups in Eastern Europe and the USSR during the Cold War, and continues to support democratic causes there. Critics have said that Soros is merely acting as an agent of American foreign policy interests.-Ed.

5   The Colour Revolutions was a term coined by the international media to describe various uprisings that took place in the nations of the former Soviet Union and the Balkans during the early 2000s, and later for various Middle Eastern revolutions as well. In each case, mass demonstrations of a peaceful nature succeeded in overthrowing leaders perceived as authoritarian, such as in Serbia, Georgia and Ukraine. Many of these revolts were associated with a specific colour (such as the Orange Revolution in Ukraine), hence the name. Opponents have often claimed that these revolutions were backed by the US government or the Soros Foundation.-Ed.

accelerated de-sovereignisation of what are now more or less independent states; and in the promotion of supposedly 'universal' values reflecting the values of the Western world, i.e. liberal democracy, parliamentarianism, free markets, humans rights, and so on.

Therefore we face a contemporary world in a strong and seemingly permanent geopolitical arrangement where the US is the core, and where the rays or spokes of its influence (strategic, economic, political, technological, informational and so on) permeate all the rest of the world, depending on the strength of the societal willof the various countries, as well as ethnic and religious groups, to accept or reject it. It is a kind of imperial network operating on a planetary scale.

This US-centric global geopolitical arrangement can be described on several different levels:

Historically: The USA considers itself to be the logical conclusion and peak of Western civilisation. At one time, this was presented in terms of the 'Manifest Destiny' of America,[6] and then in terms of the Monroe Doctrine.[7] Now they speak in terms of enforcement of 'universal' human rights norms, promotion of democracy, technology, free market institutions and so on. But in essence, we are simply dealing with an updated version and continuation of a Western universalism that has been passed down from the Roman Empire, Medieval Christianity, modernity in terms of the Enlightenment and colonisation, up to the present-day phenomena of postmodernism and ultra-individualism. History is considered to be a univocal and monotone process of technological and social progress, the path of the growing liberation of individuals from all kinds of collective identities. Tradition and conservatism are thus regarded as obstacles to freedom and should be rejected. The USA is in the vanguard of this historical progress, and has the right, obligation, and historical mission

6   Manifest Destiny was a term coined by an American journalist, John L. O'Sullivan, in 1845 in an article which called for the annexation of the then-independent territories of Texas and Oregon. The term refers to the belief that it was the natural destiny of the United States to expand across the North American continent. The term was picked up by those who shared O'Sullivan's view, and was used by Democrats to justify the 1846-48 Mexican-American War.-Ed.

7   The Monroe Doctrine was proclaimed by US President James Monroe in 1823, just after most of the nations of Latin America had proclaimed their independence from Spain. Fearing that other colonial powers might try to move in, Monroe declared that the United States would regard any European intervention in the American hemisphere as an act of aggression against itself. President Theodore Roosevelt added a corollary in 1904, stating that the US also reserves the right to intervene in the case of 'wrongdoing' by any Latin American government. The Monroe Doctrine has continued to be invoked by the US up to the 1980s, when it was used to justify American intervention in Nicaragua.-Ed.

to move history further and further along this path. The historical existence of the US coincides with the course of human history. So, 'American'
means 'universal'. The other cultures either have an American future or
no future at all.

Politically: There are very important trends in global politics that
define the transition. The peak of the political thought of modernity was
the victory of liberalism over the alternative political doctrines of modernity: fascism and socialism. Liberalism has gone global and become the
only possible political system. It is now progressing further towards a
postmodern and post-individual concept of politics, generally described
as post-humanism. The USA again plays the key role in it. The form
of politics promoted globally by the USA is liberal democracy. The US
supports the globalisation of liberalism, thus preparing the next step to
political postmodernity as described in *Empire*, the famous book by Hardt
and Negri.[8] There remains some distance between liberal ultra-individualism and properly postmodern post-humanism, promoting cybernetics,
genetic modification, cloning and chimeras. [9]But the world's periphery
still faces the universalising process — the accelerated destruction of all
holistic social entities, and the fragmentation and atomisation of society,
including via technology (the Internet, mobile phones, social networks),
where the principal actor is strictly the individual, divorced from any
organic and collective social context.

An important testimony to the dual use of the promotion of democracy has been explicitly described in an article by the American military
and political expert, Stephen R. Mann,[10] who affirmed that democracy
can work as a self-generating virus, strengthening existing and historically ripe democratic societies, but destroying and causing traditional
societies that are not prepared for it to descend into chaos. So democracy is thought to be an effective weapon to create chaos and to govern
the dissipating world cultures from the core, emulating and installing the
democratic codex everywhere. Evidence of this process can be seen in the
chaotic aftermath of the heady events of the so-called 'Arab Spring'. After

---

8   Michael Hardt and Antonio Negri, *Empire* (Cambridge: Harvard University Press,
    2000). In the book it is postulated that the world is in the process of moving away
    from the traditional relations between various nation-state and into a new world domi-
    nated by the United States and NATO, as well as multinational corporations, with
    everything else in the world in a subservient relationship to them.-Ed.

9   In genetic engineering, a chimera is a genetic hybrid between animal and human
    DNA.-Ed.

10 Stephen R. Mann, "Chaos Theory and Strategic Thought," *Parameters* (Autumn
    1992), available at www.dtic.mil/cgi-bin/GetTRDoc?AD=ADA528321.-Ed.

accomplishing the full fragmentation of these societies into individualisation and atomisation, the second phase will begin: the inevitable division and dissolution of the individual human itself via technology and genetic tinkering to create a 'posthumanity'. This 'post-politics' can be seen as the last horizon of political futurism.

Ideologically: There is a tendency for the US to increasingly link ideology and politics in their relations with the periphery. In earlier times, American foreign policy acted on the basis of pure pragmatic realism. If the regimes were pro-American, they were tolerated without regard for their ideological principles. The longstanding US-Saudi Arabian alliance represents the perfect example of this realist foreign policy in practice. Thus, some features of this schizophrenic and dual morality were ideologically accepted. However, It seems that recently the US has begun to try to deepen its promotion of democracy, supporting popular revolts in Egypt and Tunisia despite the fact that their leaders were trusted allies of the US as well as corrupt dictators. The double standards in the US's political ideology are slowly vanishing, and the deepening of the promotion of democracy progresses. The climax will be reached in the case of probable unrest in Saudi Arabia. When this happens, this ideological pro-democracy stance will be tested in politically difficult and inconvenient circumstances.

Economically: The US economy is challenged by Chinese growth, energy security and scarcity, crippling debt and budget deficits, and the critical divergence and disproportion between the financial sector and the zone of real industry. The overgrowth, or bubble, of the American financial institutions and the delocalisation of industry have created a discontinuity between the sphere of money and the sphere of the classical capitalist balance of industrial supply and consumer demands. This was the main cause of the financial crisis of 2008. The Chinese political economy is trying to reestablish its independence from US global hegemony and may become the main factor of economic competition. The control that Russia, Iran, Venezuela and some other relatively independent countries have over large reservoirs of the world's remaining natural resources puts a limit on American economic influence. The economy of the EU and Japanese economic potential represent two possible poles of economic competition to the US inside the economic and strategic framework of the West.

The USA attempts to solve these problems using not only purely economic instruments, but also political and, at times, military power as well. We could thus interpret the invasion and occupations of Iraq and Afghanistan, as well as the interventions both overt and covert in Libya, Iran and Syria from a geoeconomic and geopolitical perspective. Promotion of domestic political opposition and insurgents in Russia, Iran and China are another, similar method towards the same goal. But these are only technical solutions. The main challenge is how to organise the post-modern and finance-centric economy around continuing growth, overcoming the widening critical gap between the real economy and the financial sector whose logic and self-interest become more and more autonomous.

It has been asserted that the USA is the main and asymmetric actor in the centre of the present transition state of world affairs. As Védrine[11] has noted, this actor is a true hyperpower, and the present geopolitical arrangement that includes all the levels and networks examined above is structured around this American core. The question then raised is: is this actor fully conscious of what it does and does it fully understand what it will obtain at the end, that is, which form of international system or world order is it going to establish? Opinions on this important point are divided. The neocons proclaiming the New American Century[12] are optimistic as to the future American Empire, but in their case it is obvious that they have a clear, if not necessarily realistic, vision of an American-dominated future. In this case, the world order will be an American imperial order based on unipolar geopolitics. At least theoretically, it has one redeeming point: it is clear and honest about its goals and intentions.

The multilateralists are more cautious, and insist on the necessity of inviting the other regional powers to share the burden of global hegemony with the USA. It is obvious that only societies similar to the USA can be partners, so the success of the promotion of democracy becomes an essential feature. The multilateralists act not only in the name of the USA but also in the name of the West, whose values are, or must be made, universal. Their vision of a future world order dictated by global democracy, but led by the US, is foggier and not as clearly defined as the neocons' American Empire.

---

11 Hubert Védrine (b. 1947) is a French politician of the Socialist Party. An opponent of the unilateral action of the United States in Iraq, he popularised the term 'hyperpower' to describe the unprecedented influence of the US in the world in the Twenty-first century.-Ed.

12 The Project for the New American Century was a private institute established in 1997 which served as a mouthpiece for neoconservative thought until it was disbanded in 2006. The Project sought to develop ways to maintain and extend American supremacy into the Twenty-first century, and many of its members were either part of or influential upon the administration of President George W. Bush.-Ed.

Even hazier is the extreme vision of global governance envisaged by promoters of accelerated globalisation. It might be possible to effectively overthrow the existing order of sovereign nation-states, but in many cases, this will only open the door to more archaic, local, religious or ethnic forces and conflicts. The vision of a single open and, by necessity, largely homogenous society encompassing the Earth is so fantastic and utopian that it is much easier to imagine the total chaos of Hobbes' 'war of all against all'[13] in the state of nature of a world without states.

The visions of possible future world orders from the perspective of the US and the West differs among competing factions of American elites, ideologists, and decision-makers. The most consequent and well-defined strategy, the neocons' unipolar world order, is at the same time more ethnocentric, openly imperialistic and hegemonic. The other two versions are much more dimly conceived and uncertain. Thus, it is as likely they could lead to an increase in global disorder, as order. Richard Haass[14] has termed the paradigms of an international system according to these two visions as being characterised by 'non-polarity'.

So the *transition* in question is, in any case, American-centric by its nature, and the global geopolitical arrangement is structured so that the main global processes would be moderated, orientated, directed, and sometimes controlled by the unique hyperpower actor performing its work alone or with the help of its Western allies and regional client states.

The World Order from the Non-American Point-of-View

The Americano-centric world perspective described above, despite being the most important and central global tendency, is not the only one possible. There can be and there are alternative visions of world political architecture that can be taken into consideration. There are secondary and tertiary actors that are inevitable losers in the case of the success of the American strategies; the countries, states, peoples, and cultures that

---

13 Thomas Hobbes (1588-1679) was an English political philosopher who laid many of the theoretical foundations for modern liberal societies. In his book *Leviathan* (1651), the 'war of all against all' would be the condition of the human race in a theoretical world without any form of government.-Ed.

14 Richard N. Haass (b. 1951) is an American diplomat and has been the President of the Council on Foreign Relations since 2003. He served as an advisor to President George H. W. Bush during the Persian Gulf War of 1991. He described his view of non-polarity in an essay, 'The Age of Nonpolarity: What Will Follow U.S. Dominance', in *Foreign Affairs* (May/June 2008).-Ed.

would lose everything, even their own identity, and gain nothing if the USA realised its global aspirations. They are both multiple and heterogeneous, and can be grouped into several different categories.

The first category is composed by the more or less successful nation-states that are not happy to lose their independence to a supranational exterior authority — not in the form of open American hegemony, nor in the Western-centric forms of world government or governance, nor in the chaotic dissolution of a failed international system. There are many such countries — foremost among them are China, Russia, Iran, and India, but it also includes many South American and Islamic states. They do not like the transition at all, suspecting, with good reason, the inevitable loss of their sovereignty. So, they are inclined to resist the main trends of the global American-centric geopolitical arrangement or adapt to it in such a manner that it would be possible to avoid the logical consequences of its success, be it via an imperialist or globalist strategy. The will to preservation of sovereignty represents the natural contradiction and point of resistance in the face of American/Western hegemonic or globalist trends. Generally speaking, these states lack an alternative vision of the future international system or world order, and certainly do not have a unified or common vision. What they all want and share in common is a desire to preserve the international status quo as enshrined in the UN Charter, and thus their own sovereignty and identity as nation-states in their present form, adjusting and modernising them as an internal and sovereign process as necessary.

Among this group of nation-states seeking to preserve their sovereignty in the face of US/Western hegemonic or globalist strategies are:

1) Those states who try to adapt their societies to Western standards and to keep friendly relations with the West and the USA, but to avoid direct and total de-sovereignisation; this includes India, Turkey, Brazil, and up to a certain point Russia and Kazakhstan.

2) Those states who are ready to cooperate with the USA, but under the condition of non-interference in their domestic affairs, such as Saudi Arabia and Pakistan.

3) Those states who, while cooperating with the USA, strictly observe the uniqueness of their society by filtering those elements of Western culture that are compatible with their domestic culture from those which are not, and, at the same time, trying to use the dividends received by this cooperation to strengthen their national independence, such as China, and, at times, Russia.

4) Those states who try to oppose the USA directly, rejecting Western values, unipolarity, and US/Western hegemony, including Iran, Venezuela, and North Korea.

However, all of these groups lack an alternative global strategy that could be symmetrically comparable with American visions of the future, even if taken without consensus or a clearly defined goal. All these states generally act individually on the world stage and in their own direct interests. The difference in foreign policy among them consists only in the amount of radicalism in their rejection of Americanisation. Their position can be defined as reactive. This strategy of reactive opposition, varying from rejection to adaptation, is sometimes effective, and sometimes not. In short, it offers no kind of alternate future vision. Instead, the future of the world order or international system is considered as eternal conservation of the status quo, i.e. modernity, nation-states, the Westphalian system of state sovereignty, and strict interpretation and preservation of the existing UN Charter and UN configuration.

The second category of actors who reject the transition consists of sub-national groups, movements, and organisations that oppose American dominance of the structures of the global geopolitical arrangement for ideological, religious, and/or cultural reasons. These groups are quite different from one another and vary from state to state. Most of them are founded on an interpretation of religious faith that is incompatible with the secular doctrine of Americanisation, Westernisation, and globalisation. But they can also be motivated by ethnic or ideological (for example. socialist or Communist) considerations or doctrines. Others may even act on regionalist grounds.

The paradox is that in the process of globalisation, which aims to universalise and make uniform all particularities and collective identities on the basis of a purely individual identity, such sub-national actors easily become transnational — the same religions and ideologies often being present in different nations and across state borders. Thus, among these non-state actors we could potentially find some alternative vision of the future world order or international system that can stand opposed to the American/Western-led transition and its structures.

We can roughly summarise the different ideas of some of the more important sub-national/trans-national groups as follows:

• The most recognised form at present is the Islamist world vision, which aspires toward the utopia of an individual state based upon a strict interpretation of Islamic law, or else a Universal Caliphate which will bring the entire world under Islamic rule. This project is as much opposed to the American-led transitional architecture as it is to the existing status quo of modern nation-states. Osama bin Laden's Al Qaeda remains symbolic and archetypal of such ideas, and the attacks which brought down the towers of the World Trade Centre in New York on 9/11, and which are supposed to have 'changed the world', are proof of the importance of such networks and the seriousness with which they must be taken.

- Another such project can be defined as the transnational neo-socialist plan represented in the South American Left, and personally by Hugo Chávez. This is roughly a new version of the Marxist critique of capitalism, strengthened by nationalist emotion, and, in some cases, such as the Zapatistas and Bolivia, in ethnic sentiments or Green ecological critiques. Some Arab regimes, such as the Libyan Arab Jamahiriya under Gaddafi until recently, can be considered in the same vein. The vision of the future world order is here presented as global socialist revolution proceeded by anti-American liberation campaigns in every country across the globe. The US/Western-led transition is envisioned by this group as an incarnation of the classic imperialism criticised by Lenin.[15]

- A third such example can be found in the Eurasianist (aka multipolarity, Great Spaces, or Great Powers) project, proposing an alternative model of world order based on the paradigm of unique civilisations and Great Powers. It presupposes the creation of different transnational political, strategic, and economic entities united regionally by the community of common geographic areas and shared values, in some cases religious and in others secular and/or cultural. They should consist of states integrated along regionalist lines and represent the poles of the multipolar world. The European Union is one such example; the nascent Eurasian Union proposed by Russia's Vladimir Putin and Kazakhstan's President Nursultan Nazarbayev, another. An Islamic Union, a South American/Bolivarian[16] Union, a Chinese Union, an Indian Union,

---

15 Lenin outlined his concept of imperialism in his book *Imperialism, the Highest Stage of Capitalism* (1917), in which he theorised that capitalist nations eventually exhaust the possibilities for economic growth in their own lands and will inevitably resort to war and colonialism to secure additional resources for continued growth.-Ed.

16 Bolivarianism refers to political ideologies derived from the doctrines of Símon Bolívar, the Nineteenth-century Venezuelan General who fought for the independence of the Latin American colonies from Spain. In today's world this refers to the

or a Pan-Pacific Union are other possibilities. The North American Great Space, covering today's NAFTA, would be regarded as just one among several other more or less equal poles, nothing more.

This is not an all-inclusive list of such non-state actors or theories with alternate visions of world order. There are others, but they are of smaller scale and thus beyond the scope of this work.

In the present state of world affairs, there is a serious divide between the nation-states and the sub-state or transnational actors and ideological movements operating on different levels, mentioned above. The nation-states lack vision and ideology, and the alternative movements lack sufficient infrastructure and resources to put their ideas into practice. If, in some circumstance, it were possible to bridge that gap, taking into consideration the increasing demographic, economic, and strategic weight of the non-Western world, or 'the Rest', an alternative to the American/Western-led transition could obtain realistic shape and be regarded seriously as a consequential and theoretically sound alternate paradigm for world order.

---

desire for a Latin American union dedicated to defending the interests of all peoples on the continent. It is especially influential in Hugo Chávez's Venezuela.-Ed.

6

CONSERVATISM AND POSTMODERNITY

We Are in Postmodernity

The process that, in fact, has a global character is the process of once-victorious modernism's movement into postmodernity. There are centres, foci, loci and regions where this process proceeds logically and sequentially. These are the West, Western Europe, and especially the United States of America, where there was a historical opportunity to create in laboratory conditions the optimal society of modernity, on the basis of those principles that were developed by Western European thought; to create from a blank page, without the burden of European traditions, in an 'empty' place — Native Americans, as is known, were not reckoned as people. Michael Hardt and Antonio Negri show in their book *Empire* that the American Constitution looked at African-Americans from the start as second-class people, while the Native Americans were not thought of as people at all. In such a way, the specific American system was an ideal place for the realisation of a maximum of freedom, but only for White people, and at the cost of a determinate exclusion of all others. In any case, the United States of America is the avant-garde of freedom and the locomotive of the transition to postmodernism.

The Liberty Pole and the Freedom to Choose TV Stations

We spoke of the pole that is Western European civilisation, but within the spaces of thought, in philosophy, and in the geography of the human soul, the pole of a unipolar world is nothing other than the United States and Europe, as a purely geopolitical organisation, and specifically the idea of maximal freedom. And the movement toward the realisation of this freedom is the significance of human history, as Western European humanity understands it. Western European society managed to bind the rest of humanity to this conception of the significance of history.

Thus, there exists the pole of a unipolar world — that is, the pole of freedom, which arrived at modernity and is now moving to a new stage, to postmodernity, in which a man begins to free himself from himself, insofar as he encumbers, interferes with and is bored of himself. He disintegrates into 'schizo-masses', as is written in Deleuze's *Anti-Oedipus*.[1]

People have become contemplators upon television, having learned to change the channel better and more quickly. Many do not stop at all: they click the remote, and it no longer matters what is on — a comedy or the news. The spectator of postmodernism basically understands nothing of what happens; there is just a stream of pictures, which amuse. Television viewers are drawn into micro-processes, they become those who have not got their fill of the spectacle, 'sub-spectators', who never watch an entire programme from start to finish, but only bits and pieces of various programmes. To demonstrate this, the ideal film is Rodriguez's *Spy Kids 2*.[2] It is made in such a way that there is no meaning in it. But distraction from it is impossible, because as soon as our consciousness becomes bored of it, a flying pig suddenly appears, and we must continue watching to see to where it flies. And exactly in the same way, the moment the flying pig bores us, a little dragon climbs out of the hero's pocket. This production of Rodriguez's is faultless. In principle, the man who indefatigably changes channels will find approximately the same effect here. The only channel that works according to a different rhythm is that dedicated to 'culture', because there one can still find unhurried histories of composers, artists, scholars, theatre — that is, the remnants of modernity. If it were removed from the bill, then one could calmly click through the channels not expecting to find anything that goes against the rhythm in which one must live.

The Paradoxes of Freedom

And so, postmodernity arrives. What can oppose it? And can one say 'no' to it? This is the fundamental question.

Incidentally, emerging from that same liberal thesis which contends that man is free, it follows that he is always free to say 'no', to say this to

---

1   Gilles Deleuze and Félix Guattari, *Anti-Oedipus: Capitalism and Schizophrenia* (New York: Penguin Books, 2009).-Ed.

2   *Spy Kids 2: The Island of Lost Dreams* was released in 2002, directed by the American director, Robert Rodriguez.-Ed.

whomever he will. This, in fact, constitutes the dangerous moment of the philosophy of freedom, which under the aegis of absolute freedom begins to remove the freedom to say 'no' to freedom itself. The Western liberal model says: you want to oppose us? Please, you have the right; but, look: you will not want to give your washing machine back, right? The washing machine is the absolute argument of the supporters of progress. After all, everyone wants a washing machine — Black people, native peoples, conservatives and the orthodox. Communists, too, according to a different logic, spoke of the necessity and irreversibility of structural change. They said that socialism would come after capitalism. Socialism came, although we plainly never had capitalism. It stayed around for some time, destroyed quite a lot of people, and then disappeared. It is exactly thus with the washing machine. If one thinks about the metaphysics of the washing machine, to what extent it is coupled with the real values of a philosophical system, one will be able to come to the conclusion that, in general, human life is possible, and perhaps even has the potential to be entirely happy, without the washing machine.

But for a liberal society, this is a terrifying thing, almost sacrilege. We can understand everything, but life without the washing machine? That's already a really unscientific saying: life without the washing machine is impossible. There is no such thing. Life is the washing machine. In this resides the effect of the force of the liberal argument, which takes on a totalitarian character. There is always an element of some kind of constraint in liberation — this is the paradox of freedom. At the very least, there are the constraints of having to think that freedom is the highest value. Imagine that one person says, 'Freedom is the highest value.' Another responds, 'No, it isn't.' Then the first answers, 'You're against freedom? I will kill for freedom!'

The idea is contained in liberalism that there can be no alternatives to it. And in this there is some truth. If logos put itself onto the path of freedom, if the social logos was pulled into the adventure of total liberation, where was the first shove in this direction? It must be sought not in Descartes, Nietzsche or the Twentieth century, but back with the Pre-Socratics. Heidegger saw this moment in the conception of physis[3] and in the way it was disclosed in Plato's teaching of the idea. But what is important is something else: the movement of logos to freedom is not accidental, but nevertheless one can say 'no' to it.

---

3   Classical Greek: 'nature'.-Ed.

Conservatism as the Repudiation of the Logic of History

There is, nevertheless, the ontological possibility of saying 'no'. And from this begins conservatism.

First, what is conservatism? It is a 'no' said to that which is around one. In the name of what? In the name of something that came earlier. In the name of that which, properly speaking, was overcome at some point during sociopolitical history. That is, conservatism is the pursuit of an ontological, philosophical, sociopolitical, individual, natural, religious, cultural, and scientific position that repudiates the movements of things that we are at this time encountering, and which we identified and described earlier.

We are speaking now of conservatism and that with which one can deny the very course of history, pushing away from the sort of social-political topography that has driven us to modernity and postmodernity. This means the new age of modernity, with its linear vectors of progress and with its postmodern contortions, which are taking us away into the labyrinths of the disintegration of individual reality and to the rhizomatic subject or post-subject. But one can include here also earlier stages, which made this tendency possible and dominant. Conservatism builds its position on an opposition to the logic of the unfolding of the historical process. The phenomenology of modernity — as, in our time, of postmodernity — the rot of which conservatism seeks to reject, serves as an argument in this opposition. But conservatism as a structure does not lead to an impugning of phenomena. Negatively valued phenomenology here is not more than a pretext. Conservatism constructs a topography that rejects the logic, work and direction of historical time.

Conservatism can build up its opposition to historical time in different ways. It has three fundamental possibilities for relating to the conceptual trends of modernity and postmodernity. And from this begins the systematisation or structuralisation of conservatism. This is a systematisation without any preferences whatsoever, because the discussion is of scientific, and not of valuated judgements.

Fundamental Conservatism: Traditionalism

The first approach is so-called traditionalism. Conservatism could well be traditionalism. In some models of political science, traditionalism and conservatism differ; as, for instance, in Mannheim's.[4] But nevertheless, the aspiration to leave everything as it was in traditional societies, to preserve that way of life, is, undoubtedly, conservatism.

A more logical traditionalism — substantial, philosophical, ontological and conceptual — is one that criticises, not various aspects of modernity and postmodernity, but that rejects the fundamental vector of historical development — that is, one that essentially opposes time. Traditionalism is that form of conservatism which contends the following: what is bad are not those separate fragments here and there within a larger system that call out for our repudiation. In the contemporary world, everything is bad. 'The idea of progress is bad; the idea of technological development is bad; Descartes' philosophy of the subject and object is bad; Newton's metaphor of the watchmaker is bad;[5] contemporary positive science, and the education and pedagogy founded upon it, are bad.' 'This episteme', reasons the conservative traditionist, 'is no good. It is a totalitarian, false, negative episteme, against which one must fight.' And further, if we think his thought through: 'I like only that which existed before the start of modernity.' One could go further and subject those tendencies to criticism that in traditional society itself made possible the appearance of modernity, all the way up to the idea of linear time.

Such traditionalist conservatism, after the fall of monarchs, the separation of Church and State, and the taking up of the baton of modernity by all sociopolitical, cultural and historical nations, was thought to be non-existent. In Russia, it was exterminated by atheist militants. From a certain point of view, it is certainly so. Inasmuch as it was thought to have been completely eliminated, people almost stopped talking about it; of social groups that stood on these positions, practically none remained, and it soon enough disappeared even from some models of political science (e.g., Mannheim's). For that reason, we do not see it nor begin from it. And this is unjust. If we want to trace genuine conservatism and construct a completed topography of conservative positions, we must, as a

---

4   Karl Mannheim (1893-1947) was a Hungarian sociologist whose most important work was *Ideology and Utopia* (1936). Here Dugin is referring to his book *Conservatism: A Contribution to the Sociology of Knowledge* (New York: Routledge & Kegan Paul, 1986), although it should be noted that Mannheim used the term 'traditionalism' after Max Weber, in the sense of one who clings to the customs established in previous times within one's own society, and not in the sense of Guénon.-Ed.

5   Isaac Newton believed that the physical laws he had uncovered revealed the mechanical perfection of the workings of the universe to be akin to a watchmaker, wherein the watchmaker is God. However, Newton also believed that, like a watchmaker, God was forced to intervene in the universe and tinker with the mechanism from time to time to ensure that it continued operating in good working order.-Ed.

first priority, study precisely such an approach. In traditionalism we have a full-blown and mostly complete complex of the conservative relationship to history, society and the world.

In the Twentieth century, when, it would seem, no social platform remained at all for such a conservatism, there suddenly appears a whole galaxy of thinkers: philosophers who begin to defend this traditionalist position. What is more, they do so with radicalism, consistency and persistence, and not with the thoughts of the Nineteenth or Eighteenth centuries. These are René Guénon, Julius Evola, Titus Burckhardt, Leopold Ziegler, and all those who are called 'traditionalists' in the narrow sense of the word. It is significant that in the Nineteenth century, when there were still monarchs and churches, and when the Pope still decided something, there was no one who held such radical opinions. Traditionalists advanced the programme of fundamental conservatism, when matters concerning Tradition approached their nadir. In this way, fundamental conservatism was able to be formulated into a philosophical, political and ideological model once modernism had practically conquered all positions, but not while there were definite political and social forces still actively struggling against it.

A number of political scientists in the Twentieth century attempted to identify or to tie together the influence of fundamental conservatism with fascism. Louis Pauwels and Jacques Bergier, the authors of the book *The Morning of the Magicians*,[6] wrote, 'It could be said that Hitlerism, in a sense, was "Guénonism" plus tanks.'[7] This, of course, is definitely not so. Fascism is sooner the philosophy of modernity, which, to a significant degree, is contaminated with elements of traditional society, though it does not protest against modernity nor against time. Moreover, both Guénon and Evola harshly criticised fascism.

In their works, Guénon and Evola gave an exhaustive description of the most fundamental conservative position. They described traditional society as a super-temporal ideal, and the contemporary world of modernity and its foundational principles as a product of the Fall, degeneration, degradation, the blending of castes, the decomposition of hierarchy, and the shift of attention away from the spiritual[8] to the material, from heaven to earth, from the eternal to the ephemeral, and so on. The positions of the traditionalists are

---

6   *The Morning of the Magicians* (New York: Stein & Day, 1964). This is the book which first gave rise to many of the false myths which persist today about a supposed 'occult conspiracy' at the heart of National Socialism.-Ed.

7   *The Morning of the Magicians*, p. 180.-Ed.

8   The original word used by Dugin in Russian, духовного, also has the connotation of 'moral', 'ecclesiastical', 'noetic' and so on.-Ed.

distinguished by perfect orderliness and scale. Their theories can serve as a model of the conservative paradigm in its pure form.

Of course, some of their evaluations and prognoses turned out to be incorrect. In particular, both anticipated the victory of 'the fourth caste', in other words, the proletariat (as represented by the Soviet Union) over 'the third caste' (the capitalist camp), which proved incorrect. They opposed Communism, not completely understanding how much there was in it of traditional elements. A few of their appraisals need correction. At one congress in Rome, commemorating the twentieth anniversary of Evola's death, I delivered a lecture called 'Evola — Visto Da Sinistra' (Evola — The View From The Left), in which I suggested having a good look at Evola from Leftist positions, though he considered himself to be on the Right, even on the far Right.

Fundamental Conservatism in Our Time

There is also fundamental conservatism in our society. First, the Islamic project is fundamental conservatism. If we peel it away from the negative stereotypes and look at how, theoretically, those Muslims who lead the battle against the contemporary world would have to feel and think, we will see that they stand on the same typical principles of fundamental conservatives. They must believe in the letter of every word of the *Qur'an*, ignoring any attacks from the proponents of tolerance, who censure their opinions, finding them cruel and out of date. If a fundamentalist comes across such a commentator on television, he comes to a simple conclusion: he must throw out the television, together with the commentator.

There is a similar kind of orientation in America, too, among fundamentalist Protestant groups. And, as is not surprising, approximately the same views are held by a significant percentage of the Republican electorate in the USA. And television programmes featuring these Protestant fundamentalists, who, from a Protestant point of view, criticise everything one can criticise in modernity and postmodernity, leaving no stone unturned, are watched by millions of American viewers. There are a great number of televangelists, like the late Jerry Falwell, who criticise, essentially, the contemporary world in all its fundamentals, and interpret all events from the point of view of the Protestant version of Christianity.

Such people are also found in both Orthodox and Catholic circles. They reject modernity structurally and entirely, considering the teachings and regulations of their religion to be absolutely real, while seeing modernity and its values as an expression of the rule of the Antichrist, in which there can be nothing good by definition. These tendencies are developed among the Russian Old Believers.[9] There is still a Paraclete Union in the Urals that does not use electric lamps. Lamps are 'the light of Lucifer'; thus, they use only torches and candles.

Sometimes this reaches the point of a very deep penetration into the essence of things. One of the Old Believer authors maintains that, 'He who drinks coffee will cough himself to death; he who drinks the tea leaf, will fall from God in despair'. Others affirm that one ought never to eat boiled buckwheat because it is 'sinful'.[10]

Coffee is strictly forbidden in such circles. This may sound stupid, but stupid for whom? For rational, contemporary people. Indeed, 'the sin of boiled buckwheat' is stupid. But imagine that in the world of fundamentalist conservatives, room is found for such a figure as 'the sin of boiled buckwheat'. Some Old Believer congress might be dedicated to 'the sin of boiled buckwheat'. At this congress, they would seek to ascertain to what order of demons it belongs. After all, there were 'trouser councils'. When a group of young Old Believers, sometime in the Eighteenth century, took on the habit of wearing chequered trousers, the Fedoseyans[11] gathered a council in Kimry, sometimes called the 'trouser councils', where it was discussed whether to separate from good relations those who wear chequered trousers, because it seemed at that time that it was indecent for a Christian to wear chequered trousers. Part of the council voted to separate; another part voted against. And these investigations are not really all that delirious. Old Believers seem 'outdated' to us, but they are not that outdated. They are different. They operate within the range of a different topography. They deny that time is progress. For them, time is regress, and modern men are a sacrificial offering to the devil.

Here we can bring in the ideas of Claude Lévi-Strauss. He proves that the 'pre-rational peoples', of whom Lévy-Brühl and the evolutionist scholars spoke, who studied 'primitives', do not exist, and that aboriginal society or the structure of Indian myths were as complex in their rational connections, enumerated taxonomies and juxtaposed themes and happenings, and just as dramatic, as modern European forms. They are simply different. We do not here have an example of a 'pre-*logos*' but of a different logos,

9   The Old Believers are a sect of the Russian Orthodox Church which underwent a schism from the main branch of the Church in 1666, after its adherents objected to certain reforms by the Patriarch of the time.-Ed.

10 In Russian, the root of the word 'buckwheat' sounds similar to the root for 'sin'.-Ed.

11 The Fedoseyans were a sect of the Old Believers that emerged in Russia in the Eighteenth century, favouring strict asceticism and abolishing the institution of marriage.-Ed.

where the system of relations, nuances, differences, diversities and con-structed models work in a different system of hypotheses, but by its own complexity and the parameters of its structures (structuralism proceeds from here) it is absolutely comparable with the consciousness, thought and social models of socialisation and adaptation of other nations.

In fundamental conservatism, the renunciation of modernity has a per-fectly rational and systematic form. If we observe from that point of view, we see that absolutely everything comes together, everything is logical and rational, but arises from a different logos. It is a logos in the space of which 'the sin of buckwheat', the Paraclete Union, living by candlelight — all that which calls forth a scornful smile from the modern man — does not call forth a smile. This is an utterly different regime of existence.

Status Quo Conservatism — Liberal Conservatism

There is a second type of conservatism, which we have called status-quo or liberal conservatism. It is liberal because it says 'yes' to the main trend that is realised in modernity. But at each stage of this trend it attempts to step on the brakes: 'Let's go slower, let's not do that now, let's postpone that.'

Liberal conservatives reason approximately thus: it is good that there is the free individual, but this free post-individual, that's a little too much. Or take the question of 'the end of history'. Fukuyama at first believed that politics had disappeared, and that it would eventually be entirely replaced by 'the global marketplace', in which nations, governments, ethnicities, cultures and religions disappear. But later he decided that one would have to slow the process down and implement postmodernity more calmly, without revolutions, because in revolutions there could appear something undesirable, which could disrupt the plan of 'the end of history'. And then Fukuyama started to write that it is necessary to temporarily strengthen national governments. This is already liberal conservatism.

Liberal conservatives do not like Leftists. They also do not like Right-wingers, such as Evola and Guénon, either, but these they do not notice at all. But as soon as they see Leftists, they immediately square up.

Liberal conservatives are distinguished by the following qualitative structural characteristics: agreement with the general trends of modernity, but disagreement with its more avant-garde manifestations, which seem excessively dangerous and unhealthy. For instance, the English philoso-pher, Edmund Burke,[12] at first sympathised with the Enlightenment, but

---

12 Edmund Burke (1729-1797) was an Irish politician and philosopher who sat in the House of Commons as a member of the Whig party. He was opposed to democracy

after the French Revolution, he pushed away from it and developed a liberal-conservative theory with a front-end criticism of revolution and Leftists. Hence the liberal conservative programme: to defend freedom, rights, the independence of man, progress and equality, but by other means — through evolution, not revolution; lest there be, God forbid, a release from some basement of those dormant energies which with the Jacobins issued in the Terror,[13] and then in the anti-Terror, and so on.

In this way, liberal conservatism principally does not protest against those tendencies which constitute the essence of modernity and even postmodernity, although liberal conservatives before the face of postmodernity will press down more strongly on the brake pedal than before. That is, here at some point they can even shout out: 'Halt!' Seeing what postmodernity carries with itself, and having their eyes on Deleuze›s rhizome, they manifestly feel themselves out of their element. Besides, they are afraid that the quickening dismantlement of modernity, which is being unwrapped into postmodernity, might liberate the pre-modern. They write of this frankly.

For instance, the liberal Habermas,[14] who was once a Leftist, says that if 'We do not now preserve the hard spirit of the Enlightenment, or belief in the ideals of the free subject and moral liberation. If we do not hold man on this precipice, then we will fly off not only into chaos, but we will return to the shadow of tradition, and the sense of the war against it, which was, in fact, represented by modernity.'[15] That is, he fears that fundamental conservatives will come.

Bin Laden as Sign

The figure of bin Laden, independent of whether he is real or whether he was thought up in Hollywood, has a fundamental philosophical

and the French Revolution, although he did believe in the importance of representative government and supported the cause of the American Revolution. He was also involved for many years in addressing injustices perpetrated by the British East India Company in India.-Ed.

13 The Jacobin Club was the most powerful group among the French revolutionaries in the years immediately following the 1789 Revolution. Robespierre and those around him who were responsible for the murderous Reign of Terror of the 1790s were all Jacobins.-Ed.

14 Jürgen Habermas (b. 1929) is a German Marxist philosopher.-Ed.

15 Jürgen Habermas, 'Modernity: An Incomplete Project', in Maurizio Passerin d'Entrèves and Seyla Benhabib (eds.), Habermas and the Unfinished Project of Modernity: Critical Essays on the Philosophical Discourse of Modernity (Cambridge: MIT Press, 1997), pp. 38-55. (This quote does not exist in the English version of the essay.-Ed.)

significance. This is a formulated caricature of the transition within the framework of postmodernity to the pre-modern. It is an ominous warning that the pre-modern (tradition), meaning a belief in those values that were gathered into a heap and taken to the junkyard at the very start of modernity, can still arise. The physiognomy of bin Laden, his gestures, his appearance on our screens and in newspapers and magazines — this is a philosophical sign. This is a sign of warning to humanity, coming from the side of liberal conservatives.

The Simulacra of Che Guevara

Liberal conservatives as a rule do not perform that analysis concerning the relation between liberalism and Communism that we performed, and they continue to fear Communism. We already said that the events of 1991 — the end of the Soviet Union — possess colossal philosophical and historical significance, and have few analogues. There are only a few such events in history, as in 1991 liberalism proved its exclusive right to the orthodox inheritance of the paradigm of modernity. All other versions — including the most important, Communism — proved to be deviations on the path of modernity; offshoots, leading to another goal. Communists thought that they were travelling the paths of modernity in the direction of progress, but it became clear that they were moving toward some other goal, set in a different conceptual space. But a few liberals suppose even today that 'Communists gave up their positions only temporarily' and might yet return.

Extrapolating false fears, contemporary anti-Communism, to a larger degree, probably, than contemporary anti-fascism, gives birth to chimeras, spectres, and simulacra. Communism is no longer present (as fascism has long ceased to be) — in its place there remains a plaster-cast imitation, a harmless Che Guevara, advertising mobile telephones or adorning the shirts of idle and comfortable petty-bourgeoisie youth. In the epoch of modernity, Che Guevara was the enemy of capitalism; in the epoch of postmodernity, he advertises mobile connections on gigantic billboards. This is the style in which Communism can return — in the form of a simulacra. The meaning of this commercial gesture consists in the postmodern laughing off of the pretensions of Communism to be an alternative *logos* within the framework of modernity.

Nevertheless, liberal conservatism, as a rule, is a stranger to this irony, and is not inclined to joke with either 'Reds' or 'Browns'. The reason for this is that liberal conservatism fears the relativisation of logos in postmodernity, being uncertain that the enemy has been completely defeated. It dreams that the prostrate carcass still stirs, and therefore it does not recommend approaching it too closely or mocking it, seeing this as flirting with danger.

The Conservative Revolution

There exists yet a third kind of conservatism. From a philosophical point of view, it is the most interesting. This is a family of conservative ideologies that it is customary to call the Conservative Revolution (CR). This constellation of ideologies and political philosophies considers the problem of the correlation between conservatism and modernity dialectically.

One of the theorists of the Conservative Revolution was Arthur Moeller van den Bruck, whose book was recently translated into Russian.[16] Other thinkers who belonged to this tendency were Martin Heidegger, the brothers Ernst and Friedrich Jünger, Carl Schmitt, Oswald Spengler, Werner Sombart, Othmar Spann, Friedrich Hielscher, Ernst Niekisch and a whole constellation of mostly German authors, who are sometimes called 'the dissidents of National Socialism', because the majority of them, at some stage, supported National Socialism, but soon found themselves in a state of internal emigration, or even in jail. Many of them participated in the anti-fascist underground and helped to save Jews. In particular, Friedrich Hielscher, a first-rate Conservative Revolutionary and a supporter of the German national renaissance, helped the famous Jewish philosopher, Martin Buber,[17] hide from the Nazis.

Conservatives Must Head the Revolution

One can describe the general paradigm of the Conservative Revolutionary worldview in the following manner. There exists an objective process of degradation in the world. This is not simply the striving of 'evil forces' to perpetrate their chicanery; it is the forces of freedom, the forces of the market, which lead humanity along the path of degeneration. The peak of degeneration, from the point of view of Conservative Revolutionaries, is modernity. So far, everything overlaps with the traditionalist position. But, in contrast to it, Conservative Revolutionaries begin to ask themselves: why did it happen that belief in God, who created the world, in

---

16 Arthur Moeller van den Bruck, *Germany's Third Empire.*

17 Martin Buber (1878-1965) was an Austrian Jew who, as a Zionist, later moved to Israel. He is best-known for having formulated a form of Jewish existentialism.-Ed.

divine providence, in the sacred, in myth, transforms in a specific moment into its own opposite? Why does it slacken and why are the enemies of God victorious? A further suspicion arises: maybe that remarkable golden age, which the fundamentalist conservatives defend, carried in itself some kind of gene of future perversion? Maybe things were not all that great even in religion? Maybe those religious, sacral and sacred forms of traditional society, which we can still catch a glimpse of up until the onset of modernity, carried in themselves a certain element of decay? And then the Conservative Revolutionaries say to the conservative fundamentalists: 'You offer to return to a condition when man exhibited only the first symptoms of illness, when there first began the hacking cough. Today this man lies dying, but you speak of how good things were for him earlier. You contrast a coughing man with a dying one. But we want to dig down to discover from whence came the infection and why he started to cough. The fact that, in coughing, he does not die, but goes to work, does not convince us that he is whole and healthy. Somewhere that virus must have nested even earlier...' 'We believe', continue the Conservative Revolutionaries, 'that in the very Source, in the very Deity, in the very First Cause, there is drawn up the intention of organising this eschatological drama.' In such a vision, the modern acquires a paradoxical character. It is not merely today's sickness (in the repudiated present), it is a disclosure in today's world of that which yesterday's world prepared for it (so precious for traditionalists). Modernity does not become better from this; and tradition, meanwhile, loses its unequivocal positivity.

One of the most important formulas of Arthur Moeller van den Bruck was: 'Earlier conservatives attempted to stop the revolution, but we must lead it.' This signifies that, having come together in solidarity, in part for pragmatic motives, with the destructive tendencies of modernity, one must uncover and espy that bacillus which, from the beginning, engendered the tendency to future decline — that is, to modernity. Conservative Revolutionaries want not only to slow time down, like the liberal conservatives, or to return to the past like traditionalists, but to pull out from the structure of the world the roots of evil, to abolish time as a destructive quality of reality, and in so doing fulfilling some kind of secret, parallel, non-evident intention of the Deity itself.

Dasein and Ge-stell

The Heideggerian history of philosophy is built on a similar model. *Dasein*, as the final and localised being of man, began the raising of the question of

being — that is, of itself and its surroundings — at the daybreak of philosophy. The concept of physis became one of the first conceptions expressing
this kind of questioning, likening being to nature and conceptualising it
as a sequence of 'ascents'. The second conception was the agrarian metaphor of logos, a concept formed from the verb legein — that is, 'to har-
vest', and later receiving the sense of 'to think', 'to read', 'to speak'. The pair,
physis-logos, according to Heidegger, describing being, embraced it in
excessively narrow frameworks. These frameworks were narrowed down
further in Plato's teaching about ideas. Furthermore, European thinking
only aggravated alienation from being through increasing rationalism,
up to the oblivion of thoughts about being altogether. At the cusp of the
Nineteenth and Twentieth centuries, this oblivion spilled over into nihilism. In general terms, the definitive essence of the increasing domination
of technique in Heideggerian philosophy is *Ge-stell*, that is *po-stav*,[18] the
organisation of all new alienating and nihilistic models.

But for Heidegger, *Ge-stell* is not an accident. It expresses by itself that
which, on the other side of being, is nothing, as its internal measure. In
authentic *Dasein*, being and nothing must be present together. But if a
man accents being as 'the universal' (*koinon*) — that is, only as that which
is (the idea of *physis*) — he lets out of sight nothingness, which reminds
him of himself, leading philosophy to nihilism — through *Ge-stell*. Thus,
contemporary nihilism is not only evil, but so is news of being turned
towards *Dasein* given by such complex means. Therefore, the task of
Conservative Revolutionaries is not simply to overcome nothingness and
the nihilism of modernity, but to untangle the tangle of the history of
philosophy and to decipher the message contained in *Ge-stell*. The nihilism of modernity, thus, is not only evil (as for the traditionalists), but also
a sign, pointing to the deep structures of being and the paradoxes lying
within them.

The Gloomy End of the Show

Conservative Revolutionaries despise the actual to such a degree that they
are not content to oppose it merely with the past. They say: 'The actual is disgusting, but one must live it through, drive it forward, pull it to its final end.'

The liberal postmodernist offers 'an endless end'. Fukuyama's 'end of
history' is not simply a disappearance: after the end of history, economic
transactions continue to occur; markets continue to operate; hotels, bars

---

18 In Russian, roughly, 'the on-or-alongside-placed'.

and nightclubs shimmer invitingly; exchanges function; dividends are paid according to their price in the paper; computer screens and televisions shine; stocks are issued. History is not, but the market and TV *are*.

Everything is different with Conservative Revolutionaries. At the end of history, they count on making their appearance on the other side of *Dasein*, from the troubled space of 'that side', and to transform the postmodernist game into a non-game. The spectacle ('the society of the spectacle' of Guy Debord)[19] will end with something very unpleasant for viewers and actors. In its time, according to just such a logic, there operated a group of Surrealist-Dadaists: Arthur Cravan, Jacques Rigaut, Julien Torma and Jacques Vache, who glorified suicide. But critics thought of this as empty bragging. In one moment, the group publicly did themselves in, proving that art and Surrealism were, for them, a matter of such gravity that they gave their lives for it. Here we can recall Kirilov from Dostoevsky's *Demons*,[20] for whom suicide became an expression of the complete freedom that opened up after 'the death of God'.

Recently in Russia there occurred events no less horrendous. For instance, *Nord-Ost*.[21] The obscene and raunchy comic actor, Sasha Tsekalo, puts on a performance, at which an impressive Moscow public is present. Then Chechen terrorists arrive, and at first people think that this is a part of the performance. Only later, with horror, do they understand that something not right is happening on stage, and then there begins a real, nightmarish tragedy.

Conservative Revolutionaries present themselves in an approximately similar manner: let the buffoonery of postmodernism have its turn; let it erode definite paradigms, the ego, super-ego and *logos*; let it join up

---

19 The 'society of the spectacle' is a term coined by Guy Debord (1931-1994), a French Marxist philosopher and the founder of the anarchist Situationist International. The spectacle, as described in his principal work, *The Society of the Spectacle*, is one of the means by which the capitalist establishment maintains its authority in the modern world — namely, by reducing all genuine human experiences to representational images in the mass media, thus allowing the powers-that-be to determine how individuals experience reality. The Situationists were very influential in the mass protests and strikes in France in 1968.-Ed.

20 Fyodor Dostoevsky, *Demons* (Cambridge: Penguin Classics, 2012).-Ed.

21 *Nord-Ost* is a popular Russian musical that, in part, celebrates the triumph of Soviet soldiers in the Second World War. On 23 October 2002, a group of Chechen suicide terrorists stormed a Moscow theatre during a performance of the musical and took the entire audience and company hostage. They standoff continued for three days until Russian forces attacked the theatre, first pumping in toxic gas to disable the terrorists. Although most of the terrorists were killed or captured during the attack, some of the hostages were executed by the terrorists, but most were killed by the gas, and more than 130 hostages died in all.-Ed.

with the rhizome, schizo-masses and splintered consciousness; let nothing carry along in itself the substance of the world — then secret doors will open, and ancient, eternal, ontological archetypes will come to the surface and, in a frightful way, will put an end to the game.

Left-Wing Conservatism (Social Conservatism)

There is still another tendency, so-called Left-wing conservatism or social conservatism. The typical representative of social conservatism is Georges Sorel[22] (see his *Reflections on Violence*).[23] He held back his Leftist views, but at a specific moment discovered that both the Left and the Right (monarchists and Communists) fight the same enemy: the bourgeoisie.

Left-wing conservatism is close to the Russian National Bolshevism of Ustrialov, who detected Russian national myths under the purely Left-wing Marxist ideology. This is even more distinctly set forth in the National Socialism of Strasser,[24] and in the National Bolshevism of Niekisch. Such Left-wing conservatism can be brought to the family of the Conservative Revolution, or it can be separated into a distinct school.

It is interesting that the party United Russia[25] adopted social conservatism as its informing ideology. This orientation is now being developed by Andrei Isayev. At the other pole of United Russia is the liberal conservatism of Pligin.

Eurasianism as an Episteme

Eurasianism is not a political philosophy, but an episteme. It concerns itself with the class of conservative ideologies and shares some

22 Georges Sorel (1847-1922) was a French philosopher who began as a Marxist and later developed Revolutionary Syndicalism. He advocated the use of myth and organised violence in revolutionary movements. He was influential upon both the Communist and Fascist movements.-Ed.

23 Georges Sorel, *Reflections on Violence* (Cambridge: Cambridge University Press, 1999).

24 Gregor Strasser (1892-1934) was an early leader of the National Socialist movement in Germany who emphasised the element of socialism more strongly than did Hitler. Perceived as a rival to Hitler's authority, he was executed during the infamous 'Night of the Long Knives' in June 1934. His brother Otto attempted to revive the notion of a 'Left-wing National Socialism' in the post-war era.-Ed.

25 United Russia is a centre-Right party that was founded in Russia in 2001. It has always been strongly supportive of Vladimir Putin, and Putin was the party's leader during the period 2008-2012. As of this writing (2012), United Russia is the largest party in the country.-Ed.

characteristics with fundamental conservatism (traditionalism) and with the Conservative Revolution (including the social conservatism of the Leftist Eurasianists). The one thing in conservatism that is not acceptable to Eurasianists is liberal conservatism.

Eurasianism, recognising the pretence of the Western *logos* to universality, refuses to recognize this universality as an inevitability. This is the specific character of Eurasianism. It considers Western culture as a local and temporary phenomenon, and affirms a multiplicity of cultures and civilisations which coexist at different moments of a cycle. For Eurasianists, modernity is a phenomenon peculiar only to the West, while other cultures must divest these pretensions to the universality of Western civilisation and build their societies on internal values. There is no single historical process; every nation has its own historical model, which moves in a different rhythm and at times in different directions.

Eurasianism, in itself, is gnoseological plurality. The unitary episteme of modernity — including science, politics, culture and anthropology — is opposed by the multiplicity of epistemes, built on the foundations of each existing civilisation — the Eurasianist episteme for Russian civilisation, the Chinese for the Chinese, the Islamic for Islam, the Indian for the Indian, and so on. And only on these foundations, cleansed of Western-mandated epistemes, must long-term sociopolitical, cultural and economic projects be built.

We see in this a specific form of conservatism, which differs from other, similar conservative versions (with the exception of liberal conservatism) in that its alternative to modernity is not taken from the past or from unique revolutionary-conservative ideologies, but from societies historically co-existing with Western civilisation, but geographically and culturally different from it. In this, Eurasianism approaches, in part, the traditionalism of Guénon, who also thought that 'contemporiety' was a 'Western' notion, while forms of traditional society were preserved in the East. It is not accidental that among Russian authors, the first to refer to Guénon's book *East and West*[26] was the Eurasianist N. N. Alekseev.

Neo-Eurasianism

Neo-Eurasianism, which appeared in Russia in the late 1980s, completely apprehended the fundamental points of the previous Eurasianists'

---

26 René Guénon, *East and West* (Hillsdale, New York: Sophia Perennis, 2001). (First published in 1924, it is considered the first full formulation of Guénon's doctrines.-Ed.)

episteme, but it supplemented them with attention to traditionalism, geopolitics, structuralism, the fundamental-ontology of Heidegger, sociology,
and anthropology, and likewise carried out the gigantic task of producing
concord between the basic conditions of Eurasianism and the realities of
the second half of the Twentieth century and the beginning of the Twenty-
first, with an enumeration of new scientific developments and studies.
Today, Eurasianist journals are circulated in Italy, France, and Turkey.

New-Eurasianism is founded upon the philosophical analysis of the
theses of modernity and postmodernity. Detachment from Western culture allows for distance, thanks to which it is possible to embrace with a
glance all of modernity, and to say to all of that a fundamental 'no'.

In the Twentieth century, modernity and Western civilisation were
systematically subjected to an analogical critique by Spengler, Toynbee,
and especially the structuralists—in the first place, Lévi-Strauss, who
founded structural anthropology. This structural anthropology is based
on the principal equality between various cultures, from the primitive
to the most developed, which deprives Western European culture of any
kind of superiority over the most 'wild' and 'primitive' non-literate tribes.
Here we must recall that the Eurasianists Roman Jakobson[27] and Nicolai
Trubetskoy,[28] the founders of phonology and eminent representatives of
structural linguistics, were the teachers of Levi-Strauss and trained him
in the practice of structural analysis, which he himself willingly acknowl-
edges. In this way, an intellectual chain is retraced—Eurasianism, structuralism, and Neo-Eurasianism. In this sense, Neo-Eurasianism becomes
the restoration of a broad spectrum of ideas, insights and intuitions,
which the first Eurasianists outlined and into which entered organically
the results of the scientific activity of various schools and authors (for the
most part, those with a conservative orientation) that developed in parallel throughout the entire course of the Twentieth century.

---

27 Roman Jakobson (1896-1982) was a Russian linguist who was one of the founders
    of what came to be called Structuralism. He fled the Soviet Union just prior to the
    Second World War and lived for the remainder of his life in the United States.
    According to the original footnote, Dugin is referring to his book *Selected Writings*,
    vol. 7: *Contributions to Comparative Mythology* (New York: Mouton, 1985).-Ed.

28 Nikolai Trubetskoy, *The Heritage of Genghis Khan* (Moscow, 2000).

7

'CIVILISATION' AS AN IDEOLOGICAL CONCEPT

The Demand for a More Exact Definition

There is no agreement today as to the meaning of the concept 'civilisation' in intellectual and scientific circles — as, by the way, is the case with other fundamental terms. This springs from the fundamental meaning of our epoch, shifting from modernity to postmodernity, which essentially affects semantic fields and linguistic forms. And, inasmuch as we find ourselves in the stage of an unfinished transition, an inconceivable confusion reigns in our ideas: someone uses customary terms in their old sense; someone feels the necessity for semantic displacement and glances into the future (which has not yet come); someone fantasises (perhaps coming closer to the future, or simply falling into individualistic, irrelevant hallucinations); someone else gets completely confused.

Whatever the case might be, for the correct use of terms, especially key terms, to which, undoubtedly, the concept of civilisation belongs, it is necessary today to carry out, let it be elementarily, a deconstruction, tracing[1] the meaning to its historical context, and retracing its basic semantic shifts.

'Civilisation' as a Phase of the Development of Societies

The term 'civilisation' received wide circulation in the epoch of the rapid development of the theory of progress. This theory proceeded from two fundamental, paradigmatic axioms of modernity: the progressive and unidirectional character of human development (from minus to plus) and the universality of man as a phenomenon. In this context, 'civilisation', for

---

1   Also 'elevating' and 'raising'.-Ed.

L. H. Morgan,[2] defines the stage in which 'humanity' (in the Nineteenth
century, everyone uncritically believed as one in the evident existence of
such a concept as 'humanity') commences after the stage of 'barbarity',
while that, in turn, replaces with itself the stage of 'savagery'.

Marxists adopted such an interpretation of civilisation easily, having
written it into the theory of the evolution of economic systems. According
to Morgan, Taylor and Engels,[3] 'savagery' characterises tribes engaged in
gathering and primitive kinds of hunting. 'Barbarity' relates to non-literate
societies, occupied with the simplest kinds of rural economy and cattle-
breeding, without a clear division of labour or development of sociopolitical institutions. 'Civilisation' signifies by itself the stage of the appearance
of letters, sociopolitical institutions, cities, crafts, technological improve-
ments, the division of society into classes, and the appearance of developed theological and religious systems. 'Civilisations' were thought of as
historically steady and able to be preserved; developing, but with their
primary features remaining constant over the course of millennia (such as
the Mesopotamian, Egyptian, Indian, Chinese, and Roman civilisations).

'Civilisation' and 'Empire'

However, together with the purely historical-phase meaning in the concept
of 'civilisation', a territorial sense was also included, though less explicitly.
'Civilisation' offered a vast enough area of diffusion; that is, in addition
to a considerable temporal dimension, a broad spatial diffusion was also
presumed to characterise it. In this territorial sense, the borders of the
term 'civilisation' in part coincided with the meaning of the word 'empire',
in the sense of a 'world power'. 'Empire' in this civilisational sense pointed
not to the peculiarity of a political and administrative arrangement, but to
the fact of an active and intense spread of influence, proceeding from the

2 Lewis Henry Morgan (1818-1881) was a lawyer who also conducted research into
   ethnology. He became fascinated with the Native Americans and was initiated into the
   Iroquois tribe. In his book *Systems of Consanguinity and Affinity of the Human Family*,
   he compared his studies of the Native Americans with the tribal life of other cultures,
   and developed his theory of the Unity of Origin of Mankind, in which he believed he
   had identified the universal primordial social structure of humanity. He also came to
   believe in the necessity for continual progress in societies in order for them to survive,
   which he identified in modern times with technological progress, as described in his
   Ancient Society (New York: Henry Holt & Co., 1877). This is the book cited by Dugin
   in his original footnote. Marx and Engels were heavily reliant on Morgan's work when
   discussing tribal societies and social progress in their own theories.-Ed.

3 Friedrich Engels, *The Origins of the Family, Private Property, and the State, in the Light
   of the Researches of Lewis H. Morgan* (New York: International Publishers, 1972).

centres of civilisation to the surrounding territory, supposedly populated by 'barbarians' or 'savages'. In other words, in the very concept of civilisation one can already espy the character of expansion and the export of influence characteristic of empires (ancient and modern).

Civilisation and the Universal Type

Civilisation worked out a new universal type, qualitatively differing from the models of 'barbarian' and 'savage' societies. This type was most often built on the 'globalisation' of that ethno-tribal and/or religious centre that stood at the source of a given civilisation. But in the course of this 'globalisation', that is, through the equating of the concrete ethnic, sociopolitical and religious pattern to the 'universal standard', the very important process of transcending the *ethnos* itself occurred, transferring its natural and organic, most often unconsciously imparted, tradition into the rank of a man-made and conscious, rational system. The citizens of Rome, even in the first stages of the Empire, already differed essentially from the typical residents of Latium, while a variety of Muslims, praying in Arabic, went far beyond the Bedouin tribes of Arabia and their direct ethnic descendants.

In this way, at the time of the move to 'civilisation', social anthropology qualitatively changed: man, turning to 'civilisation', had a collective identity imprinted on a fixed body of spiritual culture, which he was obliged to assimilate to a certain degree.

Civilisation assumed a rational and volitional force from the side of man; that, which in the Seventeenth century, after Descartes, philosophers started to call 'the subject'. But the necessity of such a force, and the presence of a model, abstracted and fixed in the culture, equalised itself, to a certain extent, with both the representatives of the core ethnos (of religion), lying at the foundation of 'civilisation', and those who ended up in the zone of influence from other ethnic contexts. To adopt the foundations of civilisation was qualitatively easier than to be accepted into a tribe, inasmuch as there was for this no demand to organically absorb the gigantic reservoirs of unconscious archetypes, but to perform a series of rational, logical operations.

Civilisation and Culture

In some contexts (depending on the country or the author) in the Nineteenth century, the concept of civilisation was identified with the concept of culture. In other cases, hierarchical relations were established between them — most often, culture was thought of as the spiritual filling of civilisation, while civilisation properly meant the formal structure of society, answering to the main points of the definition.

Oswald Spengler, in his famous book *The Decline of the West*, even contrasted civilisation and culture, considering the second an expression of the organic, vital spirit of man, but the first a product of the cooling off of that spirit in mechanical and purely technical boundaries. According to Spengler, civilisation is a product of cultural death. However, such a sharp-witted observation, correctly interpreting some qualities of contemporary Western civilisation, did not receive general acknowledgement; and most often today the terms civilisation and culture are used as synonyms, although each researcher can have his own opinion on this point.

Postmodernism and the Synchronistic Understanding of Civilisation

Even the most cursory survey of the meaning of the term civilisation shows that, in using it, we are dealing with a concept saturated with the spirit of the Enlightenment, progressivism and historicism, which was characteristic for the epoch of modernity in its uncritical stage; that is, until the fundamental reconsiderations of the Twentieth century. Faith in the progressive development of history, in the universality of the human path according to a common logic of development from savagery to civilisation, was the distinguishing feature of the Nineteenth century. But already with Nietzsche and Freud, the so-called 'philosophers of suspicion', this optimistic axiom started to be doubted. And over a period of the Twentieth century, Heidegger, the existentialists, traditionalists, structuralists, and at last postmodernists smashed it to bits.

In postmodernity, criticism of historical optimism, universalism and historicism acquired a systematic character and established the doctrinal premises for a total revision of the conceptual apparatus of Western European philosophy. This revision itself has not yet been carried out to its conclusion, but what has been done (by Levi-Strauss, Barthes, Ricoeur, Foucalt, Deleuze, Derrida, and others) is already enough to convince one of the impossibility of using the dictionary of modernity without a thorough and rigorous deconstruction. Paul Ricoeur, summarising the theses of the 'philosophers of suspicion', paints the following picture: man and man's society consist in rational-conscious components (*kerigma*, according to Bultmann; 'superstructure', according to Marx; 'ego', to Freud) and the unconscious (properly, 'structures' in the Structuralist understanding;

'bases'; 'the will to power' of Nietzsche; 'the unconscious').[4] And although externally it seems that the path of man leads directly from the captivity of the unconscious to the kingdom of reason, and that this exactly represents progress and the content of history, in fact, under the closest scrutiny, it becomes clear that the unconscious ('myth') proves much stronger and, as before, considerably predetermines the work of the intellect. Moreover, reason itself and conscious, logical activity is almost always nothing other than a gigantic work of repressing unconscious impulses — in other words, an expression of complexes, strategies of displacement, the substitution of projection, and so on. In Marx, the unconscious is played by 'the forces of production' and 'industrial relations'.[5]

Consequently, civilisation does not merely remove 'savagery' and 'barbarism', entirely overcoming them, but itself is built precisely on 'savage' and 'barbaric' grounds, which transfer to the sphere of the unconscious, but there is not only nowhere to escape from this, but, on the contrary, they acquire unlimited power over man, to a large extent precisely because they are thought to be overcome, and even non-existent. This explains the striking difference between the historical practices of nations and societies, full of warfare, oppression, cruelty, and wild outbursts of terror, abounding in aggravating psychological disorders, and the pretensions of reason to a harmonious, peaceful and enlightened existence under the shadow of progress and development. In this respect, the modern era is not only not an exception but also the peak of the intensification of this discrepancy between the pretensions of reason and the bloody reality of world wars, ethnic cleansing, and the historically unprecedented mass genocides of entire races and *narodi*[6]. And in terms of savagery, modernity possesses the most perfect technical means invented by civilisation, right up to weapons of mass destruction.

Thus, the critical tradition, structuralism and the philosophy of postmodernity force one to move from the mainly diachronic (phased) interpretation of civilisation, which was the norm for the Nineteenth century and which, by inertia, continues to be widely in use, to the synchronic. The synchronic approach assumes that civilisation comes not instead of savagery or barbarity, not after them, but together with them and continues to coexist with them. One can imagine civilisation as the numerator, and savagery-barbarism as the denominator of a conditional fraction.

4   Paul Ricoeur. *Hermeneutics and Psychoanalysis: Religion and Belief* (Moscow, 1996).

5   Karl Marx, *Capital* (London: Penguin Books, 1986).

6   Dugin uses the term *narodnik* as synonymous with the German term *volk*, or peoples.-Ed.

Civilisation affects consciousness, but the unconscious, through the unceasing 'work of dreams' (Freud),[7] constantly misinterprets everything in its favour. Savagery is that which explains civilisation, and is the key to it. It turns out that man hurried to proclaim 'civilisation' as that which already actually happened, while it remains not more than an incomplete plan, constantly suffering disruption under the onslaught of the cunning energies of the unconscious (however we might understand it: as Nietzschean 'will to power', or psychoanalytically).

The Deconstruction of Civilisation

How, in practice, can one apply the structuralist approach for the deconstruction of the concept of civilisation? In compliance with the general logic of this operation, one should subject to doubt the irreversibility and novelty of that which constitutes the basic characteristics of civilisation, in contrast with savagery and barbarity.

The main characteristic of civilisation is often thought to be an inclusive universality; that is, the theoretical openness of the civilisational code for those who would like to join it from without. Inclusive universality is, at first glance, the complete antithesis of exclusive particularity, the primary characteristic of tribal and ancestral societies of the pre-civilisational period. But the historical pretensions of civilisation to universality — ecumenicalism, and, correspondingly, uniqueness — constantly pushed against the fact that, besides the 'barbarian' nations, beyond the borders of such a civilisation, there existed other civilisations, with their own unique and different variants of universalism. In this case, a logical contradiction was placed before civilisation: either one must admit that the pretension to universality proves groundless, or one must include the other civilisation(s) in the category of barbarians.

While recognising this groundlessness, various decisions can also follow: either to try to find a syncretic model of the unification of both civilisations (at least in theory) into a general system, or to admit the correctness of the other civilisation. As a rule, in confronting such a problem, 'civilisation' acts on the basis of an exclusive (not inclusive) principle, and considers the other civilisation defective; that is, 'barbaric', 'heretical', or 'particular'. In other words, we are dealing with the transfer of the previously tribal ethnocentrism to a higher level of generalisation. Inclusivity

---

7   Sigmund Freund, *The Interpretation of Dreams* (Oxford: Oxford University Press, 1999). (Freud believed that the purpose of dreams was to interpret one's unconscious desires in symbolic or allegorical form.-Ed.)

and universalism, in practice, turn into a familiar exclusivity and particularism that is usually attributed to savagery.

This is easy to recognise in the following, striking examples: the Greeks, considering themselves as a civilisation, numbered everyone else among the barbarians. The origin of the word 'barbarian' is the onomatopeic pejorative, signifying him whose speech makes no sense and is a bundle of animal sounds. Many tribes have a similar relationship to members of a different tribe: not understanding their language, they think the others have no language at all; consequently, they do not consider them people. From here, incidentally, is derived the Slavic tribal name *nemtsie* (Germans), that is *nemie* (dumb, silent, mute), for those who do not know what anyone calling himself a man should know: the Russian language.

Among the ancient Persians, who represented precisely a civilisation with pretensions to the universality in the form of their Mazdian religion, this was expressed even more clearly: division into *Iran* (people) and *Turan* (demons) was drawn on the level of religion, cults, rites and ethics. The matter came to the point of the absolutising of endogenous relations and the normalisation of incest, in order that the solar sun of the *Iranians* (Ahura Mazda) would not be profaned by the impurities of the sons of Angra-Mainyu.

Judaism as a world religion, having pretensions to universalism and having laid the theological foundations of monotheism — both for Christianity and for Islam, which were developed by a few civilisations simultaneously — is, to this day, almost ethnically limited to the blood-tribes by the *Halakhah*.[8]

The tribal system is based on initiation, in the course of which the neophyte is informed about the foundations of the tribal mythology. On the civilisational level, this same function is played by religious institutions; and in comparatively later epochs, by the system of common education, made deliberately ideological. Neophytes learn the myths of modernity in other conditions and under another veneer, but their functional value remains constant, while their foundation (if one takes into account the Freudian analysis of the substitution-repression actions of reason and the 'ego') has not strayed far from legend and tradition.

In a word, even a rough deconstruction of civilisation shows that the claims to overcoming previous phases are illusions, while in practice, big and 'developed' collectives of people, united in a civilisation, in essence simply repeat, on a different level, the archetypes of the behaviour and moral systems of 'savages'. Hence, endless and ever bloodier wars, double

---

8   *Halakhah* refers to the totality of Jewish law.-Ed.

standards in international politics, fits of passion in private life, and the constantly broken ethical and normative codes of moderate and rational societies. Developing Rousseau's idea of the 'noble savage' (Rousseau, by the way, sharply criticised civilisation as a phenomenon and thought of it as the source of all evil), one can say that the 'civilised' man is none other than the 'wicked savage', a defective and perverted 'barbarian'.[9]

The Synchronic and Plural Understanding of Civilisation Prevails Today

With these preliminary observations, we can at last turn to that which we include today in the concept of civilisation, when we develop Huntington's[10] thesis about 'the clash of civilisations' or raise objections to it with the ex-President of Iran Khatami, insisting upon 'a dialogue of civilisations'.

The very fact that there is hardly any consensus in the use of the term 'civilisation' evidently shows that the phased (purely historical or progressive) interpretation of that concept, prevailing in the modern epoch, and generally accepted in the Nineteenth and first half of the Twentieth centuries, has clearly lost its relevance today.

Only the most outdated researchers, who are stuck in the uncritical modernity of Kant or Bentham,[11] can contrast 'civilisation' and 'barbarity' today. Although it is comfortable to use the term civilisation instrumentally in a historical analysis in the description of ancient types of societies, still, it clearly lost its ideological charge as a global positive in comparison with a global negative (barbarism and savagery). Universalism, gradualness of development, the anthropological unity of human history — on the philosophical level, all of this has long been put into question. By his studies in structural anthropology, based on the richest ethnographic and

---

9   Jean-Jacques Rousseau, *The Social Contract and Other Later Political Writings* (Cambridge: Cambridge University Press, 1997).

10 Samuel Huntington (1927-2008) was an American political scientist who became infamous for serving as an advisor to authoritarian regimes, such as South Africa in the 1980s. He famously postulated that nations in the process of transitioning into modernity must be cautious about not introducing democracy too quickly into their societies, and that repressive measures can actually be necessary and beneficial in the short term. More recently, he became well-known for his 1993 essay 'The Clash of Civilizations' published in *Foreign Affairs*, which was later expanded into a book of the same name, in which he theorized that the changing world order following the collapse of Communism would be defined by conflicts between cultural blocs, such as the West and the Islamic world.-Ed.

11 Jeremy Bentham (1748-1842) was an English jurist, social reformer and Utilitarian philosopher.-Ed.

mythological material of the life of North and South American tribes, Levi-Strauss convincingly showed that the conceptual and mythological systems of those same 'primitive' societies, by their complexity, richness of nuance, connections and functional elaborations of differentiations, are in no way inferior to those of more civilised countries.

In political discourse, there is still talk of 'the privileges of civilisation', but even this already looks anachronistic. We confronted such a spike of uncritical ignorance when liberal-reformers tried to present the history of Russia as a continuous chain of unchecked barbarity in the face of 'flourishing', 'resplendent', and 'established' Western civilisation. However, even this was not only an extrapolation of the bravado-based, propagandistic pretensions of the West itself and a result of the network of influence's induction, but also a form of Russian cargo-cults: the first McDonald's, private banks and clips of rock bands shown on Soviet television were perceived as 'sacral objects'.

With the exception of these propagandistic symbols or the hopeless backwardness of uncritical philosophers, in the framework of an even distant familiarity with contemporary philosophy, still the concept of civilisation, in discourse that does not contradict the mainstream, is interpreted without any moral charge whatsoever, but is used as a technical term, and implies not something opposed to barbarism and savagery, but to another civilisation. In Huntington's famous and aforementioned article, there is not a word about barbarism; he speaks exclusively of the borders, structures, peculiarities, frictions and differences of various civilisations which are opposed to each other. And this feature is one of not only those of his positions or lines of argument stemming from Toynbee, whom Huntington clearly follows. The use of this term in the contemporary context already suggests a blatant pluralism, comparativism, and, if you like, synchronism. Here, philosophical criticism and the reconsideration of modernity, implemented in a thousand different ways in the course of the whole Twentieth century, are immediately impactful.

And so, if we dismiss the recurrences of uncritical liberalism and the narrow-minded naïvety of pro-American and pro-Western propaganda, we will see that today the term civilisation, in operational and active political analysis, is used above all synchronically and functionally, in order to designate wide and stable geographical and cultural zones, united by approximately common spiritual, moral, stylistic and psychological arrangements and historical experience.

Civilisation in the context of the Twenty-first century signifies precisely this: a zone of the steady and rooted influence of a definite social-cultural style, most often (though not necessarily) coinciding with the borders of the diffusion of the world religions. And the political formation of separate segments entering into a civilisation can be rather different: civilisations, as a rule, are broader than one government, and can consist of some or even many countries; moreover, the borders of some civilisations cross countries, dividing them in parts.

If, in Antiquity, 'civilisations' most often coincided with empires, and were in one way or another politically united, then today their borders correspond to invisible lines, irrelevantly superimposed onto the administrative borders of governments. Some of these governments were never a part of a single empire (for instance, Islam spread almost everywhere in the conquests of the Arabs who built the world Caliphate). Others did not share a common statehood, but were united among themselves in different ways: religiously, culturally or racially.

The Crisis of Classical Models of Historical Analysis (Classical, Economic, Liberal, Racial)

We have established that, in the use of the term civilisation in the Twentieth century and in the framework of criticisms of modernity, there occurred a qualitative shift to the side of synchronicity and plurality. But can one take a step further and attempt to understand why, in fact, this word usage became so topical in precisely our time? Indeed, the earlier concept of civilisation was not a subject of deliberate problematisation, while it was customary only for humanitarian and academic circles to think in terms of such a category. Other approaches — economic, national, racial, class-based — dominated in political and, closely related to it, political science discourse. Today we see that to think only in terms of economics, to speak of national governments and national interests, and more so, to put class analysis or the racial approach at the head of one's analysis, is less and less acceptable. And on the contrary, it is rare that some statement or speech of a political actor passes by without a mention of the word civilisation, to say nothing of political and analytic texts, where this term is perhaps most prevalent.

With Huntington, in fact, we see the attempt to make civilisation the central moment of political, historical and strategic analysis. We are clearly on our way to thinking in terms of civilisations.

Here we should look more attentively at that which, precisely in the main versions of political science discourse, substitutes itself for 'civilisation'. To speak seriously of races is not acceptable after the tragic history of European fascism. Class-based analysis in the mainstream became irrelevant after the fall of socialism and the break-up of the USSR. And at that moment, it seemed that the sole paradigm of political science would be liberalism. Meanwhile, the impression grew that the national borders of homogenous, essentially liberal-democratic governments, no longer confronting any kind of systematic alternatives laying claim to a planetary scope (after the fall of Marxism), would soon be abolished, and a world leadership and a one-world government would be established with a homogenous market economy, parliamentary democracy (world parliament), a liberal system of values and a common infrastructure of information technology. In 1990, Francis Fukuyama emerged as the herald of such a wonderful new world in his policy book, *The End of History and the Last Man*. Fukuyama brought the development of the phased interpretation of the concept of civilisation to its logical conclusion: the end of history, in his version, signified the final defeat of civilisation over barbarism in all its forms, guises and variants.

Huntington argued with Fukuyama, advancing as his main argument the fact that the end of the opposition of the clearly-defined ideologies of modernity (Marxism and Liberalism) in no way signified the automatic integration of humanity into a unified liberal utopia, inasmuch as under the formal constructions of national governments and ideological camps were found deep tectonic plates; as it were — continents of collective unconsciousness, which, as soon became clear, were by no means overcome by modernisation, colonisation, ideologisation and enlightenment, and as before, predetermined the most important aspects of life — including politics, economics and geopolitics — in one or another segment of human society according to their belonging to a civilisation.

In other words, Huntington proposed to introduce the concept 'civilisation' as a fundamental ideological concept, and called for the replacement not only of the class-based analysis, but also of the liberal utopia, which took too earnestly and uncritically the propagandistic demagoguery of the Cold War, and thus became, in its turn, its victim. Capitalism, the market, liberalism, and democracy seem universal and commonly human only externally. Each civilisation reinterprets its substance in accordance with its own unconscious templates, where religion, culture, language and psychology play a massive and often decisive role.

In this context, civilisation acquires a central significance in the analysis of political science, stepping into first place and replacing with itself the clichés of the liberal Vulgate.

The unfolding of events in the 1990s shows that Huntington proved in this argument to be closer to the truth, and Fukuyama himself is obliged in part to reconsider his views, having admitted that he evidently spoke too soon. But this very revision by Fukuyama of the thesis of 'the end of history' demands a more thorough reconsideration.

The Step Back of the Liberal Utopians: State Building

The problem is that Fukuyama, analyzing the discrepancy of his predictions about 'the end of history' through the prism of the global victory of liberalism still tried to stay in the framework of that logic, from which he at first proceeded. Consequently, he needed to implement a one-time reality check and to turn aside from that, in order to admit the correctness of his opponent Huntington, who, in his forecast, proved by all signs closer to the truth. Then Fukuyama made the following conceptual move: he proposed to defer the end of history to an indefinite date, and meanwhile to engage in the strengthening of those socio-political structures that were the nucleus of the liberal ideology in its previous stages. Fukuyama advanced a new thesis: 'state-building'. As an intermediate stage for the transition to global government and world leadership, he recommended strengthening national governments with a liberal economy and democratic system of rule, in order to more fundamentally and profoundly work the soil for the final victory of world liberalism and globalisation. This is not a rejection of the perspective; this is its postponement until the indefinite future with a concrete proposition concerning the intermediate stage.

Fukuyama says almost nothing about the concept of civilisation, but clearly takes into account Huntington's theses, indirectly responding to him: the steady development of national governments, which proved cramped both in the epoch of colonisation, in the epoch of national-liberation movements, and in the epoch of the ideological opposition of the two camps, must now proceed in due course. It is this which will lead gradually to different societies adopting the market, democracy and human rights, uprooting the remains of the unconscious and preparing a more fail-safe (than now) soil for globalisation.

Thomas Barnett's *The World as Network*

In American political science and foreign policy analysis, there also exists a new promulgation of a purely global theory, presented this time in the essays of Thomas Barnett.[12] The meaning of this conception comes down to this: that technological development establishes a zonal division of all territories on Earth into three regions: the core, the zone of connectedness, and the zone of disconnectedness. Barnett thinks that network processes freely penetrate through borders, governments and civilisations, and structure the strategic space of the world in their own way. The USA and European Union are the core; there are concentrated all the codes of the new technologies and the decision-making centres. The majority of other countries, doomed to a 'user' relationship to the network, constitute the 'zone of connectedness' (they are compelled to use ready-made technological means and to adjust to the rules that are worked out by the core). To the 'zone of disconnectedness' belong the countries and political forces that have stood up in direct opposition to the USA, the West and globalisation.[13]

For Thomas Barnett (as for Daniel Bell), 'technology is fate'; in it is embodied the quintessence of civilisation, understood purely technologically, almost as with Spengler, but with a positive sign.

The American View of the World System (Three Versions)

In American political analysis — and we must recognise that it is precisely the Americans who set the tone in this region — all three conceptions of the separation of subjects on the map of the world co-exist. Globalism and civilisation (in a singular sense), in the spirit of Fukuyama's earlier ideas, are reflected in Barnett's constructions. Here, only the core is recognised as a subject; the rest is subject to external direction, that is, to de-subjectivisation and de-sovereignisation.

Fukuyama himself, critically examining his earlier, optimistic statements, takes an intermediate position, insisting that one must, for some time longer, recognise 'national governments' as a subject, the development of which must prepare a more secure ground for the coming globalism.

12 Thomas P. M. Barnett (b. 1962) is an American geostrategist who was worked for the US Navy and the Department of Defense. Dugin is referring to his book *The Pentagon's New Map: War and Peace in the Twenty-first Century* (New York: G. P. Putnam's Sons, 2004), and its sequels.-Ed.

13 Thomas P. M. Barnett, *The Pentagon's New Map: War and Peace in the Twenty-first Century*.

And finally, Huntington and the supporters of his approach think that civilisations are excessively grand and foundational realities, which can well lay claim to the status of being the global subjects of world politics. When the previous ideological models collapsed, national governments started to lose, in leaps and bounds, the real stuff of sovereignty under the influence of the separate, effective aspects of globalisation, but globalisation itself, while breaking old borders, was and is unable to actually penetrate into the depths of societies with settled traditional components.

It is significant that those forces in the world which strive to slip away from globalisation, Westernisation and American hegemony in order to preserve and strengthen anew their traditional identity hold to precisely Huntington's thesis. Only in place of the gloomy, catastrophic discourse of Huntington concerning 'collision' and 'conflict', they started talking about 'dialogue'. But this almost propagandistic, moralistic nuance should not lead us into a misunderstanding concerning the most important task of those who largely accept Huntington's model. In the first place, this is the Iranian President Khatami's. juxtapositioning of 'collision' or 'dialogue' — the question is secondary and practical; much more important is the principled agreement that precisely civilisation becomes today the foundational, conceptual analytic subject of international politics.

In other words, in contrast to both globalist-maximalists (like Barnett) and to moderate liberal-statists, the supporters of the civilisational method explicitly or implicitly take their stand on the position of a structuralist, philosophical approach to the understanding of world processes.

The marking out of civilisation as the foundational subject, pole and actor of contemporary world politics is the most promising ideological approach, both for those who want to objectively evaluate the real state of affairs in world politics, for those who are striving to select an adequate toolkit for political science's generalisations of the new epoch, the epoch of postmodernity, and for those who are striving to defend their own unique identity in the conditions of a progressive blending and also of the real attacks of network globalisation. In other words, the appeal to civilisations allows one to organically fill the ideological vacuum that was formed after the historical crisis of all theories that had opposed liberalism, and also after the internal crisis of liberalism itself, which was unable to handle the guardianship of the contemporary world space, as the unfortunate experience of Fukuyama's utopia confirms.

Civilisation as a concept construed in the contemporary philosophical context proves to be the centre of a new ideology. This ideology can be described as multi-polarity.

The Scantiness of the Ideological Arsenal of Opponents of Globalism and the Unipolar World

Opposition to globalism, which announces itself ever more loudly on all levels and in all corners of the planet, has not yet formed into a concrete system of views. In this is the weakness of the anti-globalist movement; it is unsystematic and deprived of ideological orderliness; patchy and chaotic elements prevail in it, most often representing an inarticulate mixture of anarchism, irrelevant Leftism, ecology and even more extravagant and marginal ideas. In it, third-rate losers of Western gauchism[14] lay claim to the leading roles. In other cases, globalisation collides with resistance from the side of national governments, which do not wish to give over part of their sovereign authority to external control. And finally, the representatives of traditional religion, as well as supporters of ethnic and religious independence, actively resist globalisation and its Atlantic-Western liberal-democratic code, its networked nature and its value system (individualism, hedonism, laxity); we see this especially clearly in the Islamic world.

These three existing levels of opposition to globalisation and American hegemony are unable to lead to the development of a general strategy and distinct ideology, which would be able to unite different and disconnected forces, at times incomparable in scale and oriented in contrary ways in relation to local problems. The anti-globalist movement suffers from 'the disease of infantile Leftism' and is blocked by the experience of a whole series of defeats suffered by the global Leftist movement in the last century. National governments, as a rule, do not have enough of a scope to throw down a challenge to the highly developed technological might of the West; besides, their political and especially economic elites are completely involved in transnational projects, dependent on that very West; while local, ethnic and religious movements and communities, although they can, at certain moments, prove to be an effective opposition to globalisation, are too uncoordinated to count on in earnest for a change in the foundational trends of the world, or even for a correction of course.

The Meaning of the Concept 'Civilisation' in Opposition to Globalisation

In such a situation, the concept of civilisation comes to help as a fundamental category for the organisation of a full-blown alternative project on a

---

14 Dugin discusses this at length in Chapter Eight.-Ed.

world scale. If one puts this concept at the centre of attention, then one can find a basis for a harmonic resonance of alignment of broad governmental, public, social and political forces into a general system. One can unite under the banner of a multiplicity of civilizations, peoples, and religious and ethnic communities living under various governments, offering them a common, centralised idea (in the framework of a concrete civilisation) and leaving them many choices for the hunt for identity inside it, allowing for the coexistence of civilisations, differing according to their fundamental parameters.

And such a perspective absolutely does not necessarily lead to a 'clash of civilisations', Huntington notwithstanding. Here both conflicts and alliances are possible. The most important thing is that a multi-polar world, emerging in such an instance, will create the real preconditions for the continuation of the political history of mankind, inasmuch as it will normatively affirm a variety of sociopolitical, religious, moral, economic and cultural systems. Otherwise, simple and sporadic opposition to globalism on a local level or on behalf of an ideologically amorphous mass of anti-globalists (and that in the best case) will only postpone this 'end', and will put the brakes on its onset, but will not become a real alternative.

Toward 'Large Spaces'

The selection of civilisation as the subject of world politics in the Twenty-first century will allow one to conduct 'regional globalisation', a unification between themselves of countries and *narodi*, relating to one and the same civilisation. This will allow one to make use of the benefit of social openness, not in relation to everyone simultaneously, but rather in the first place to those who belong to a common civilisational type.

An example of such integration along civilisational criteria is afforded by the new supra-national political organisation of the European Union. It is a prototype of 'regional globalisation', including in its boundaries those countries and cultures that have a common culture, history and value-system. But, having admitted the undoubted right of Europeans to form a new political subject on the basis of their own civilisational differences, it is rather natural to admit an analogical process in the Islamic, Chinese, Eurasian, Latin American, and the African civilisations.

After Carl Schmitt, it is customary in political science to call analogical projects of integration 'large spaces'.[15] In economics, even before Schmitt,

---

15 Carl Schmitt. *Völkerrechtliche grossraumordnung mit interventionsverbot für raum-fremde mächte: Ein beitrag zum reichsbegriff im völkerrecht* (Berlin: Dunker and Humbolt, 1991).

this was theoretically understood and employed in practice with colossal success by the creator of the model of the German 'customs union', Friedrich von List.[16] The 'large space' is a different name for that, which we understand by 'civilisation' in its geopolitical, spatial and cultural senses. The 'large space' differs from other existing national governments precisely in that it is built on the foundation of a common value system and historical kinship, and it also unifies a few or even a multitude of different governments, tied together by a 'community of fate'. In various large spaces, the integrating factor can vary; somewhere it will be religion; somewhere ethnic origin; somewhere, cultural form; somewhere, the sociopolitical type; somewhere, geographic position.

An important precedent: the creation of a European Union shows that the embodiment of the 'large space' in practice, the transition from a government to a supra-governmental establishment, built on the foundation of civilisational commonality, is possible, constructive and, despite all internal problems, positively unfolds in reality.

A Register of Civilisations

In contrast to national governments, it is possible to argue about the number and borders between civilisations. Huntington separates out the following:

1. Western,

2. Confucian (Chinese),

3. Japanese,

4. Islamic,

5. Indian,

6. Slavic-Orthodox,

7. Latin American, and possibly,

8. African civilisations.

However, some considerations force themselves on us. Huntington includes the USA and Canada in Western civilisation with Europe. Historically this is accurate, but today, from a geopolitical point of view,

---

16 Friedrich von List (1789-1846) was a German philosopher and economist. In his own footnote, Dugin references Friedrich von List, *National System of Political Economy* (Moscow, 2005). Von List has never been translated into English. -Ed.

they constitute in relation to one another two different 'large spaces', the strategic, economic and even geopolitical interests of which diverge ever more and more. Europe has two identities: the 'Atlantic' (for which it is entirely fair to identify Europe and North America) and the 'Continental' (which, on the contrary, is strongly attracted to the construction of independent policies and to the return of Europe to history as an independent player, and not as a mere military beachhead for its North American 'younger brother').

Euroatlantism has its headquarters in England and the countries of Eastern Europe (which are moved by an inertial Russophobia), while Eurocontinentalism has its in France and Germany, with the support of Spain and Italy (this is classic Old Europe). The civilisation is, in any case, one, Western, but its 'large spaces', it may be, will be organised somewhat differently.

By Slavic-Orthodox civilisation it is more accurate to understand Eurasian civilisation, to which belong historically, organically and culturally not only the Slavs and not only the Orthodox, but also other ethnicities (including the Turks, Caucasians, Siberians, and so on) and a significant portion of the population professing Islam.

The Islamic world itself, undoubtedly, united religiously with the constantly growing awareness of its own identity, in its turn is separated into a few 'large spaces': 'the Arab world', 'the zone of continental Islam' (Iran, Afghanistan, Pakistan) and the diffusion of Islam in the Pacific region. A special place in this picture is occupied by the Muslims of Africa, but also by the constantly growing communities of Europe and America. And, nevertheless, Islam is precisely a civilisation, more and more recognising its peculiarity and its difference from other civilisations, and in the first place from liberal-Western civilisation, which has been actively treading upon the Islamic world in the course of globalisation.

It is complicated to establish borders between the zones of influence of Japanese and Chinese civilisation in the Pacific region, whose civilisational identity remains open to a significant degree.

And, of course, it is difficult for now to speak of a common consciousness of the inhabitants of the African continent, although in the future this situation might change, inasmuch as in the present process there is at any rate historical precedent, such as in the African Union,[17] but also in the existence of a Pan-African idea.

---

17 The African Union was established in 2002 and consists of 54 African nations, and is an attempt to organise a united front among the various countries to addresses problems that are specific to their continent.-Ed.

The growing intimacy between the countries of Latin America in recent years is evident, especially considering the fact of North American pressure, although it is too early for now to speak of processes of integration.

There are no existing barriers at all to the integration of the Eurasian expanse around Russia, inasmuch as these zones were politically, culturally, economically, socially and psychologically united during the course of many centuries. The Western border of the Eurasianist civilisation goes somewhat more East of the Western border of the Ukraine, making that newly-formulated government *a fortiori* fragile and not viable.

Essentially, the enumeration of civilisations gives us an idea of the quantity of poles in a multi-polar world. All of them — besides the West — dwell, so far, in a potential condition, but at the same time each of these civilisations has serious, impressive grounds to move toward integration and to become a full-fledged subject of the history of the Twenty-first century.

The Multi-polar Ideal

The idea of a multi-polar world, where the poles will be as many as there are civilisations, allows one to propose to humanity a broad choice of cultural, paradigmatic, social and spiritual alternatives. We shall have a model with the availability of 'regional universalism' in concrete 'large spaces', which will give to enormous zones and significant segments of humanity an unavoidable social dynamic, characteristic of globalisation and openness, but without those shortcomings that globalisation has taken on a global scale. Moreover, in such a system, regionalism and the autonomous and independent development of local, ethnic and religious communities can be developed at full speed, inasmuch as the more unifying pressure, characteristic of national governments, weakens considerably (we see this in the European Union, where integration considerably facilitates the development of local communes and so called Euroregions).[18] In addition, we shall be able at last to decide the fundamental contradiction between exclusivism and inclusivism of the 'imperial' identity: the planet

---

18 Euroregions are those areas which extend over the territory of several different sovereign states who border upon each other. Euroregions allow for the citizens of these regions to address common problems, although their power is restricted to the local level and have no national power.-Ed.

will present itself not as one, sole *oecumene*[19] (with the inherent 'cultural racism' of this solitariness in the distribution of the titles of 'civilised nations', as opposed to 'barbarians' and 'savages') but as a few *oecumenes*, a few 'heavens', where there will live side-by-side in their rhythm, in their context, in their own time, with their own consciousness and unconsciousness, not one 'humanity', but a few.

It is impossible to say beforehand how relations between them will turn out. Surely, both dialogue and collisions will emerge. But something else is more important: history will continue, and we will return from that fundamental historical dead-end to which uncritical faith in progress, rationality and the gradual development of humanity drove us.

Something in man changes with time, but something remains eternal and invariable. Civilisation allows one to strictly develop everything in its place. Reason and the philosophical, social, political, and economic systems created by it will be able to develop according to their own lines, while the collective unconscious will freely preserve its archetypes, its basis and inviolability. Moreover, in every civilisation, both rationality and the unconscious can affirm their own standards, secure their correctness, and strengthen them or change them according to its own discretion.

There will be no universal standard, neither in the material nor in the spiritual aspect. Each civilisation will at last receive the right to freely proclaim that which is, according to its wishes, the measure of things. Somewhere that will be man, somewhere religion, somewhere ethics, somewhere materialism.

But in order that the project of multi-polarity can realise itself, we must still survive more than a few skirmishes. And in the first place, it is necessary to get the better of the first and foremost enemy: globalisation, the striving of the Atlantic Western pole to hang its unipolar hegemony on all the nations and countries on Earth. Despite the deep and sure observations of its own best intellectuals, many representatives of the political establishment of the USA continue as before to use the term 'civilisation' in a singular sense, understanding by it 'American civilisation'. This is the real challenge, to which all nations of the Earth, and Russians most of all, must give an adequate response.

---

19 First coined in its modern usage by Lewis Mumford in his *Technics and Civilization* (1934), the term refers to a theoretical unified nation consisting of all the countries of the world.-Ed.

8

THE TRANSFORMATION OF THE LEFT IN THE TWENTY-FIRST CENTURY

The Leftist Philosophy in Crisis

In contrast to the situation that ruled in the sphere of political ideas and projects one hundred years ago, to speak of the presence of some kind of clearly determined space for Leftist (socialist or Communist) projects is now impossible. The problem is that, at the end of the Twentieth century, there occurred a fundamental crisis of expectations, connected with Leftist movements, Leftist ideas, Leftist philosophy and Leftist politics. This is above all connected to the breakup of the Soviet Union and the falling apart of the socialist camp, and also to the loss of influence and prestige of European Marxism, which at a specific time practically became 'the reserve ideology' of Western Europe.

Moreover, even at the best of times, the Leftist project was not something uniform and universal, and the fate of Leftist ideas in the concrete political practice of various peoples showed that, even from a purely theoretical point of view, within the Leftist political philosophy itself, various foundational tendencies exist, which one should study separately.

Leftist political philosophy from the beginning was thought of as a fundamental, general and systematic criticism of liberal capitalism. In the middle of the Twentieth century, there arose the phenomenon of a systematic critique of the Leftist project (both from the side of liberals — Hayek, Popper, Aron, and so on, as well as from the side of neo-Marxists and Freudian-Marxists); with the Leftist ideology itself, the philosophical schools carried out the same thing that the Leftist ideology carried out concerning liberal capitalism 100, or 150 years ago.

Three Varieties of Leftist Ideology

From the position of today's historical experience, one can identify three foundational directions in Leftist political philosophy, which either continue along a new branch of previous ideological development, rethink the past, or offer something radically new. They are:

- The Old Left (French: *vetero-gauche*);

- Left Nationalists (National Communists, National Bolsheviks or National Gauchists);

- New Left (neo-Gauchists, Postmoderns).

The first two tendencies existed at the end of the Nineteenth century and throughout the Twentieth century, and to some degree they are present in today's world. The third orientation appeared in the 1950s and 1960s and developed out of a criticism of the Old Leftists, which gradually appeared in the course of postmodernity and influenced the aesthetics, stylistics and philosophy of modern Western society to a great extent.

The Old Left Today (The Blind Alley of Orthodoxy; Perspectives of Evolutionary Strategy and Pro-Liberal Revisionism)

The Old Left are now divided into a few orientations:

- Orthodox Marxists;

- Social Democrats;

- Post-Social Democrats (adherents of the Third Way, along the lines of Giddens);[1]

- European Orthodox Marxists.

By inertia, they exist in European countries and also in the United States and Third World countries, continuing to defend the foundational premises of Marxist thought. They are often embodied in Communist parties,

---

1   Anthony Giddens (b. 1938) is a British sociologist. He envisions the Third Way as a post-Marxist phenomenon which will deal with the effects of globalisation, changes in personal life wrought by modernity and postmodernity, and humanity's connection to nature. He outlines these ideas in a number of books, especially *The Third Way* (Cambridge: Polity, 1998).-Ed.

professing the corresponding ideology. In the majority of cases, those Orthodox Marxists soften (in the spirit of Eurocommunism)[2] the radicality of Marx's teaching, rejecting the call to a revolutionary uprising and the establishment of a dictatorship of the proletariat. The most lasting form of Orthodox Marxism turned out to be the Trotskyite movement (the Fourth International), which was almost untouched by the fall of the USSR and the breakup of the Soviet system, so far as it initially originated from a hard critique of that system.

It is characteristic that the more orthodox followers of Marx meet in those countries where the proletarian, socialist revolutions did not occur, although Marx himself predicted that, precisely in the more developed industrial countries with a working capitalist economy, these revolutions were destined to take place. European Marxism in some sense accepted the fact that Marx and Engels' predictions were realised, not where by all logic they should have been realised, but on the contrary, where it was thought that they could never be realised under any conditions, such as Russia. Rejecting the Soviet experience as a historical stretch, this variety of old Leftists in practice does not believe in the success of Marxist prophecies, but continues to defend their views rather as being faithful 'in the moral sense' and 'to the ideological tradition', rather than seriously counting on the revolutionary uprising of the proletariat (who, in the modern Western world, it seems, no longer exist as a class, to such a degree has it merged with the petty bourgeoisie).

The most important shortcoming of Western Orthodox Marxists consists in their continuing to operate using the terms of the industrial society at a time when Western European and especially American society have moved to a qualitatively new stage, the post-industrial (information) society, of which almost nothing is said in classical Marxism, excluding the troubled intuitions of the young Marx about 'the real domination of capital'. In the absence or failure of the socialist revolutions, this can come as a replacement of 'the formal domination of capital', characteristic of the industrial age. But even these fragmentary observations of the Orthodox Marxists, as a rule, do not spark great interest and are not at the centre of attention.

Gradually, the prognostic and political meaning of such Orthodox Marxist discourse comes to nought, and this means that to speak of their ideas as a 'project' — even 'a Leftist project' — is not possible. At the same

---

2   Eurocommunism was a term coined in the 1970s to describe an attempt to develop a form of Communism specifically suited for Western European nations, and not dependent on alignment with the Soviet Union.-Ed.

time, their critical observations concerning the capitalist system, moral views, solidarity with the unfortunate and the criticism of liberalism can arouse definite interest and sympathy. The adherents of this persuasion almost always relate only with distrust to other anti-liberal theories, and are typically closed to dialogue and are degenerating into a sect.

European Social Democracy

European Social Democrats differ slightly from Orthodox Communists. This political current also derives from Marxism, but already in the epoch of Kautsky[3] it selected not a revolutionary, but an evolutionary path, repudiating radicalism and placing its goal in influencing politics in the Leftist manner (social justice, the 'welfare state', etc.) by parliamentary means and through organised labour movements. This version of the old Left achieved considerable results in European countries, having prede-termined to a large degree the sociopolitical aspect of European society, in sharp contrast to the United States, where, on the contrary, the Right liberal doctrine undoubtedly prevails.

The purpose of the Social Democratic orientation of the old Left in our time comes down to economic theses, which oppose liberal tendencies. Social Democrats come out in favour of:

1) Progressive income tax (liberals: for flat tax);

2) The nationalisation of large monopolies (liberals: for privatisation);

3) The broadening of government responsibility in the social sector;

4) Free medicine, education, guaranteed pension plans (liberals: for reducing government influence in the economy, private medicine, education and pension plans).

Social Democrats try to realise these demands through parliamentary electoral mechanisms and, in critical situations, through the mobilisation of labour unions and social organisations, right up to strikes.

It is significant that for Social Democrats, the characteristic slogans are libertarian (not to be confused with liberal!):

---

3   Karl Kautsky (1854-1938) was a Czech-German Marxist philosopher who was the leading European Marxist theoretician between the death of Engels and the Russian Revolution. He was an opponent of the Bolshevik revolution, claiming that Lenin was attempting to impose reforms on Russia for which it did not have the correct economic or social basis.-Ed.

- The legalisation of light narcotics;

- The protection of sexual and ethnic minorities and homosexual marriages;

- The broadening of individual rights and civic freedom;

- The development of the institutions of civil society;

- Ecology;

- The softening of criminal penal codes (repealing capital punishment), and so on.

Classical Social Democrats combine the demands of Leftist economics (social justice, strengthening the role of government) with the broadening of personal rights and civic freedoms ('human rights'), the development of democracy, and internationalism (today it is accepted to speak of 'multiculturalism' and 'globalisation').

The project of classical Social Democrats, directed toward the future, is the continuation of such a politics of concrete steps along a sociopolitical evolution, in argument with the Right — both with liberals in economics, and with national conservatives in politics. Most often, classical Social Democrats are also:

- For progress;

- For the battle against archaic and religious prejudices;

- For science and culture.

At the same time, there are no serious theoretical developments regarding the new conditions of post-industrial society discussed in this camp, and both the criticism of classical Marxism and the thematisation of capitalism on the new historical stage (in contrast to the postmodernists and 'the New Left') are almost entirely absent from them.

Socialists of 'the Third Way'

One more version of the Old Left is an orientation of Social Democrats, which in the face of the evident upsurge of liberal ideas in 1990-2000 decided to compromise with liberals. The theoreticians of this orientation (in particular, the Englishman Anthony Giddens) called it the Third Way, something between classical European Social Democracy and

American (more generally, Anglo-Saxon) liberalism. Proponents of the Third Way propose to find a compromise between Social Democrats and liberal democrats on the basis of their common ideological roots in the Enlightenment, and their common dislike both of conservatism and of Leftist extremism. The platform for compromise is constructed in terms of give-and-take relating to concrete arrangements concerning the extent to which Social Democrats agree to lower the progressive tax in the direction of the flat tax, while liberals raise the latter in the direction of the former. Concerning the rights of man, there are no principal disagreements between them about guaranteeing minority rights or about multiculturalism (if we do not consider liberal conservatives, who combine the idea of a flat income tax with conservative principles of the family, morals, and religion as American rights, such as the Republicans and 'neocons').

The purpose of the Third Way project, according to Giddens, consists in the cooperation of Social Democrats and liberals in the construction of a European society, founding itself on a broadening of personal rights, preservation of the institutions of private ownership, and a modification of the ability of government to intervene and the mechanism of redistribution in each concrete instance, in deliberately established limits. In contrast to classical Social Democrats and even European Communists, the adherents of the Third Way relate sympathetically to the USA and insist on strengthening the Atlantic alliance (whereas typical Leftists — both old and new — harshly criticise America and American society for its liberalism, inequality and imperialism).

If there are real renegades among the Leftist movements, then these are precisely the followers of the Third Way. Next come former Trotskyites (such as certain Americans — the theoretical founders of neoconservatism — or Europeans, for instance the head of the European Commission, the Portuguese Barroso),[4] who changed their views from extreme Communism and revolutionary socialism for a no less radical defence of liberalism, the market and economic inequality.

The Leftist project in the case of Third Way socialists is to preserve the status quo.

---

4   José Manuel Barroso (b. 1956) was the Prime Minister of Portugal between 2002 and 2004, and became President of the European Commission in 2004 (and still occupies this position, as of 2012). During the 1970s, Barroso was an outspoken Maoist, but by the 1980s had moved to the Right.-Ed.

National Communism (Conceptual Paradoxes, Ideological Imbalances, Subterranean Energies)

National Gauchism should be understood as a perfectly unique phenomenon. In contrast to Orthodox Marxism and Social Democracy, this orientation is studied much less, and its correct deciphering is a matter for the future. The problem is that National Gauchism almost never parades its national component, covering it up or even repudiating it. Consequently, the study of the direct and honest discourse of the National Communist movements, parties or regimes themselves most often becomes more difficult because of the fact that the theses they discuss either correspond to reality only in part, or else not at all. We meet deliberate, open and unbroken National Gauchist discourse only on the periphery of those regimes and political parties that, in themselves, profess and realise this ideological model, refusing, however, to admit this. For that reason, National Gauchism dodges direct, rational study, preferring to safeguard half of the phenomenon; whatever is tied to the 'national' is in the shade.

National Communists themselves reckon themselves as being 'simply Communists' and 'Orthodox Marxists', strictly following the teachings of the Communist classics. In order to understand what the discussion is really about, it suffices to propose the following criterion: socialist (proletarian) revolutions were victorious only in those countries that Marx thought were entirely unprepared for them by virtue of the following:

- Their agrarian character;

- Underdevelopment (or lack) of capitalist relations;

- A paucity of urban proletarians;

- Weak industrialisation;

- The preservation of the fundamental social conditions of traditional societies (in virtue of their belonging to pre-modernity).

And this is the fundamental paradox of Marxism: where socialism was supposed to be victorious, and where all conditions came together to this end, it was not victorious; although purely theoretically it was there that Orthodox Marxist parties and trends existed, and are in part still preserved. But in those places where, according to Marx, the socialist revolution could in no way win, they won triumphantly. The victorious Communists, in the first place the Russian Bolsheviks, carefully tried to cover up and retouch this obvious lack of correspondence to the prognosis of their teacher, never subjecting it to careful analysis, preferring to arbitrarily build a reality under their speculative constructions — driving society, politics and economics under abstract criteria, artistically and mechanically. And only foreign observers (sympathisers or critics) noticed this National Communistic character of successful Marxist revolutions, recognising nationalistic elements as a driving factor and virtue, providing these revolutions with success and stability via archaic national stories of the mobilisation of Marxism as a nationally interpreted eschatological myth. Sorel was one of the first to notice this; Ustrialov noticed a little later. (Savitskiy, the Germans Niekisch, Petel, Lauffenburg, Wolfheim and others — from the side of the sympathisers; Popper, Hayek, Cohn, Aron — from the side of the critics.)

National Communism ruled in the USSR, Communist China, North Korea, Vietnam, Albania, Cambodia, and also in many Communist movements of the Third World, from the Mexican Chiapas and Peruvian Sendero Luminoso (The Golden Path) to the Kurdish Workers' Party and Islamic socialism. Leftist — socialist — elements were found in the Fascism of Mussolini and in the National Socialism of Hitler, but in these cases, these elements were fragmentary, not systematised and superficial, exhibited more in marginal or sporadic phenomena: Left Italian Fascism only occurred in its early Futurist[5] phase and in the Italian Social Republic;[6] and the Leftist anti-Hitler National Socialism of the Strasser brothers, or the anti-Hitler underground of the National Bolsheviks Schultz-Boysen and so forth, neither of which was permitted any place within the regime of the Third Reich. Although, it would seem, according to the formal signs and title, we should relate National Socialism to this category, there

---

5   Futurism was an Italian art movement which was founded by the writer F. T. Marinetti in 1909. Futurism loathed anything conventional or traditional, and embraced speed, technology, youthfulness and violence, as well as Italian nationalism. Although Futurism had already reached its apex by 1918, Marinetti himself became an ardent Fascist, and attempted, unsuccessfully, to convince Mussolini that Futurism should become the official art of Fascism. Marinetti continued to nurse such ambitions, by bringing Futurism closer to mainstream Italian culture, until the late 1930s, when Fascism, following German National Socialism, ultimately condemned all Modernist art as degenerate.-Ed.

6   The Repubblica Sociale Italiana, also sometimes known as the Salò Republic due to its being headquartered there, was the government of Fascist exiles which was set up in northern Italy following the coup against Mussolini in July 1943. Once rescued by the Germans and instated as its head of state, Mussolini returned to his socialist roots, and said that he had been prevented from realising the genuine Fascist revolution by political contingencies, and pledged to create a new Fascist state that was much more socialist in nature. He claimed to advocate workers' rights, and while the original Fascist regime had defended private property, he now nationalised all companies within his sphere of influence.-Ed.

was no pure socialism as such there—rather statism, multiplied by the invocation of the archaic energies of the *ethnos* and 'race'. But in Soviet Bolshevism, very precisely indicated by the *Smena vekh*[7] author Nikolai Ustrialov as National Bolshevism, very evidently both beginnings are present: the social and the national, although this time around, the 'national' did not receive a conceptual formulation.

Up to the present day, many political movements, for instance in Latin America, are inspired by this complex of ideas, while the political regimes of Cuba, Venezuela or Bolivia (Evo Morales is the first South American leader of native Indian heritage), or Ollanta Humala,[8] the supporters of whom are close to seizing power in Peru, and other National Communist movements are full-blown political realities. Either a governmental system is already founded on them, or else this could happen in the near future. And everywhere where Communism has a realistic chance, there we face Leftist ideas that have been multiplied by national (ethnic, archaic) energies and are implemented along the lines of traditional society. Basically, this is neo-Orthodox Marxism, *sui generis*[9] National Marxism (however it would characterise itself). But where there are all the classical prerequisites, according to Marx, for its realisation (industrial society, the development of heavy industry, an urban proletarian, and so on), socialist revolutions did not occur (with the exception of the ephemeral Bavarian Republic),[10] are not occurring, and most likely will never occur.

The meaning of Leftist nationalism (National Gauchism) consists in the mobilisation of archaic foundations—local, as a rule—in order to break away to the surface and exhibit itself in sociopolitical creativity. Here, socialist theory comes into play, serving as a sort of 'interface' for those energies, without which it would be forced to remain a strictly local phenomena, but thanks to Marxism—however understood and interpreted—these national energies receive the possibility of communicating with other energies, analogical by nature but different structurally, and can

---

7   *Smena vekh* (Change of Landmarks) was a collection of articles published by Ustrialov in 1921, stating the basic principles of National Bolshevism.-Ed.

8   Ollanta Humala (b. 1962) is the leader of the Peruvian Nationalist Party. He was elected President of Peru in July 2011.-Ed.

9   In philosophy, it refers to an idea that is unique and cannot be included in a wider concept.-Ed.

10 The Bavarian Social Republic was a short-lived attempt to establish a Soviet state in Bavaria, Germany. Formed on 6 April 1919, it lasted for slightly less than a month, when elements of the German Army and the paramilitary Freikorps entered Munich on 3 May and defeated the Communists.-Ed.

even claim universality and planetary breadth; transforming, thanks to a socialist rationality warmed up by nationalism, into a messianic project.

The grandiose experience of the USSR shows how large-scale the National Communist initiative can be, having produced for almost a century a fundamental headache for all the world's capitalist systems. China, meanwhile, even today in a new context, accentuating more and more the national component of its sociopolitical model, proves that this foundation, in good time and delicately worked, can remain competitive, even after the global triumph of liberal-capitalism. The experience of Venezuela and Bolivia, for its part, illustrates that National Communist regimes arise even in our time, and demonstrate their capacity for life in the face of great pressure. North Korea, Vietnam and Cuba, as before, maintain their political systems from Soviet times, not adopting such market reforms as China adopted, and not giving up their positions, as the USSR did.

From a theoretical point of view, in the phenomenon of National Gauchism we are faced with Marxism, interpreted in the spirit of archaic eschatological expectations and deep national mythologies, connected to the expectation of 'the end of times' and the return of 'the golden age' (cargo cults, millenarianism). The thesis of justice and 'government rights' on which the socialist utopia is built is recognised as religious, which awakens the fundamental tectonic energies of the *ethnos*.

Does National Gauchism today have a project for the future? In its completed form, no. It is hampered by a series of factors:

- The persisting shock of the dissolution of Soviet National Communism (Russian Eurasianists even in the 1920s predicted this downfall if the Soviet leadership did not recognise the importance of minding the national and religious myths directly, face to face);

- The lack of a conceptualisation and rationalisation of the national component in the general ideological complex of National Communist movements and ideologies (the absolute majority of supporters of this ideological orientation truly reckon themselves to be 'simply Marxists' or 'socialists');

- The weak institutional communication of National Bolshevik circles between themselves on a global scale (there are no serious, large-scale conferences on this theme, no theoretical journals are published, or, if they are, they remain marginalized, and there are no philosophical developments).

Nevertheless, in my opinion, National Gauchism could certainly have a global future, insofar as among many segments of humanity archaic, ethnic and religious energies are far from being spent, whatever can be said of the citizens of the modern, enlightened and rational West.

The New Left (Anti-Globalism, Postmodern Paths, Labyrinths of Freedom, to the Advent of Post-humanity)

More than anything today, that which is called the 'New Left' (neo-Gauchism) or 'postmodernism' fits the word combination 'Leftist project'. Amidst the whole spectrum of Leftist ideas at the start of the Twenty-first century, precisely this orientation is not only the most bright and blazing, but also the most thought out, intellectually adjusted and systematised.

New Leftists appeared in the 1950s and 1960s in Europe on the periphery of the Leftist flank of Marxists, Trotskyites and anarchists. Marx was the *sine qua non*[11] for them, but they also actively used other theoretical and philosophical sources, in contrast to the 'Old Leftists', bringing imported elements into their own theory without disturbance. For that reason, Marxism in this form actively broadened, while constantly juxtaposing with other philosophical conceptions, developed itself, rethought itself, subjected itself to criticism — in short, became an object of concentrated reflection. Such an unrestricted relation of the New Left to Marxism produced two results: on one hand, it became diluted; on the other, it modernised essentially.

The 'philosophers of suspicion', drawing not only on Marx but also on Freud and Nietzsche, exerted a great influence upon the philosophy of the New Leftists. Through Sartre, one of the classic theorists of the New Leftists, the deep influence of Martin Heidegger and the existential problem penetrated into the Leftist movement. Structuralism had a colossal significance, from the most important theoreticians of structuralism, Ferdinand de Saussure to Levi-Strauss. In a philosophical sense, New Leftists were themselves structuralists, while in the second half of the 1980s, developing this philosophical impulse further, they moved on to 'post-structuralism', having exposed to systematic critical reflection their own views of the 1960s and 1970s.

The New Leftists approached Marxism from a structuralist position — that is, they thought that Marx's most important idea of Marx's

---

11 Latin: 'a thing that is essential'.-Ed.

concerned the fundamental influence of understructures (in the usual case, bourgeois society, carefully hidden from ideological consciousness) in relation to a superstructure. The Marxist analysis of ideology as 'false consciousness' became, for the New Leftists, the key to the interpretation of society, philosophy, man and the economy. But that same train of thought they discovered from Nietzsche, who had raised the whole spectrum of philosophical ideas to the primordial 'will to power' (this was its very basis, according to Nietzsche), and from Freud, for whom the base was the subconscious and unconscious impulses, rooted in the mineral foundations of man's sexuality and the habitual structures that form in early childhood. To this was added the Heideggerian model, where the base is the fact of pure existence, *Dasein*. All the various decipherings of the 'base' were aggregated by the New Leftists into a general scheme, where the role of 'the base' as such — regardless of a concrete philosophical tendency — was carried over into the notion of structure. Structure — that is, simultaneous industrial forces reproduced in industrial relations, the subconscious, 'the will to power', and *Dasein*.

The basic idea of the New Leftists is that bourgeois society is a result of many-faceted violence and oppression by the 'superstructures' (of the bourgeoisie political system, ordinary consciousness, the rule of elites, generally accepted philosophical systems, science, society, the market economy, and so on), 'bases' and 'structures' (also understood very broadly, including 'unconscious', 'proletariat', 'corporeity', 'mass', the experience of authentic existence, freedom and justice). By such means, the New Leftists, in contrast to the Old Leftists, mount a systematic, critical attack on capitalist society simultaneously from all directions, from the political (the events of May 1968 in European capitals) to the cultural, philosophical, artistic, the very presentation of man, reason, science, and reality. In the course of this massive intellectual work (to which, incidentally, neither the Old Leftists nor the National Gauchists paid the slightest attention), the New Leftists came to the conclusion that capitalism is not only sociopolitical evil, but the fundamental expression of a global lie concerning man, reality, reason, and society, and consequently, in capitalist society, as in the resulting moments, is concentrated the whole history of alienation. The New Leftists re-animated Rousseau's idea of the 'Noble Savage' and proposed an extensive panorama of an ideal society without exploitation, alienation, lies, suppression, or exclusion, by analogy with the archaic groups which are motivated by the 'economy of the gift' (M. Mauss).[12]

---

12 Marcel Mauss (1872-1950) was an influential French sociologist. In his 1923 book *The Gift*, he studied archaic societies and discovered that their economies were

The analysis of the New Leftists showed that modernity not only did not realise in practice its 'liberation' slogans, but made the dictatorship of alienation even more rigid and repulsive, although hidden behind democratic and liberal facades. In this manner was the theory of postmodernism assembled, founded on the fact that, at the very foundation of the picture of the world, science, philosophy and political ideologies, which had been assembled at the dawn of the epoch of modernity or in the course of its development, are strained interpretations, infelicities, delusions and 'racist' presuppositions, which even theoretically block the possibility of liberating 'the structure' ('the base') from 'superstructures'. This led to the reconsideration of the philosophical tradition of modernity with the unmasking of those mechanisms that concentrate the nodes of alienation in themselves. This practice received the name 'deconstruction', which proposes a careful and thorough structural analysis of the context from which one or another idea proceeded, with a detailed ex-articulation of the substantial nuclei from out of the layer of pathos, moralism, rhetorical figures and conscious juggling. Foucault, in *History of Madness*[13] and *The Birth of the Clinic*,[14] showed that the contemporary relation to psychological disorders, and, more broadly, to disease as such, carries all the signs of intellectual racism, apartheid, and other totalitarian prejudices, that become evident in the equation of the sick with the criminal and in the structural identity of penitential and therapeutic establishments, having been one and the same in the early stages of modernity.

Bourgeois society, despite its mimicry and democratic facade, proves to be a totalitarian and disciplinarian society. What is more, at the centre of this liberal dictatorship, the New Leftists recognise the deep and almost never doubted normative notions of reason, science, reality, society and so on, and not only one or the other political and economic mechanisms, which are themselves consequences of the deep mechanisms of alienation.

In this consists the main difference between the New Leftists and the Old Leftists: the New Leftists doubt the structure of reason, they contest the basis of our conception of reality, disrobe positive science as a mystification and dictatorship of the academic circles (Feyerabend, Kuhn)[15], and sharply criticise the concept of man as a totalitarian abstraction. They

based on a principle of reciprocal exchange, rather than wealth accumulation as in modern societies.-Ed.

13 Michel Foucault, *History of Madness* (London: Routledge, 2006).-Ed.

14 Michel Foucault, *The Birth of the Clinic* (New York: Pantheon Books, 1973).-Ed.

15 Paul Feyerabend (1924-1994) and Thomas S. Kuhn (1922-1996) were both philosophers of science who argued against the notion that modern science represented a form of objective truth, free from ideological or other prejudices.-Ed.

do not believe that it is possible to change something by the path of evolution in the Leftist manner of the existing system, but also contest the
effectiveness of radical Marxism, noting that it did not overcome what
it was supposed to; and that where it did, it was not Orthodox Marxism
(they borrow from Trotsky the criticism of Stalinism and the Soviet experience).

And so the New Leftists formulate a vast project of 'the correct' future,
in which the central place is occupied by:

- The rejection of reason (the call to the conscious adoption of schizophrenia by Deleuze and Guattari);

- The renunciation of man as the measure of all things ('the death of
  man' of Levi, 'the death of the author' of Barthes);

- The overcoming of all sexual taboos (freedom to choose one's orientation, renunciation of the prohibition on incest, a refusal to recognise perversion as perversion, and so on);

- The legalisation of all kinds of narcotics, including the hard ones;

- A move to new forms of spontaneous and sporadic being (the 'rhizome' of Deleuze);

- The destruction of structural society and government in the service of new, free and anarchical communes.

The book *Empire* by Negri and Hardt, in which are given the theses of
the New Leftists, can be read as a political manifesto of these tendencies,
simplified to the point of primitiveness. Negri and Hardt call the global
capitalistic system 'Empire' and identify it with globalism and American
world government. In their opinion, globalism creates the conditions for
a universal, planetary revolution of the masses, who, using the common
character of globalism and its possibilities for communication and the
wide, open spread of knowledge, create a network of world sabotage, for
the shift from humanity (standing out as the subject and object of oppression, hierarchical relations, exploitation and disciplinarian strategies) to
post-humanity (mutants, cyborgs, clones, and virtuality), and the free
selection of gender, appearance and individual rationality according to
one's arbitrary rule and for any space of time. Negri and Hardt think that
this will lead to the freeing up of the creative potential of the masses and
at the same time to the destruction of the global power of 'Empire'. This
theme is endlessly repeated in the cinematography in such films as *The
Matrix*, *The Boys' Club*, and so on.

The anti-globalisation movement in whole is oriented precisely to such a project of the future. And such actions as 'the Conference in São Paulo',[16] where anti-globalists first tried to aim at a common strategy, attest that the New Leftist project is discovering forms of concrete political realisation. Many concrete actions — gay parades, anti-globalisation protests, Occupy Wall Street, the disturbances in immigrant suburbs of European cities, the rebellions of 'autonomous ones' in defence of squatters' rights, broad social protests of new labour unions (all reminding one of a carnival), the movement for the legalisation of drugs, ecological actions and protests and so on — are included in this orientation.

Moreover, postmodernism as an artistic style, having become the mainstream of contemporary Western art, expresses this very New Left political philosophy, entering our way of life through pictures, design or the films of Tarantino and Rodriguez, without preliminary political-philosophical analysis, outrunning our conscious selection, hooking itself into our minds without our knowledge or will. This is attended by both a general broadening of virtual communication technologies, which in their own system carry an implicit invitation to postmodernity, and the dispersion into post-human, hedonistic fragments. SMS and MMS messages, Internet blogs and video blogs, flash mobs and other habitual engagements of contemporary youth, in essence represent the realisation of separate sides of the New Left project, while, it is true, being controlled by the bourgeoisie system, willingly profiting from a fashion that this time is not its own, but that of its hidden enemy.

Here we should say a few words about the relations of the new Leftists and anti-globalists to contemporary liberals and globalists. As Marx thought in his time that capitalism, despite its horrors, was more progressive than feudalism and the Middle Ages (since it brings closer the onset of socialism), so contemporary postmodernists and new Leftists, while harshly criticising 'Empire', stand in solidarity with it to some degree, as it, in their opinion, while aggravating alienation and strengthening its planetary dictatorship, latently prepares the world revolution of the masses.

Leftists in Contemporary Russia

In conclusion we will say a few words about the state of affairs of Leftist forces in contemporary Russia. In practice, we see that we have no 'Old Leftists' in the full sense of the word, just as we had none in Soviet times. A

---

16 Presumably, this is a reference to the World Social Forum, an anti-globalist organisation which had its founding meeting on 9 April 2001 in São Paulo.-Ed.

group of Soviet Marxist-dissidents (Zinoviev, Schedovits, Medvedev) are of no account, inasmuch as they were unable to start any sort of ideological school.

National Communists, on the other hand, afford by themselves a broad formation — social, psychological and political — the leaders of which, in our time, are the Communist Party of the Russian Federation. Inasmuch as all Soviet history, marked by the victory of socialism (the true sign of a work that has an archaic foundation), is the history of unconscious National Gauchism, such a steady tendency is not surprising.

In the first stages of Zyuganov's creation of the Communist Party of the Russian Federation[17] (not without some participation on my part, as well as Prokhanov,[18] which was expressed in the opinion of the newspaper *Zavtra* [Tomorrow] at the start of the 1990s), efforts were made to interpret and conceptually appraise the presence of the national component in the Soviet worldview (National Bolshevism), but this initiative was abandoned by the leadership of the CPRF, which had occupied itself with some other matters — which were apparently more important for it. However, on the level of rhetoric and first reactions, Russian Communists in all senses present themselves as confirmed national conservatives — sometimes even as 'Orthodox Monarchists.'

Indeed, average Russians — especially the middle aged and older generations — are in large part unconscious National Gauchists. They support this complex of ideas whenever the opportunity is afforded them (the party Rodina),[19] and construe in this vein much that has no relation whatsoever to that complex (the social conservatism of United Russia, and even Putin himself). Those same marginalised groups, who, imitating European neo-Nazism, attempt to bring out an amalgam 'national social-

---

17 Gennady Zyuganov (b. 1944) is the First Secretary of the Communist Party of the Russian Federation (CPRF), which, at present, is the second-largest party in Russia. Founded in 1993, it has attempted to formulate a new form of Communism with a more nationalist bent. It declared itself to be the successor to the Communist Party of the Russian Soviet Federative Socialist Republic, which was established in 1990 to provide a republican-level branch of the Soviet Union's Communist Party for Russia, which had always been the only one of the USSR's republics to lack a republican organisation of its own. It was abolished in 1991 following the coup against Gorbachev.-Ed.

18 Alexander Prokhanov (b. 1938) is a Russian writer and novelist who became an ultra-nationalist following the collapse of the USSR. He is the Editor-in-Chief of *Zavtra*.-Ed.

19 Rodina, or Motherland-National Patriotic Union, was a coalition of nationalist and Leftist groups which was created in 2003. The party generated some controversy when it was accused of promoting anti-Semitism and racism. In 2006, Rodina merged into a new party, A Just Russia.-Ed.

ism' by name, were never National Gauchists; insofar as they imitate (as a rule, from a deficiency of intellect) the gadgets of Hitler's regime, as it were continuing to play at soldiering in the sandbox or while watching the programme *Seventeen Moments of Spring,*[20] delighting in the black as the crow's wing uniform of Bronevoy as Müller.[21] The project of the National Bolshevik Party, which I, in my time, was preparing to transform into an authentic, Russian, conscious National Gauchism on the foundations of the theories of Ustrialov, Niekisch and the Leftist Eurasianists, alas, degenerated at the end of the 1990s into hooliganism and senseless organisation, and later started to serve the anti-Russian, Orange[22] ultra-liberal powers, fed by the West (which completely contradicts the fundamental premises of National Bolshevism, which represents, both in theory and in practice, the conscious Left — being thus a strictly anti-liberal, Russian patriotic — and consequently anti-Western — project).

The New Left and the postmodernists in Russia›s political spectrum are practically not represented: the philosophical discourse of postmodernism is too complicated for them. A tiny group of conscious (representative) anti-globalists exists, but it is known more in the West and constitutes nothing serious, neither in an organisational nor in a theoretical sense. In Russian art — in particular, in the Guelman gallery at Winzavod,[23] and also in Russian film — postmodern tendencies, on the contrary, are rather clearly evident, and their artistic expressions are at times impressive. The books of Sorokin[24] or Pelevin[25] present postmodernism in a literary form.

Moreover, the average artistic or even technological — which is more important! — product of the West carries in itself a not insignificant charge of latent postmodernity, occupying therewith the Russian cultural space with actively functioning signs, which are hammered out in the creative laboratories of the New Left, and are then put on the production line of global industry, which derives a short-term benefit from them (and

---

20 *Seventeen Moments of Spring* was a Soviet television miniseries aired in 1973, about a Soviet spy who has infiltrated the Nazis' high command and is tasked with disrupting negotiations ongoing between the Third Reich and the United States for a separate peace, aligned against the Soviet Union, during the Second World War.-Ed.

21 Leonid Bronevoy played the part of Gestapo officer Heinrich Müller in the series.-Ed.

22 The Orange Revolution took place in the Ukraine in 2004-05, and was seen as a victory for liberal forces over the traditional political establishment.-Ed.

23 The Moscow Contemporary Art Centre in Moscow.-Ed.

24 Vladimir Sorokin (b. 1955) is a popular Russian writer and playwright of the postmodernist school.-Ed.

25 Victor Pelevin (b. 1962) is a Russian writer, also a postmodernist.-Ed.

gradually sharpens its own foundations). Russia here performs the role of an inert consumer, not understanding the political and ideological meaning of that which it is buying automatically — following fashions or global trends, and forgetting that every trend has, as the postmodernists say, trend-setters: those who establish a determinate trend for a specific goal.

9

Liberalism and Its Metamorphoses

In 1932, the German National Bolshevik, Ernst Niekisch, whose ideas were remarkably similar to both the Russian National Bolsheviks (Ustrialov) and the Eurasianists, wrote a book with a revealing title: *Hitler: Disaster for Germany*.[1] The book went almost unnoticed, but after a few years led him straight to the concentration camps. He turned out to be absolutely right — Hitler had, in fact, appeared to be precisely such a fateful figure for Germany. Fateful, meaning not accidental; well-founded, engrained in the course of things, joined with the logic of Fate, but embodying her darker aspect. And in this book, as in others of his works, Niekisch repeated, 'In human society there are no fatalities such as those inherent in nature — the changing of the seasons, natural disasters. The dignity of man consists in the fact that he can always say 'no'. He can always rebel. He can always rise and fight against even that which seems inevitable, absolute and unbeatable. And even if he loses, he gives an example to others. And others take his place. And others say 'no'. That's why the most fateful and fated occurrences can be defeated with the strength of the soul.'

Niekisch fought against Nazism and the Nazis, and predicted earlier and more precisely than most others what would be the consequences of their bloody rule for Germany and mankind. He did not give up. He threw down a challenge to 'evil fate', not putting down his fists. Most importantly: he resisted a strength that seemed invincible with a handful of like-minded anti-Nazis. A group of Niekisch's followers — one of them the National Bolshevik Harro Schulze-Boysen[2] — became the core of the

---

1   Ernst Niekisch, *Hitler: ein deutsches Verhängnis* (Berlin: Widerstands-Verlag, 1932). No English translation exists.-Ed.

2   Harro Schulze-Boysen (1909-1942) was a Left-leaning nationalist who fought against the French occupation of the Ruhr, and was later a member of Volksnationale Reichsvereinigung (People's National Imperial Union). He was friendly with both nationalists and Communists, and helped to begin the anti-Nazi activities of the 'Red Orchestra' group. He joined the Luftwaffe as a pilot and eventually became an officer. He was arrested and executed in 1942.-Ed.

'Red Orchestra'.[3] It was him, almost blind by then, that the Soviet troops freed from a concentration camp in 1945. He did not see the physical victories for which he gave his life, but until the end of his days he remained convinced that it is necessary to stand opposed to the evil fate of human history, even if it arises from its deepest flywheels.

Today the same could be said about liberalism as an ideology, which was victorious in the West and which spreads its influence — using many old and new methods — across the entire world, supported by superpower number one, the United States. It seems once again that this might is inevitable, not accidental, and follows the same fundamental fateful law which seems to suggest that to argue with this power is useless. But again, as in the case of Ernst Niekisch, people are found who are ready to carry out that same programme, only this time not as regarding a separate country, but rather all mankind: 'Liberalism is the evil fate of human civilisation.' The battle with it, opposition to it, and refutation of its poisonous dogmas — this is the moral imperative of all honest people on the planet. At all costs, we must, argumentatively and thoroughly, again and again, repeat that truth, even when to do so seems useless, untimely, politically incorrect, and sometimes even dangerous.

Liberalism as a Summary of Western Civilisation, and Its Definition

In order to adequately understand the essence of liberalism, we must recognise that it is not accidental, that its appearance in the history of political and economic ideologies is based on fundamental processes, proceeding in all of Western civilisation. Liberalism is not only a part of that history, but its purest and most refined expression, its result. This principal observation demands from us a stricter definition of liberalism.

Liberalism is a political and economic philosophy and ideology, embodying in itself the most important force-lines of the modern age and of the epoch of modernity:

- The understanding of the individual as the measure of all things;

- Belief in the sacred character of private property;

- The assertion of the equality of opportunity as the moral law of society;

---

3   Red Orchestra was the name given by the Gestapo to a spy ring in Berlin that was passing information to the United States and the Soviet Union. Beginning its activities in 1936, the Gestapo destroyed it in 1942.-Ed.

- Belief in the 'contractual' basis of all sociopolitical institutions, including governmental;

- The abolition of any governmental, religious and social authorities who lay claim to 'the common truth';

- The separation of powers and the making of social systems of control over any government institution whatsoever;

- The creation of a civil society without races, peoples and religions in place of traditional governments;

- The dominance of market relations over other forms of politics (the thesis: 'economics is fate');

- Certainty that the historical path of Western peoples and countries is a universal model of development and progress for the entire world, which must, in an imperative order, be taken as the standard and pattern.

It is specifically these principles which lie at the base of historical liberalism, developed by the philosophers Locke, Mill, Kant, and later Bentham and Constance, right up to the neo-liberal school of the Twentieth century, such as Friedrich Hayek[4] and Karl Popper. Adam Smith,[5] the follower of Locke,[6] on the basis of the ideas of his teacher, analysed business activity and laid the foundations for political economy, having written the political and economic Bible of the modern epoch.

'Freedom From'

The principles of the philosophy of liberalism and the very name 'liberalism' are based on the thesis of 'freedom equals liberty'. At the same time, the liberal philosophers, in particular Mill, underscore that the freedom they stand for is a strictly negative freedom. Moreover, they separate

---

4   Friedrich Hayek (1899-1992) was an economist who was crucial to the development of the Austrian school of economics. He opposed collectivism and state control of the economy in favour of classical liberalism, holding that only the free market and limited government were the only effective method of organizing societies.-Ed.

5   Adam Smith (1723-1790) was a Scottish economist who helped to lay the foundation for modern-day capitalism. He advanced the idea that individual self-interest was ultimately good for all of society.-Ed.

6   John Locke (1632-1704) was an English philosopher of the Enlightenment who is regarded as the most important theorist of liberalism, as his works were extremely important to the development of modern democracy.-Ed.

freedom from and freedom to and suggest using for these things two different English words: 'liberty' and 'freedom'. Liberty implies freedom from something. It is from here that the name liberalism is derived. Liberals fight for this freedom and insist on it. As for 'freedom to' -that is, the meaning and goal of freedom — here liberals fall silent, reckoning that each individual can himself find a way to apply his freedom, or that he can neglect altogether to search for a way to use it. This is a question of private choice, which is not discussed and which has no political or ideological value.

On the other hand, 'freedom from' is defined precisely and has a dogmatic character. Liberals propose to be free from:

- Government and its control over the economy, politics and civil society;

- Churches and their dogmas;

- Class systems;

- Any form of common areas of responsibility for the economy;

- Any attempt to redistribute, with one or another government or social institutions, the results of material and non-material labour (the formula of the liberal philosopher Philip Nemo, a follower of Hayek: 'Social justice is deeply immoral');

- Ethnic attachments;

- Any collective identity whatsoever.

One can think that we have some version of anarchy here, but that is not exactly right. Anarchists — at least those like Proudhon[7] — consider, as an alternative to government, free, communal labour, with a complete collectivisation of its products, and they come out strongly against private ownership; while liberals, on the other hand, see in the market and in the sacredness of private property a pledge for the realisation of their optimal socio-economic model. Besides, theoretically considering that the government must sooner or later die out, opening up a place for the world market and world civil society, liberals, for pragmatic reasons, support the government if it is bourgeois-democratic, facilitates the development

---

7   Pierre-Joseph Proudhon (1809-1865) was a French politician and philosopher who opposed capitalism and did not believe in state ownership of property, instead believing that property should belong to workers' groups.-Ed.

of the market, guarantees to 'civil society' safety and protection against aggressive neighbours, and staves off 'the war of all against all' (Hobbes).

In everything else, liberals go rather far, repudiating practically all sociopolitical institutions, right up to the family and sexual differentiation. In extreme cases, liberals support not only the freedom of abortions, but even the freedom from sexual differentiation (supporting the rights of homosexuals, transsexuals, and so on). The family, as another form of society, is thought by them to be a purely contractual thing, which, as with other 'enterprises', is conditioned by legal agreements.

On the whole, liberals insist not only on 'freedom from' tradition and sacrality (not to mention previous forms of traditional society), but even on 'freedom from' socialisation and redistribution, on which Leftist — socialist and Communist — political ideologies insist (to speak of political forms that are contemporaries of liberalism, or even pretenders to its throne).

Liberalism and the Nation

Liberalism was engendered in Western Europe and America in the epoch of bourgeois revolutions and strengthened as Western political, religious and social institutions that preceded the imperial-feudal periods gradually weakened: monarchy, the church, estates. In its first stages, liberalism dealt with the idea of the creation of contemporary nations, when in Europe they conceived the 'nation' as a uniform political formation founded on a contractual basis, opposing the more ancient imperial and feudal forms. 'The nation' was understood as the totality of citizens of a state; a totality in which is embodied the relationship of a population of individuals connected by a common territorial residence and a common level of economic development. Neither ethnic, nor religious, nor class factors had any significance. Such a 'nation-state' (*état-nation*) had no common historical goal and no determinate mission. It conceived of itself as a corporation or business that is founded through the reciprocal agreement of its participants and that can theoretically be dissolved on those same bases.

The European nations kicked religion, ethnic identity and classes to the curb, believing these to be remnants of the 'dark ages'. This is the difference between liberal nationalism and other versions thereof: here, no values of ethno-religious or historical communities are taken into consideration; the accent is put only on the benefits and advantages of the collective agreement of the individuals concerned, who have established a government for concrete, pragmatic reasons.

The Challenge of Marxism

If, with the dismantling of feudal-monarchic and clerical regimes, everything was going smoothly for liberalism, and no ideological alternatives stemming from the European Middle Ages were able to oppose liberals, then in the depths of the philosophy of the modern era there appeared a movement contesting with liberals for the right to first place in the process of modernisation, and coming out with a powerful conceptual critique of liberalism derived not from positions of the past (from the Right), but from positions of the future (the Left). Such were socialist and Communist ideas, receiving their most systematic expression in Marxism.

Marx carefully analysed the political economy of Adam Smith, and, more broadly, of the liberal school, but he drew from these ideas an absolutely original conclusion. He recognised their partial correctness — in comparison to feudal models of traditional societies — but he offered to go further, and in the name of the future of mankind, to refute what are for liberals the most important postulates.

In liberalism, Marxism:

- Denied the identification of the subject with the individual (thinking instead that the subject has a collective-class nature);

- Recognised the unjust system of the appropriation of surplus value by capitalists in the process of a market economy;

- Reckoned the 'freedom' of bourgeois society a veiled form of class supremacy, masking under new clothes the mechanisms of exploitation, alienation and oppression;

- Called for a proletarian revolution and abolition of the market and private property;

- Pinned its hopes on aiming for the social collectivisation of property (expropriation of the expropriator);

- Claimed creative labour as the social freedom of the Communist future (as the realisation of man's 'freedom to');

- Criticised bourgeois nationalism as a form of collective violence over the poorest layers of its respective societies, and as an instrument of international aggression in the name of the egoistic interests of the national bourgeoisie.

Thus, over two centuries, Marxism transformed into the most important ideological opponent and competitor of liberalism, attacking its system, and ideologically following and sometimes scoring important successes, especially in the Twentieth century, with the appearance of a world socialist system. At a certain point, it seemed as though precisely those Leftist powers would win the argument over the heritage of modernity and for the 'orthodoxy' of the new age, and many liberals began to believe that socialism was the unavoidable future, which would correct the liberal political system, and perhaps abolish it altogether. From here, the tendencies of 'social-liberalism' begin, which, recognising certain 'moral' theses of Marxism, strove to smooth over its revolutionary potential and to combine two foundational ideologies of the new era at the price of rejecting their cruelest and most pointed affirmations. Revisionists on the side of Marxism, in particular Right-wing Social Democrats, moved in the same direction from the opposite camp.

The question about how to relate to socialists and Leftists reached its most difficult moments for liberals in the 1920s and 1930s, when the Communists first proved the importance of their historical intentions and the possibility of their seizing and holding power. In this period, the neo-liberal school arose (von Mises, Hayek, and a little later, Popper and Aron), formulating a very important ideological thesis: liberalism is not a transitional stage from feudalism to Marxism and socialism, but rather an ideology that is complete in itself, holding an exclusive monopoly on the heritage of the Enlightenment and the modern era. In this view, Marxism itself is no development of Western thought, but rather a regressive return, using modernist slogans, to the feudal epoch of eschatological uprisings and millenarian cults. Neo-liberals proved this by the systematic critique of the German conservative philosopher, Hegel, as well as by references to the totalitarian Soviet experience, and called for a return to the roots, to Locke and Smith, standing firmly on their principles; and by criticising social-liberals for their concessions and compromises.

Neo-liberalism as a theory was most clearly formulated in Europe (Austria, Germany, and Great Britain), but its large-scale realisation happened in the United States, where liberalism dominated in politics, ideology and economic practice. And although at the time of Roosevelt there were strong social-liberal tendencies even in the USA (the New Deal era, the influence of Keynes, and so on), the indisputable advantage was with the liberal school. In a theoretical sense, this tendency received its greatest development in the Chicago school (M. Friedman, F. Knight, G. Simons, J. Stigler, and others).[8]

After the Second World War, the decisive stage of the battle for the heritage of the Enlightenment began: liberals supported by the USA fought the final battle with Marxism, personified by the USSR and its allies. Europe occupied the third place in the ideological war: social-liberal and Social Democratic tendencies prevailed there.

The Definitive Victory of the Liberals in the 1990s

The fall of the USSR and our defeat in the Cold War signified, from an ideological point of view, the final distribution of roles in the fight for the heritage of the Enlightenment and for the way of the future. Exactly on the strength of the fact that the USSR lost and fell apart, it became obvious that historical right was on the side of the liberals, especially of the neo-liberals, who prevented socialism and Communism from claiming the future as 'the progressive tomorrow'. Soviet society and other socialist regimes turned out to be carefully disguised versions of archaic structures, having interpreted in their own way the 'mystically', 'religiously' understood Marxism.

This all-important moment in the political history of mankind first of all put the dot on the i with respect to the most important question of the times: which of the two central ideologies of the Twentieth century would follow the past (the spirit of the Enlightenment) and automatically receive the future (the right to dominate, by ideological means, the coming days). The question of the goal of the historical process was principally settled.

In the middle of the Twentieth century, the French philosopher, a Hegelian of Russian origin, Alexandre Kojève, suggested that the Hegelian 'end of history' would mark a Communist world revolution. The traditionalists (René Guénon, Julius Evola), who rejected the Enlightenment, defending Tradition and foretelling 'the end of the world' through the victory of 'the fourth caste' (the *Shudras*,[9] or proletarians) thought similarly. But in 1991, with the dissolution of the USSR, it became clear that 'the end of history' would carry not a Marxist, but a liberal form, about

---

8   The Chicago school of economics was so named because most of those who developed it were on the faculty of the University of Chicago. They favor total deregulation of the economy.-Ed.

9   In the Vedic (Hindu) caste system, the *Shudras are the lowest class, consisting of the servants and labourers.-Ed.*

which the American philosopher Francis Fukuyama hurried to inform humanity, proclaiming 'the end of history' as the planetary victory of the market, liberalism, the USA and bourgeois-democracy. Marxism as a possible alternative and project of the future became a meaningless episode of political and ideological history.

From that moment, there not only began the take-off of liberalism in its most orthodox, fundamentalist Anglo-Saxon and anti-socialist forms, but also the laying bare of the fundamental fact of the ideological history of man: liberalism is destiny. But this means that its theses — its philosophical, political, social and economic principles and dogmas — should be looked at as something universal and absolute, having no alternatives.

On the Threshold of the American Century

As a result of the political history of the Twentieth century, it was discovered that liberalism had won the war for contemporary times, having beaten all its opponents on both the Right and the Left. The huge cycle of the modern era was completed with the triumph of liberal ideology, which received henceforth a monopoly on the control and direction of historical development. Liberalism was left with no symmetrical enemy, no large-scale subject with an adequate historical self-understanding, a convincing and orderly ideology, serious material and military resources, and comparable technological, economic and armed forces. All that still opposed liberal ideology showed itself as a chaotic collection of simple nuisances and mistakes; in a word, 'noises', opposing through inertia the builders of 'the new liberal order'. This was not a rivalry of alternative civilisational and geopolitical subjects, but the reactive and passive resistance of a disorganised field. Thus, soil, rain, karstic emptiness or marshland bothers the builders of roads: the discussion is not about the construction of another route that another company insists on, but about the resistance of the environment.

In this situation the USA, as the citadel of world liberalism, took on a new quality. From this time on, it became not only one of two superpowers, but the single planetary hero, suddenly pulling away from its rivals. The French critic of the United States, Hubert Védrine,[10] suggested that it should henceforth not be called a superpower but a hyperpower,

---

10 Hubert Védrine (b. 1947) was the Foreign Minister in Prime Minister Jospin's Socialist administration between 1997 and 2002. Védrine is well-known for his opposition to American hegemony and popularised the term 'hyperpower' to describe America's position in world affairs.-Ed.

underscoring its solitariness and its asymmetrical superiority. From an ideological point of view, the victory of liberalism and the rise of the USA is not an accidental coincidence, but two sides of one and the same occurrence. The USA won 'the Cold War' not because it amassed more potential and got ahead in the technological competition, but because it based itself on the liberal ideology, proving both its technological competence and its historical rightness in the ideological war, substantiating the balance of the modern era. And just as liberalism displayed its fated dimension, the USA received a concrete confirmation of its messianism, which, in the ideology of Manifest Destiny, was, since the Nineteenth century, an article of faith for the American political elite.

American neoconservatives recognised this arrangement of matters more clearly than anyone else. In the words of one of their most important ideologues, William Kristol,[11] 'The Twentieth century was the century of America's rise, but the Twenty-first century will be the American century.' Let us consider that statement: what difference is there between 'the century of America' and 'the American century'? 'The century of America' signifies that, in that period, the ideology of liberalism fought with its rivals (residual traditionalism, fascism, socialism and Communism) and smashed them to bits. America, having been one of a few world powers, transformed into the only one. And now, according to the thinking of the neoconservatives, America is due to affirm the American model, the American way of life, as a world order obligatory for all. Before one's eyes, the USA stopped being a national government and became a synonym for world government. The entire planet must henceforth become a 'World America', 'World Government', or 'World State'. This is what they call 'the American century', the project of globalising the American model to global proportions. This is not simply colonisation or a new form of imperialism, this is a programme of the total implementation of the one and only ideological system, copied from American liberal ideology. America henceforth has pretensions to the universal spreading of a unitary code, which penetrates into the life of peoples and governments in a thousand different ways — like a global network — through technology, the market economy, the political model of liberal-democracy, information systems, the model of mass culture and its media products, and the establishment of direct strategic control of Americans and their satellites over geopolitical processes.

---

11 William Kristol (b.1952) is one of the most influential neoconservative thinkers in America today. He was one of the founders of the Project for the New American Century, and is also the founder and Editor-in-Chief of the neoconservative journal *The Weekly Standard*, and is a regular contributor to the Fox News Channel.

The American century is thought of as a re-smelting of the existing world order into a new one, built up on strictly American patterns. This process is conditionally called 'democratisation', and it is directed at a few concrete geopolitical enclaves that are, in the first place, problematic from the point of view of liberalism. In this way, there came to be the projects of 'the Greater Middle East', 'Greater Central Asia' and so on. The meaning of them all consists in the uprooting of inertial national, political, economic, social, religious and cultural models and their replacement by the operational system of American liberalism. But it is not that important whether the discussion is about the enemies of the USA or their allies: both friends and enemies are subject to re-formatting, as are those who wish to remain neutral. This is the meaning of 'the American century': liberalism, having defeated its formal enemies, penetrates completely. And now it is not enough to be on the side of the USA in local conflicts (as many countries behaved that were not liberal — those like Pakistan, Saudi Arabia and Turkey). Henceforth, liberalism must penetrate into the depths of all societies and countries without exception, and the slightest resistance will be, according to the designs of the neoconservatives, broken — as happened in Serbia, Iraq and Afghanistan.

American critics of such an approach — for instance, the paleoconservative, Patrick Buchanan — declare: 'America acquired the whole world, but lost itself.' However, this does not stop neoconservatives, inasmuch as they take the US not only as a national government, but also as the avant-garde of the liberal ideology. And it was no accident that the neoconservatives emerged from Trotskyism. Just as Trotskyites sought a global Communist revolution, mercilessly criticising Stalin and the idea of building socialism in one country, contemporary neoconservatives call for a global liberal revolution, categorically rejecting the call of 'isolationists' to limit themselves to the American borders and their historical allies. Precisely the neoconservatives, setting the tone for contemporary American politics, most deeply understand the ideological meaning of the fate of political teachings at the dawn of the Twenty-first century. American neoconservative circles most adequately perceive the significance of the large-scale changes happening in the world. For them, ideology remains the most important subject of attention, although today it also turns into 'soft ideology' or 'soft power'.

Liberalism and Postmodernity

Having gone over from the formal opposition to the alternative ideologies to the new phase of introduction on the world scale, the liberal ideology changes its status. In the epoch of modernity, liberalism always coexisted with non-liberalism, which means that it was an object of choice; like with modern computer technology, where one can theoretically select a computer with a Microsoft, Mac OS or Linux operating system. After defeating its rivals, liberalism brought back a monopoly on ideological thinking; it became the sole ideology, not allowing any other alongside itself. One could say that it switched over from the level of a programme to the level of an operating system, having become something common. Notice, coming to a store and selecting a computer, we more often than not do not say, 'Give me a computer that runs Microsoft.' We simply say, 'Give me a computer.' And in accordance with our silence, we are sold a computer with a Microsoft operating system. So it is with liberalism: it is implanted in us by itself, like something standard, which it would be absurd and pointless to contest.

The content of liberalism changes, switching over from the level of expression to the level of speech. Liberalism becomes not proper liberalism, but sub-audition, silent agreement, consensus. This corresponds to the switchover from the epoch of modernity to postmodernity. In postmodernity, liberalism, preserving and even increasing its influence, ever more rarely projects an intelligent and freely adopted political philosophy; it becomes unconscious, self-understood and instinctive. This instinctive liberalism, having pretences to transform itself into the generally non-conscious 'matrix' of contemporariness, gradually acquires grotesque characteristics. From the classical principles of liberalism, which have become unconscious ('the world reserve unconscious' could be used as an analogy alongside the dollar as the 'world reserve currency'), the grotesque ways of postmodern culture are born. This is already a *sui generis* post-liberalism, following from the total victory of classical liberalism, but leading it to extreme conclusions.

Thus there arises the panorama of post-liberal grotesques:

- The measure of things becomes not the individual, but the post-individual, 'the dividual', accidentally playing an ironic combination of parts of people (his organs, his clones, his simulacra — all the way up to cyborgs and mutants);

- Private property is idolised, 'transcendentalised', and transforms from that which a man owns to that which owns the man;

- Equality of opportunity turns into equality of the contemplation of opportunities (the society of the spectacle — Guy Debord);

- Belief in the contractual character of all political and social institutions grows into an equalisation of the real and the virtual, and the world becomes a technical model;

- All forms of non-individual authorities disappear altogether, and any individual is free to think about the world howsoever he sees fit (the crisis of common rationality);

- The principle of the separation of powers transforms into the idea of a constant electronic referendum (a sort of electronic parliament), where each Internet user continually 'votes' on any decision by giving his opinion in any number of forums, which in turn cedes power to each individual citizen (each becoming, in effect, his own branch of government);

- 'Civil society' completely displaces government and converts into a global, cosmopolitan melting pot;

- From the thesis 'economy is destiny' it takes up the thesis 'the numerical code — that is destiny', so far as work, money, the market, production, consumption — everything becomes virtual.

Some liberals and neoconservatives were terrified at that prospect, which opened up as a consequence of the ideological victory of liberalism, before the transition to post-liberalism and postmodernity. Thus, Fukuyama, the author of the thesis of the liberal 'end of history' in the last decade, has called on the US and the West 'to turn back' and to hold over the previous phase of 'vintage' classical liberalism, with the market, the nation-state and its customary scientific rationalism, in order to avoid sliding into the post-liberal chasm. But in this, he is contradicting himself: the logic of the transformation from normal liberalism to the liberalism of postmodernity is neither arbitrary nor voluntary; it is written in the very structure of the liberal ideology: in the course of the gradual liberation of man from all that which is not himself (from all non-human and supra-individual values and ideals), one must sooner or later free a man from his own self. And the most frightening crisis of the individual does not begin when he is fighting alternative ideologies that deny man is the highest value, but when he attains his conclusive and irreversible victory.

Liberalism in Contemporary Russia

If we were to juxtapose all the aforementioned about liberalism with what is understood by liberalism in Russia, we would have to admit that there is no liberalism here. There are liberals, but no liberalism. Until the beginning of the 1990s, Marxist ideology formally dominated in Russia, and raised up from childhood the outright majority of those people who, in one way or another, influence the decisions of government today. The principles of liberalism, in the first place, were foreign to the instinctive foundations of Russian society; they were severely persecuted by the ideological organs in the USSR, and were either unknown or else construed in a caricatured and fragmentary way. The sole meaning of 'liberalism' in Russia in the 1990s was freedom from Russian-Soviet political-economic traditions and an uncritical, ignorant and parodic imitation of the West. Practically none of the post-Soviet elite selected liberalism consciously and deliberately: until the last moment of the fall of the USSR, the leaders of Russian liberalism eulogised the Communist Party, the ideas of Marx, the Plan and socialism, while the oligarchs made a living in the Committee of Komsomols[12] or served in the KGB. Liberalism as a political ideology interested no one; not a penny was paid for it. Such a cheap and crooked liberalism was maintained in the 1990s as an ersatz ideology for post-Soviet Russia. But instead of mastering liberal principles, its supporters and preachers engaged in careerism, privatisation and setting up their own little deals, in the best case fulfilling the guidelines of the Western curators of the breakdown of the Soviet and Russian state. This was an ideological disintegration of the previous structure without erecting anything new in its place at all. No one even really chose the dubious 'freedom from'.

When Putin came to power and attempted to turn the process of Russia's disintegration around, he encountered, to a large measure, no ideological opposition. He was challenged by concrete economic clans, whose interests he discerned, and the more active agency of influence, deeply entrenched in espionage in the service of the West. The absolute majority of liberals quickly transformed themselves into 'backers of Putin', adapting themselves under the individual patriotic sympathies of the new leader. Even iconic figures of Russian liberalism — Gaidar,[13]

---

12 Komsomol was shorthand for the Communist Union of Youth, which was the young people's branch of the Communist Party of the Soviet Union.-Ed.

13 Yegor Gaidar (1956-2009) was a Russian economist who briefly served as Prime Minister of the Russian Federation during 1992. He was the developer of the 'shock therapy' method of transitioning the Russian economy from being state-run to the free market,

Chubais,[14] etc. — behaved like banal opportunists: they could not care less about the ideological content of Putin's reforms.

In Russia, irrespective of the whole period of the 1990s, liberalism did not penetrate deeply and did not spawn a political generation of authentic, convinced liberals. It operated on Russia mainly from without, which led in the end to a worsening of relations with the US, to the obstruction of Putin and his course in the West, and, in response, to his Munich speech.[15]

But insofar as the number of conscious liberals during the critical moment of change in Russia turned out to be not more than the number of conscious Communists at the end of the 1980s, Putin did not insist on their ideological harassment, opting to control only the more unbridled of the liberal oligarchs and the direct agents of influence who became impudent through lawlessness. Intuitively striving to preserve and consolidate Russian sovereignty, Putin entered into a conflict with the liberal West and its plans for globalisation, but without forming his actions into an alternative ideology. This was mostly because there were so very few convinced liberals in Russia.

The real liberal is the one who acts in compliance with the fundamental principles of liberalism, including in those instances when to do so could lead to serious consequences, repressions and even deprivation of life. If people turn out to be liberals only when liberalism is permitted, in fashion or even out of obligation, ready at the first difficulty to repudiate these principles, such 'liberalism' has no relation to the real kind. It seems Khodorkovsky,[16] the 'icon' of contemporary Russian liberals, understood that, having spent some time in prison. But in this, it seems to me, he is an exception among the liberals who remain free.

which involved the sudden removal of state regulation and the introduction of liberal reforms. This move was controversial since it led to hardship for a great many Russians.-Ed.

14 Anatoly Chubais (b. 1955) is a Russian politician who served as Deputy Prime Minister during the Yeltsin administration. He was given the task of privatising Russian industry after the collapse of the Soviet Union.-Ed.

15 At the Munich Conference on Security Policy on 10 February 2007, President Putin criticised America's hegemony and what he said was America's unconstrained use of force to resolve international disputes, such as in Iraq, saying that such policies abrogate the value of international law and would lead to an 'arms race'.-Ed.

16 Mikhail Khodorkovsky (b. 1963) is a Russian oligarch who made billions in developing the Siberian oil fields after the collapse of the Soviet Union, becoming the richest man in Russia by 2004. An advocate of liberal policies and a critic of Putin, Khodorovsky was charged with fraud and sentenced to prison in 2003, leading to the collapse of his empire. Some have claimed that his arrest was engineered to remove one of Putin's rivals. He is currently set to be released from prison in 2017.-Ed.

The Crusade Against the West

However much liberalism today claims that there are no alternatives, there is always a choice in human history. While man exists, he is free to choose; both what everyone chooses, and what no one does. Liberalism (and, by the way, the US and the West) today does not offer itself up as an option among many to prefer; it calls this decision the only one possible. And this is not a usual arbitrariness: the logic of the political history of modernity avows the validity of such an approach.

Of course, one could imagine that many people on the planet came late to the awareness of what happened at the end of the Twentieth and the start of the Twenty-first century, and by inertia believe in socialism, Communism and even religion. Or maybe that someone does not accept liberalism for some other local or individual consideration — for instance, after realising that, in such a system, he would find himself among 'losers'. But this does not matter much: all systematic and foundational alternatives are crushed, and someone's peripheral, troubled and unintelligent dissatisfaction, plainly, in political-ideological terms, affects nothing.

Nevertheless, even in the new phase of its self-evident imposition, liberalism (and post-liberalism) may (and must — I believe this!) be repudiated. And if behind it, there stands the full might of the inertia of modernity, the spirit of the Enlightenment and the logic of the political and economic history of European humanity of the last centuries, it must be repudiated together with modernity, the Enlightenment, and European humanity altogether. Moreover, only the acknowledgement of liberalism as fate, as a fundamental influence, comprising the march of Western European history, will allow us really to say 'no' to liberalism. We should repudiate it in its capacity as a global metaphysical factor, and not as a particular, accidental heresy, or as a distortion of normal development. The path that humanity entered upon in the modern era led precisely to liberalism and to the repudiation of God, tradition, community, ethnicity, empires and kingdoms. Such a path is tread entirely logically: having decided to liberate itself from everything that keeps man in check, the man of the modern era reached his logical apogee: before our eyes he is liberated from himself.

The logic of world liberalism and globalisation pulls us into the abyss of postmodern dissolution and virtuality. Our youth already have one foot in it: the codes of liberal globalism are effectively introduced on an unconscious level — through habits, commercials, glamour, technology, the media, celebrities. The usual phenomenon now is the loss of identity, and already not simply only national or cultural identity, but even sexual, and soon enough even human identity. And defenders of human rights, not noticing the tragedy of the entire peoples that they sacrifice to their cruel plan of 'the new world order', will howl tomorrow about transgressions against the rights of cyborgs or clones.

The people's refusal to adopt liberalism is completely understandable, and can be met at every turn. But it will remain impotent and ineffective until we recognise that we are dealing not with an accident, but with something systemic; not with a temporary deviation from the norm, but with a fatal, incurable disease, the origins of which we should seek in those periods in which to many everything seemed unclouded and clear, and humanity seemed to enter into the epoch of progress, development, freedom and equal rights. But this was simply a syndrome of approaching agony. Liberalism is an absolute evil; not only in its factual embodiment, but also in its fundamental theoretical presuppositions. And its victory, its world triumph, only underscores and displays those most wicked qualities, which earlier were veiled.

'Freedom from' is the most disgusting formula of slavery, inasmuch as it tempts man to an insurrection against God, against traditional values, against the moral and spiritual foundations of his people and his culture.

And even if liberalism won all the formal battles and brought us indeed to the cusp of 'an American century', the real battle is still ahead. But it takes place only after the authentic meaning of the past will be genuinely understood, when the metaphysical meaning of liberalism and its fateful victory becomes known in the right measure and the right proportions. Only tearing it out by its roots can defeat this evil, and I do not exclude that such a victory will necessitate erasing from the face of the Earth those spiritual and physical halos from which arose the global heresy, which insists that 'man is the measure of all things'.[17] Only a global crusade against the US, the West, globalisation, and their political-ideological expression, liberalism, is capable of becoming an adequate response.

The elaboration of the ideology of this Crusader campaign, undoubtedly, is a matter for Russia not to pursue alone, but together with all the world powers, who, in one way or another, oppose 'the American century'. Nevertheless, in any case this ideology must begin with the recognition of the fatal role of liberalism, which has characterised the path of the West from the moment when it rejected the values of God and Tradition.

---

17 This statement was originally made by the Greek philosopher Protagoras (ca. 490-420 BCE). As the quote only survives as a fragment, its original context, and therefore its intended meaning, has been disputed.-Ed.

10

THE ONTOLOGY OF THE FUTURE

Is there a future? The question is legitimate because it provokes thinking about the ontology of time. *What is*, or at least, is now? Precisely because of the fact of its being now, it is considered as being proper according to the multitude of our direct, empirical perceptions. *What was*, or the facts of that which has existed previously, is certified by the historical record and other remnants. But in both cases, forgery or misunderstanding is possible. Therefore, the existence of *what has yet to be* is highly questionable, at best.

Martin Heidegger spoke about three ecstasies of time:[1] the past, the present and the future. Apparently, there are three ontological arguments relative to these three ecstasies: immediacy (there is/there is not) is related to the present; documentary (there was/there was not) is related to the past; and probabilistic (there will be/ there will not be) is related to the future. It seems that we could create a hierarchy, based on the evidence: there is, there was, there will be. 'There is' is most evident. 'There will be' is most doubtful. 'There was' is in the middle. The future is the most unreliable among the three ecstasies of time. The future cannot be taken into consideration to the same degree as 'there is' or 'there was'. 'There was,' was, or at least we believe that it was from the evidence at hand. Concerning the future, you cannot know for certain. A given event or thing could happen, but most likely will not. Thus, the future lacks 'being' compared with the other ecstasies of time.

From this point we could proceed in several different directions. For example, we could question the solidity of ontological arguments concerning the most evident moment — the present. This recalls Kant and his doubts about the inner being of the object. The fact of simply perceiving something is not enough for a definitive declaration of its being. This is the *Ding an sich* (the-thing-in-itself) conundrum of Kantian philosophy.

---

1   This is in *On Time and Being*.

Not *pure reason*, but only *practical reason* gives being to an object, based on the moral imperative. An object should have being. It would be good for it to have it. Therefore, it has to have it.

If the 'being' of the present, as the most evident of all the moments of time, can be seriously put in doubt, then we are arriving at an interesting point: all three moments of time are then ontologically unprovable and unverifiable and concern only the gnoseologic level, relating to the philosophy of knowledge and the human faculty for learning. This is pessimistic concerning the present, whose reality we habitually take for granted, but is optimistic concerning the two other moments, the past and the future. The past and the future thereby acquire equal consideration with the present. From the perspective of pure reason, the present, past and future all have equal phenomenological value. The future, in this case, *is* the phenomenon, and hence, phenomenologically speaking, it *is*. Being the phenomenon itself, the future *is* and it *is real*. The future, therefore, is actual.

Kant, analysing the *a priori* forms of sensibility, puts time nearer to the subject, and space nearer to the object. It indicates that time belongs closest to the orbit of the subject. Time is hence subjective. It is the transcendental subject that installs time in the perception of the object.

Now let us change perspective and consider time phenomenologically. Husserl proposed to study time through the use of music. The consciousness of hearing the music is not based on the strict identification of notes sounding in a concrete, discrete moment. Hearing music is something different from hearing an individual note that sounds now, in the present. The consciousness of music occurs by hearing an individual note that sounds now, in the present, as well as recalling the past notes that are dissolving little by little into nothingness. However, their resonance persists in the consciousness and gives music its aesthetic sense. Husserl calls it 'the continuous instance'. The past is present in the present. The present thus becomes continuous and includes the past as a vanishing presence.

This is the methodological key for the understanding of history. History is awareness of the presence of the past in the present. The vanishing events continue to sound in the act of recalling of them. Clio and Polyhymnia, the Muses of History and Time respectively in Greek mythology, are sisters. This recalling is necessary to give us our sense of the present. The *anamnesis*[2] of Plato has the same function. The soul

---

2   According to Plato, who discusses the concept in the Socratic dialogues *Meno* and *Phaedo*, since the soul is repeatedly incarnated in a series of bodies, each birth causes one to forget everything one knew in one's previous lives, therefore learning is actually a process of remembering what one knew previously, rather than being the acquisition of new knowledge. He terms this process *anamnesis*.-Ed.

should recall the hidden past of its previous lives in order to reconstruct the wholeness of the melody of destiny. Only thus could it be played harmoniously.

The future should, therefore, be understood in this context. The future is continuous in the present. Not the moment of *novum*,[3] but the process of the fading of the present into the past. The future is the tail-end of the present, its resonance. We live the future just now, and already now, when we play the note of the melody of life. The future is the process of the death of the present, attention to the dissolution of melody into the totality of harmony. The *novum* appears in the future only when the harmony is lost, when our attention falls asleep, and then suddenly we awaken and cannot identify the sounds that we hear. Momentarily, they simply make no sense. That is the novum: spontaneous incomprehension of what is going on in the ecstasy of time. It is the nature of discreet, discontinuous events. It is the suspended moment of being without history, and hence without a sense of awareness and consciousness.

Edmund Husserl dug much deeper into the phenomenology of time. He discovered the new instance of consciousness lying underneath the level where the nature of time, as illuminated by music, is perceived. According to Husserl, beneath this level there is another, ultimate one, which is responsible for our perception of what is now with the force of evidence, and a much more intensive taste of reality that recalls the ever-dying past. This instance is consciousness itself, the consciousness as such that precedes the intentionality and the dualist nature of apprehension, being necessarily divided into two parts — the perceived and the perceiving. In the present, the consciousness perceives itself and nothing else. That is the ultimate experience of the last source of reality. According to Husserl, the foundation of all consciousness is transcendental subjectivity, from whence it conceives itself as a kind of short circuit. This experience is self-referential. In it, there is the perception of pure being as the presence of the subjectivity of consciousness.

This short circuit causes all kinds of dualities to be born — the logical ones and the temporal ones. The necessity of stopping this trauma is manifest in the creation of time, the articulation of the three moments of time. Consciousness of time is necessary to hide the present, which is the traumatic experience of the self-referential nature of pure consciousness. Intentionality and logical judgments are all rooted in this evasion of the perception of the pain of the void whereby consciousness becomes aware of itself.

---

3   Latin: 'new thing.'-Ed.

Such an attitude to the levels of consciousness explains the origin of time as the evasion of the present, and the unbearable tension of the pure presence of the same. This tension is immediately relieved by the expansion of all the imaginable types of dualities that constitute the textures of the continuous process of time. The model of this process is the creation of the three moments of time. The logical and spatial symmetries follow — such dualities as yes/no, true/false, high/low, right/left, here/there, and so on. Before/after belongs to the same cadence. Time constitutes consciousness running from the unbearable confrontation with itself. But this confrontation is inevitable, so the present, and the high precision of its existential perception, is born.

What is most important in this interpretation of the morphology of time? The idea that time precedes the object, and that in the construction of time we should seek an *inner* depth of consciousness, rather than a consciousness rooted in *outer* phenomena constituted by the subjective process of traumatic self-awareness. The world around us becomes what it is by the fundamental action of *presencing* accomplished by the mind. When the mind sleeps, reality lacks the sense of present existence. It is fully immersed in a continuous dream. The world is created by time, and time, in its turn, is the manifestation of self-aware subjectivity, an *intrasubjectivity*.

These remarks lead us to considerations of the future — prognostication, projection, and analysis of the future.

Moving from man to society, and from anthropology to sociology, we can affirm the future as something absolutely subjective in nature, and so, in this context, it is something social. The future is social because it is a historical feature and not immanent to an object's nature. The object has no future. The Earth, animals, stones, machines — all have no future. Only that which is included in the human social context can take part in the future, and then only indirectly. Without self-referential consciousness, there can be no time. Time is that which is inside us, and what makes us what who we are. Time is man's ultimate identity.

This subjectivity of time does not mean that prognostication will be self-fulfilling prophecy, as per Robert K. Merton,[4] nor that any event is realisable a priori. The future is strictly determined, not something volun-

---

4 Robert K. Merton (1910-2003) was an American sociologist. Among the many concepts he developed was the idea of the 'self-fulfilling prophecy' in his book *Social Theory and Social Structure* (1949), by which a belief or expectation held by a social group affects their behavior. An example given by Merton is of a woman who gets married but is convinced her marriage is destined to end in divorce; her expectations will influence her actions and cause this to actually happen.-Ed.

tary. Time, being historical, is predefined precisely by its historical content. The subject is not free from its structure, and more than this, it is
absolutely enslaved by it. Time needs the future as a void for the continuous fading of the present and, partially, of the past. Without the future,
the subject will not have the space necessary to evade, running from the
impossible encounter with itself, from the short circuit mentioned above.
The frozen moment of the present without the future is that of death.

Society needs the future to run from itself further and further. The
chronicle of such a run is the sense of history. Society requires a narrative
of the past. The future is predefined by the structure of the subject. That
is why the future is strictly defined. The subject cannot stop itself from
deploying the chains of reason, it cannot *not* think, and cannot constitute
the temporal cadences. The future is in the same measure as the present
and past. Where time is, the future is also.

The future makes sense. It makes sense even before it happens. More
than this, the future makes sense *even if* it will never happen. In this lies
the semantic value of prophecy and prognosis: even if it does not occur, it
is also pregnant with meaning and helps explain the present. Prophecies
and prognosis, further, help us to discern the meaning of the future.
When the future refutes the expectations of prophecy and prognosis, the
fact of their refutation gives sense to the future, because our understanding of it consists, in part, in what was not realised. Unfulfilled prophecy
has exactly the same importance as fulfilled prophecy.

The future can be analysed with the same accuracy as the present and
the past. The only unique features of the future are the flash of the encounter of the deepest consciousness with itself, and the intensive shock that
results from a conscious understanding of the present for what it is. What
the present is — is the note that sounds now. But it is not music, and can
be analysed. The isolated note says nothing. It conveys nothing to us. It is
understandable only by taking into consideration and in the context of the
other notes of the particular piece of music. The context gives it sense. So,
in the content of time, it is something whole that is disposed a priori in
the three moments of time. We experience time in its totality. Therefore,
the future is already laid out with the sense of music. History is not only
our memory of the past. It is also the explication of the present and the
experience of the future. When we understand history and its logic well,
we can easily guess what will follow, what is going to happen, and which
note should come next. Knowing society, we could identify in its history
the harmony, the periods, the refrains, and the structure of the piece. Of
course we could encounter surprises, but most surprising would be the

possibility of one authentic moment of experiencing the self-knowledge of pure consciousness. It is possible to be awoken by the strength of this inner light of self-reflection. In this traumatic situation, we discover our identity between the most inner and outer levels of our consciousness. We live in the creation of the external world by the internal self. But that is no longer history; it is breaking through history, an intrusion to the centre of time, where time is eternally being constructed. Time springs from this point. There it exists in the undifferentiated unity of all three ecstasies — past, present and future.

Time can be constructed and organised in different ways. The past can be connected with the present and with the future by different links. This, *circular time*, is based on an eternal refrain pattern. In the centre of circular time, there is the experience of consciousness linked to itself in the manner of a short circuit. The power of this trauma rejects our awareness of life and banishes it to the periphery, where it becomes circular time, where the future becomes the past, and so on, for eternity. It is the eternal return of the same.

Time can be organised as a regressive line, *traditional time*. Here, the experience of the short circuit is placed in the past. The ear tries to capture the distant sounds of the past and truly reproduce it. In traditional society, time is based on the everlasting effort of Platonic *anamnesis*. Most important here is memory and transmission. In this organisation of time, the future and the present are constructed by the past. Reality and actuality regress into the past and are consigned to memory.

Time can also be constructed as the perpetual state of waiting for the future. This is chiliastic or messianic time. Here, the short circuit experience is projected into the future. History is going to fulfil itself in the future, where the ultimate nature of reality lies. This organisation of time is centred on that which is to come. Tomorrow is the focus of the historical sense. Being is oriented to future life.

There is another construction of time installed in the object, which is moved to the extreme periphery of the subject, where the objective world is fixed. This organisation of time is *material time*, time introduced in the substance of the physical world. This is the time of slaughter, of the death of the subject.

Consciousness can construct different forms of time and their combinations. Before creating the world filled with forms, the subject creates the form of time where the world is to be.

The histories of different societies are different. Different, too, are the pieces, the musicians, the composers, the instruments, the musical genre, and the types of notation used by them. That is why humanity as a whole cannot have a future. It has no future. To speak of the future of humanity is quite senseless because it completely lacks semantic value, as well as the sense of these different societal constructions of history and time. Every society is a separate act of consciousness, expanded in the rational and temporal horizons. All are unique and open. But before coming to an understanding of the the history of a given society, we should immerse ourselves in the depths of its identity. The fact that every people, every culture, every society has its own history, makes time a local phenomenon, grounded in geography. Every society possesses its own temporality. For a given society, all the moments of time are different — past, present, and future. Societies can cross and intersect, cross-pollinate and interact. Their sense of history, however, cannot. History is local. A shared sense of history is possible only on the basis of the domination of one society over another, and imposing its own history and, thus, its identity on the enslaved one.

That means if a given society is to have a future, it must be its own future. Its future is formed through appurtenance to the expanding forces of the constituent subject. A society is united through the structures of the collective consciousness of the individuals that comprise it. It means we should unite the semantic ranges of our respective pasts. Further, it means that in order to prove the harmonious correspondences of the notes and melodies of our own particular musical piece, the symphonic nature of a given society must be realised. The past is fading, but never extinguished. If the past were extinguished, the present would lose its sense and the future the possibility of occurring. The fading of the past is an essential characteristic of time. The fading of the past is necessary for the morphology of time at the same level as the flash of the present and the vagueness of the future.

Therefore, the members of a society should ask themselves today about their future. If they have a history, they could have a future. If they have both a history and a future, they are. If they are, the future is implicit, now, in the present. The future is being made now.

On this basis, we can establish both prognosis and projection. According to Heidegger, 'thrownness' (*Geworfenheit*) is a concept that describes the interactions of the subject with its surroundings in everyday life that cause it to act upon instincts, form immediate reactions to other people's language and actions, 'flow with the situation', and make immediate interpretations. Being 'thrown into a situation' without being able to reflect on it first, and therefore not acting is also an action, for reflection on the situation (i.e., not acting) is also something that can be interpreted as an action. One therefore must rely on instinctual interpretations, and go with the flow. The thrownness of the subject (*Dasein*) forces it to project itself into the future. Etymologically, it is clear: the subject is formed by sub-jectum (*sub-jacere*), projection — by pro-jectum (*pro-jacere*). In both cases we have the Latin verb 'to throw'. The analysis of the future is rooted in this: by apprehending the future, we are making it. Therefore, any consideration of the future is to work on history and the consciousness of time as such.

It is doubtful that one society is capable of comprehending another society at the same level as it is comprehended by its own members. Such a possibility presupposes the existence of the meta-society, the society-God, which could operate with the ultimate depths of consciousness in the same manner as consciousness operates with awareness, *noesis*,[5] intentionality, logic, time, and finally with the world. Obviously, Western society is particularly afflicted with such an ethnocentric approach and 'universal' pretensions rooted in its racist and colonialist past. But in the Twentieth century, this was proven to be completely unfounded and false. Structuralists, sociologists, cultural anthropologists, postmodernists, phenomenologist, linguists, existentialists, and so on, have all deployed convincing arguments demonstrating that the inner nature of such an attitude is rooted in the will to power and paranoid imposition of one's own identity on the Other. This illness is called Western racism.

The West is a local and historical phenomenon. It is a very acute civilisation, very particular, very arrogant, and very smart. But it is just one civilisation among many others. The West has history, and *is* because of its history. The attempt to abdicate this history in favour of pure universalism and in favour of meta-culture and meta-language is doomed. There are two possible outcomes of this:

1) either the West will lose its own identity and will turn into an automaton;

2) or it will try to impose its own history, conceived by itself as being universal, on all the other existing civilisations, destroying them in the process, and creating a new kind of global concentration camp for their cultures.

---

5   *Noesis*, or *nous*, is a Greek term which refers to the mind or the intellect. The Neoplatonists understood *nous* as the process by which the mind transmutes matter into form, form which was identified with beauty. They also believed that objects could be thus transformed by both reason and the soul (although reason was considered the more perfect method).-Ed.

The first outcome implies a struggle of automatons with humanity. The second implies an inevitable global liberation movement struggling against this neo-imperialism. It is for the West to decide how to manage the consequences of its proper history and its implications. The West can try to close its history, but it is unlikely that it will succeed in closing the history of all the others.

Now is the moment to begin the fight for the historical being of societies. This historical being is time, the sense of which is constituted subjectively. This sense can reside only in a given society itself. Time is socially and subjectively constructed. The West cannot intersect with the sense of non-Western societies. The non-Western societies, i.e. the 'Rest', cannot correctly understand the West and its values. They are in continuous error thinking that they can. It is false. They cannot. But, likewise, Western people cannot understand the Rest. The structures of the subjects, its sense of time, and its music are all different. The past, the present and the future of historical societies cannot be exposed by any meta-culture: they are lying too deep and are defended from foreign eyes by the destructive might of the self-referential moment, by the shock of this great tension. What for the West is, for the other cultures is not. So, we are dealing with different conceptions of time and with different futures.

At last, we have come to 'the end of history' and globalisation. The end of history is the logical conclusion of universalism. The end of history is the abolition of the future. History proceeds and reaches its terminal state. There is no more space to go on. By abolishing the future, the entire structure of time, such as the past and the present, are also abolished. How can this be possible? We could compare it to the simultaneous playing of all existing notes, sounds, and melodies of a musical piece, resulting in a cacophony, the gnashing and grinding of teeth. At the same time, it will provoke absolute silence, deafness and sourness. Hence there will be no space for the temporalisation of the inner tension of transcendental subjectivity; the short circuit would grow exponentially without the possibility of being dissipated. That means the igniting of a conflagration, the same fire that goes usually goes hand-in-hand with the sword.

In order to prevent the blaze and the clashing of swords that would result from closing the temporal and logical relief valve, the world will strive to trap consciousness in networks and virtuality, where it can run away from the inner pressure of self-awareness without issue. If it succeeds, the new world of the machine kingdom will be created. The global networks and cyberspace are suitable only for the existence of post-humans, post-society, and post-culture. Instead of fire we will get lightning and electricity. Some people believe Fukuyama is already a robot.

Globalisation is equivalent to the end of history. Both go hand-in-hand. They are semantically linked. Different societies have different histories. That means different futures. If we going to make a 'tomorrow' common to all societies existing on the planet, if we are going to propose a global future, then we need first to destroy the history of those other societies, to delete their pasts, to annihilate the continuous moment of the present, virtualising the realities that are constructed by the content of historical time. A 'common future' means the deletion of particular histories. But this means that no histories at all, including their futures, will exist. The common future is no future. Globalisation is the death of time. Globalisation cancels out the transcendental subjectivity of Husserl or the *Dasein* of Heidegger. There would be neither any more time, nor being.

We must deal with the bifurcation of temporal constructions. It is time to address this question with all its implicit weight. Now, on the eve of the end of history, the edge of the descent into post-history, we could make the decision to give different ontological responses.

When we construct the future, it should not be global in scope. It cannot be just one future, we must have many futures. The transcendental subjectivities, cultures, and societies can preserve space for the scattering of energies born of the encounter with oneself, the short circuit in question through its temporalisation: that will grant the existence of the outer world and the continuing of (always and necessarily) local histories. Time will continue, and the world as the experience of real *presencing*, will be supported by the structure of the deep subjectivity. History will remain local. The common history must be a symphony of the different music of local histories being created by the unique chronological rhythms of times, and not one part attempting to drown out and overwhelm the rest until it is the only sound that can be heard.

The next question is: does the formalisation of the nation-state correctly and exhaustively reflect the structure of the transcendental subject as the creator of history? Will future historical time necessarily be national (as constructed by modernity), or will it be expressed in other ways? Maybe it will return to pre-modern forms? When Huntington evokes civilisations, he admits the possibility of emergent localities and local identities being different from the existing, manufactured, nation-states. Civilisations are cultural and religious communities — not ethnic-national ones. We could imagine a step backward, in the pre-national direction (Islamic integration); or a step forward in the post-national direction (the European

Union or Eurasian Union); or we could tolerate other civilisations in the form of nation-states. The historical narratives and the way in which politics formalises time could be changed. It means there is a lot of work that should be done, historically speaking. While someone is alive, he can change not only the future but also the past. The gesture or meaningful action accomplished in the present will add a new sense to the past. Only after death does one's past become the property of another. Hence, the history of peoples, societies, and cultures is open. They have the possibility to make the amazing turn that is necessary to view their past from a new perspective. So, history is music and the work of Muses.

Are civilisations destined to clash with each other? It is not written in stone: history lacks linear rules. Difference does not automatically necessitate clash and struggle. Of course, history knows war. But history knows peace as well. War and peace have always existed. War and peace will always be. They serve to relive the tension and the stress of the present. They liberate and subjugate horror and death. Total war and total peace are equally murderous.

The continuation of the history of local societies instead of a single historical narrative will lead to the preservation of being, and hence to the possibility for the future to happen.

The second option is globalisation. It cancels the future. It requires the arrival of post-humanity. It constructs the post-world consisting of simulacra and virtual structures. In place of the transcendental subject, *Dasein*, society becomes a huge computer centre, a matrix, a supercomputer. In place of time, it creates simulacrums of the past, present and future. The simulacrum of the past is false memory, the product of artificial influence rewriting historical memory. The walling-off of the transcendental subject allows the past to be changed as if it were a pirated DVD. An alternate version of society could be loaded as a prequel. Such a substitution of the past is technically possible. Sufficient control over the present allows the past to be easily rewritten.

The substitution of the future follows from this manipulation. Two disparate tracks mixed and played over each other produce cacophonic repercussions in the future. The future is petrified, and the semantics of time blur, fork, and multiply.

Manipulating the present is a little more complicated and requires a higher degree of sophistication. To remove the present, the transcendental subjectivity must not only be walled off, but eradicated. This presumes the transition from the human to the post-human.

Developments in the human genome project, cloning, advances in robots, and new generations of cyborg all brings us close to the advent of post-humanity. The goal of this process is to produce creatures that will lack an existential dimension with zero subjectivity. Simulacrums can be made not only out of reason, but also from unconsciousness. The most important facet of this process is the abolition of the present. Such post-human creatures and inanimate objects — animals, vehicles, plants, stones, and so on — have no sense of the present.

If globalisation continues, what is the fate of subjectivity? What is the ontology of the future that will — probably — never happen? A fairly unorthodox theory could be suggested. Let us assume that multipolarity is stillborn, that history has ended, and that the project of globalisation has become a reality. How will the final exorcism of transcendental subjectivity be performed? How will 'the final decision' concerning the abolition of *Dasein* be implemented? After all, as long as mankind and societies exist, they should make this decision for themselves. It is impossible to make an appeal to the Other which could be blamed or praised for the decision and its result. Such a reference to the Other is acceptable only when the Self and the Other are one and the same. If we lose our identity, we will also lose *alterity*, the capacity for 'otherness', and thus the ability to distinguish between self and not-self, and consequently to assume the existence of any alternative viewpoint. So we are the authors of the end of history which concerns ourselves and no one else.

Thus having excluded the presence of the *Other,* an explanation is still required about how man can accomplish the last gesture of self-destruction. How can he transfer the initiatives of existence to the post-human world, a world that will disappear immediately upon the expiration of the last man — for there will be no one left to bear witness?

This is a great problem, and it requires an even deeper insight into the structure of the transcendental subject that generates time and its formulations. Nobody else can make decisions about how to reset time or to end it, an end that can only be brought about by ourselves through a final self-immolation by the exaltation of the short circuit. Hence, the subject carries within itself the possibility of such a chronocide. Globalisation and the end of history cannot be reduced to the will of someone other than he who is the source of the creation of time, at least not within the limits of immanent philosophy. Consequently, this can mean only one thing: that within the depths of transcendental subjectivity, there lies another layer which Husserl had not uncovered. Husserl was convinced that the layer he discovered was the last one. But it turns out that this is not so. There has to be another dimension yet to be found — the most hidden one.

We can designate it as the Radical Subject.

If Husserl's transcendental subjectivity constitutes reality through the experience of a manifestation of self-awareness, the Radical Subject is to be found, not on the way out, but on the way in. It shows itself only in the moment of ultimate historic catastrophe, in the traumatic experience of the 'short circuit' which is stronger, and lasts for a moment longer than it is possible to endure.

The same experience that makes the transcendental subjectivity manifest itself and deploy its content, thus creating time with its intrinsic music, is regarded by the Radical Subject as an invitation to reveal itself in another manner — on the other side of time. For the Radical Subject, time — in all its forms and configurations — is nothing more than a trap, a trick, a decoy, delaying the real decision. For the Radical Subject, it is not only virtuality and the electronic networks which are the prison, but reality itself has already become so: a concentration camp, an agony, and a torture. The slumber of history is something contrary to the condition where the Radical Subject could exist, complete itself, and become. The creation of subjectivity, being the secondary formation of temporality, is an obstacle for its realisation.

If we accept the hypothesis of the Radical Subject, we immediately confront an instance that explains who has made the decision in favor of globalisation, the suicide of humanity, and the end of history; who has conceived this plan and made it reality. It can only therefore only be the drastic gesture of the Radical Subject, looking for liberation from time through the construction of non-temporal (impossible) reality. The Radical Subject is incompatible with all kinds of time. It vehemently demands anti-time, based on the exalted fire of eternity transfigured in the radical light.

When everybody has gone, the only thing that remains is those who cannot be gone. Perhaps that is the reason for this greatest of all probations.

11

THE NEW POLITICAL ANTHROPOLOGY: THE POLITICAL MAN AND HIS MUTATIONS

Man as a Function of Politics

What man is, is derived not from himself as an individual, but from politics. It is politics, being the dispositive of violence and legitimate power, that defines the man. It is the political system that gives us our shape. Moreover, the political system has an intellectual and conceptual power, as well as a transformative potential without limitations. The answer to the anthropological question rests on the configuration of power in society. Power itself consists of two elements: first is the power to shape the paradigm, integrated in society through state institutions, and second is power as the dispositive of violence, which serves as a means to integrate the paradigm into the society. Consequently, the single, highest authority of power and its structure controls our political concept of man in a given society. The sphere of political anthropology emerges here, the study of the political concept of man. But there is also the concept of the political man. The difference between these two categories is that the political concept of man is the concept of the man *as such*, which is installed in us by the state or the political system. The political man is a particular means of correlating man with this state and political system. At first, the state or the political system installs this concept in us, and then it both grants and takes away our rights.

However, on the pre-conceptional level, on the level of political anthropology, it falls to us to give (or to take away) our own rights and to add (or remove) a political status. We believe that we are *causa sui*, generated within ourselves, and only then do we find ourselves in the sphere of politics. In fact, it is politics that constitutes us. Whether we are born in a maternity hospital or in an open field, whether we are carried into a ward with electricity or a dark, smoky hut, depends on politics. Politics grants us our political status, our name, and our anthropological structure. Man's anthropological structure shifts when one political system changes to another. Consequently, the political man and our political anthropology alike are given different shapes after the conversion from traditional to modern society. If we remain within the bounds of conventional politi-cal-anthropological structures, which were described in great detail my book, *The Philosophy of Politics*, we may stress two notions. First, we can say, 'Look how tremendous the shift in the political anthropology is, that resulted from the conversion of the traditional state to the modern state.' We may be astonished by it; we may be amazed, at how it is not only the political institutions, but also man himself that is transformed on the most fundamental level. But later, we inevitably encounter the fact that, right now, we are in the state of shifting from the political mode of modernity to postmodernity, and we realise that a completely new view surrounds us. It becomes clear, from our perspective that the parameters of both the traditional and modern society flow one into the other. In fact, *Homo politicus*, the political man, was postulated in both of these paradigms. Of course, on the pole of modernity, we have the rational, autonomous individual, and we have a particle of a certain holistic ensemble on the other pole. As for postmodernity, it declares that there are no differences as such between these two types of society, politics, and concepts of man. It matters not whether this very man is constituted according to the lib-eral, individualist approach or by the holistic *eidos*,[1] it is Man which is the outcome.

The Boundaries of Post-anthropology and the Origin of Post-politics

At this stage we are able to single out completely new symptoms of the type of man constituted by the politics of postmodernity: *depolitisation, autonomisation, microscopisation,* and *sub-* and *transhumanisation.* That is, today man is not regarded as a whole — his parts are considered to be independent. It is his desires, emotions, moods and inclinations that matter. At the same time, while on the one hand attention is transferred from the individual to the sub-individual level, on the other hand, the sub-individual level merges with other sub-individualities, that is, it enters the domain of the trans-individual. The chaos of a contemporary dance club

---

1   In Plato's theory of ideas, the *eidos* designates the essential form of something before it becomes abstractly represented by thought or language.-Ed.

can be regarded as a metaphor for this trans-individuality. It is possible to distinguish between pairs, figures, styles of expression, and sexes during quadrille or even rock dancing, which is late modernity. But, in a modern dance club, there are creatures of uncertain sex, undefined appearance, and vague identity, regularly moving to the beat of the music. Moreover, the dancing has a hyper-individualistic nature: the dancers are not moving, they are being moved. What moves each dancer, moves the others. Are they moving separately? No, their bodies are moving simultaneously, giving in to a common resonance. Something like this is happening in politics: the de-individualisation of the individual and the sub- and transindividualisation of political institutions and structures.

Thus, we are confronting a completely new politics, the essence of which is the denial of politics itself as a certain distinct, authoritative line. No matter how we solve the question of power (to whom it belongs — to the elite, to the caste, to the priests, to the warriors, or to the democratic parliament), it will still be a formalisation of political relations. Interests, positions, levels, statuses, and roles are always visible. We are dealing with a political society, be it modern or traditional. But if one proposes to remove the very question of power, if one says there is no such concept, if we are compelled to withdraw this question, if the notion of the subject of the political process is forbidden, it will be ousted by a rhizomatic entity (Gilles Deleuze and Félix Guattari use the term 'rhizome' and 'rhizomatic' to describe theory and research that allows for multiple, non-hierarchical entry and exit points in data representation and interpretation), which Hardt and Negri name a 'multitude'.[2] These 'multitudes' act for both subject and authority. Consequently, the concept of the State is replaced by the concept of the post-State. What is the post-State? It is the idea of the abolition of the State. The process of the demonisation of the State starts, the basis of which is the thesis that the state interferes with private property. The word 'the state' itself eventually becomes an invective, and after this, its abolition becomes an obvious measure. After that, everything that interferes with absolute freedom is abolished.

In the end, all forms of vertical symmetry (the orientation of a 'top to bottom' hierarchy) are subject to destruction, and everything becomes horizontal. Similarly, the vertical lines of power and the state become horizontal, and thus political anthropology, implying this or that constitution of the individual, dissipates and disperses in the space of rhizomatic dust.

---

2   According to Hardt and Negri, the 'multitude' is a collective social subject which both sustains the global empire of today, but which will also eventually bring about its destruction.-Ed.

One could call it *apoliteia*.[3] But if it really were *apoliteia*, we would observe a gradual fading of the political, its entropy. But we are not speaking about *apoliteia* or indifference towards politics. Instead we encounter a deliberate, axiological trend. That is the liquidation of political structures, or the structure of the political, if we include the structures of both political pre-modernity and modernity. That is, while confronting postmodernity, both of them are rejected. At the same time, in order to actively denounce the political, political will is required. It turns out that postmodernity is loaded with political meaning. And it is loaded with an imperious, epistemologically obsessional meaning, and an obligatory political meaning of apolitisation, at that. That is, this is not pure entropy of the political structure; it is a revolutionary counter-project, a theoretical scheme of political post-anthropology. And the core of this post-anthropology is, of course, this rhizomatic sub- and trans-individual network. It is this dispersed nebula of multitude that is deliberately destroying the structures of the will that belong to the political (*das Politische*), in its classical Schmittian meaning.

The Core Subjects of Postpolitics

Today we can sum up the situation in this way: we add the destructive, corrosive strategy of political postmodernity (possessing the same authoritative, offensive dispositive) into the sphere of the political (which is Schmitt's classical politics, including pre-modernity and modernity), and we receive politics in its widest meaning, in its absolute meaning. This is the Absolute Political (*absolut Politische*), in the boundaries of which we can place two basic anthropological models. It sounds natural: the first is 'contemporary man', constructed by the political, struggling against politics as such. He is like a dancer at a club. He has his blog, he watches TV, he pretends he votes for the opposition (that is, he latently identifies himself with the destructive, anti-state political trend, even if he lacks a well-thought-out, coherent politics). When confronting any integral political concept, he starts by saying 'no', his attitude toward it is very aggressive, and it creates a specifically-aimed influence. The other figure is the political soldier (*Das politische Soldat*). 'The political soldier' is a different concept, developed in the 1930s, which is a personality, summing up what we have called the classical approach to *das Politische*, the classical approach to the political. Its definition is very picturesque: the political soldier differs from the common man by the fact that he kills and dies for

---

3   Latin: 'apolitical'. Both Julius Evola and Ernst Jünger adopted this term to describe their own indifference to matters of practical politics later in life.-Ed.

politics. His killing and personal death become an existential element of the manifestation of the political, and thus, for him the political acquires an existential dimension. The politician, unlike the political soldier, deals with the political, but never kills or dies for it. When the politician confronts death and murder, he says, 'No, I'd better rethink my convictions.'

This is a wonderful romantic image, employed as a part of modernity and the Twentieth century, where we could see these splendid political soldiers. Nietzsche's words illustrate their role in the history of the Twentieth century. Although wars in the Nineteenth century were fought for material goals, '[a] warlike age [is] approaching that will above all restore honour to bravery! For it shall pave the way for a still higher age and gather the strength that the latter will one day need — the age that will carry heroism into the search for knowledge and wage wars for the sake of thoughts and their consequences.'[4] When is this time? It was the Twentieth century. The entirety of the Twentieth century was filled with political soldiers killing each other for their beliefs. They killed and were killed. Besides, every traditional society (for example that of Genghis Khan's) was founded by political soldiers. The Russian Empire was also built by political soldiers. Modernity was very sensitive to this figure. They say the political soldier fights only for elevated and spiritual ideas. But that is not the case. Even a liberal can become a political soldier (although there is nothing spiritual or noble in liberal ideas). He may die for quite senseless ideas, but he remains a political soldier, and that is very important. The political soldier is an instrumental notion, and should not be hyperbolised. It is a charming, but purely utilitarian element of modernity.

We believe that, on the level of political anthropology, this political soldier is confronting the decomposed, rhizomatic post-human android. We register this reading, and it may seem that we are ready to throw away our ideological differences and for the political soldier to confront the postmodern world. But my thesis is that, from the perspective of the phase shift we are in, we are living in a society where this conflict is possible, but, at the same time, its outcome is predetermined. In fact, the figure of the political man is removed. And his anthropological space is being occupied by a new personality, a very cunning and suspect personality, which is not that of the political soldier, but, at the same time, is not related to the hissing, rhizomatic, twittering sub-individual. This personality is the political man's simulacrum. It is something that imitates the political soldier, in the same way that postmodernity imitates Modernity. In the final

---

4   Friedrich Nietzsche, *The Gay Science* (Cambridge: Cambridge University Press, 2001), pp. 160-161.

analysis, the readings do not give us the 'human vs. post-human' scenario. Instead, what we see is the undisguised, rotten liberal post-human and the pseudo-human, the pseudo-soldier, within whom the general substance of this phase of history has found itself. This is why we have the phenomenon of contemporary fascism, which is an excellent illustration of this condition. Every last vestige of fascism that was embodied by political soldiers ran out in 1945. Each and every declared fascist after 1945 is a simulacrum. The liberals' fears, taking the form of fascists, is a complete parody. They do not differ much from the decomposed and half-dissolved masses. Communism, which has held out longer than fascism, created its simulacrum within itself. The late Communists were already pseudo-political soldiers. Today there are no chances for Communism to return to life. The same goes for fascism. Soon, we will see that liberalism has arrived at the same point. At least our liberals, who are not really liberals at all, demonstrate this: give them some money, and they will declare anything and everything. We are dealing with entities, lacking anything resembling the classical political anthropology.

The Fatalism of Postanthropology and *Angelpolis*

As much as can be discerned, we are dealing with Deleuze's 'fold' (the concept allows for creative thought about the production of subjectivity, and ultimately about the possibilities for and the production of non-human forms of subjectivity): we have the confrontation of post-political anthropology and the pseudo-political soldier. In this case, the antithesis of the post-human is the non-human. If we face it, we acquire a very complex and intriguing perspective. It is either phantasmagoric despair, to which Baudrillard,[5] describing the world with radical post-historical categories, gave way, or the feeling that we are not satisfied with this fold, this post-anthropological perspective. However, if we grasp the fatality of this pair, we can calmly step back and assess the situation.

Having raised the question of anthropology, we must look for a solution, and at the same time we must acknowledge this post-anthropology, that is, not wait for what is coming to arrive, but to consider, instead, that it is already here. What do we gain from this perspective? I think that Schmitt, who created the classical approach to the political, might give us some hints. He spoke about political theology. Schmitt said that all

---

5   One of Baudrillard's principal ideas is that contemporary reality is made up of concepts and symbols which have no corresponding meaning in the real world, a condition he termed 'hyperreality'. -Ed.

political ideologies and systems are integral theological models with religions, dogmas, institutions, and rites of their own. That is why, in order to understand politics, one must regard it as a religious phenomenon. But political theology presupposes the existence of the political *telos*,[6] which can be constructed by man, like Hobbes' *Leviathan*,[7] or it can be of non-human construction, such as the Catholic model of *imperium*, which was close to Schmitt's heart. Naturally, in the post-anthropological structure, in postmodernity, this appeal to *telos* as a political factor which unfolds the system into an integral theology will not help us much, as we have crossed the boundaries of political theology.

It is impossible to speak about political anthropology while describing the post-anthropological model of today's politics. We are forbidden to speak about an integral political theology because we have witnessed this fundamental mutation of 'the fold'. What are we allowed to speak about? We have political processes, sources of power and dispositives of influence, we observe paradigmatic epistemologies, which are pushed and promoted in the same way as they were in the framework of classical politics. They remain with us, which means that the political in its wider sense is here, it is simply that neither man nor God is there. Who is the actor of this post-politics? There is a certain hypothesis that I call the concept of *Angelopolis*, 'the city of Angels' or *Angelpolitia* (angelic politics) that is a turn from political theology to political angelology. What this means is that the sphere of the political is starting to be controlled by and is starting to ground itself upon the confrontation between superhuman entities. That is entities that are neither human nor divine (or not divine at all). *Angelopolis* possesses a huge potential to assign political roles without taking humanoids and post-humanoids into account. For example, one may think that a man sends an SMS, but it is actually the SMS that sends itself. Considering the growing level of standardisation and lack of originality in these messages, its over-individualistic essence is becoming more and more evident.

There really is a command centre in post-politics. There are actors and there are decisions, but they are totally dehumanised in postmodernity. They are beyond the frames of anthropology. We can find a certain proof of this hypothesis in traditional teachings and in traditional eschatologies, which state that the End Times will not be triggered by the human hand, but that it will stop just prior to the final hour. The final act will

---

6   Classical Greek: 'purpose' or 'goal'.-Ed.

7   In Hobbes' book *Leviathan*, he defends the concept of absolute monarchy on social contract principles (an agreement between the monarch and those governed).-Ed.

not depend on man. It will be a war of angels, a war of gods, a confrontation of entities, not tied by historical or economic laws and patterns, and which do not identify themselves with religions or certain political elites. And this angelic war can be thought of politically. That is *Angelopolis*, or *Politische Angelologie*, which I bring forward as a concept, devoid of mysticism and esotericism, which has the same sense and nature as Schmitt's metaphor of 'political theology'. Political angelology must be considered as a metaphor which is both scientific and rational. *Angelopolis* is a method to understand, to interpret and to hermeneutically decipher the contemporary processes which surround us and are regarded as being alienated from political anthropology, from humanity as a species, and as a politically institutionalised and constituted notion.

12

FOURTH POLITICAL PRACTICE

The adherents of the Fourth Political Theory are in need of a plan. The plan is based on the following idea: if we have the Fourth Political Theory as a set of concepts and a theoretical definition, then this theory *must* be realised, because every theoretical construction can either be brought to life, or cannot because of circumstances.

Therefore, if we theorise and talk about the Fourth Political Theory, we should also think about how it could be realised in practice. However, this should give us pause, because the Fourth Political Theory strains to conclude the political topography of modernity, with all its implicit and hidden dualistic models therein. We can develop a scheme representing the correlation between the theory and its practice in different fields of knowledge: science, metaphysics, religion, philosophy, technologies, and common use. Below is a table with these different fields of knowledge on the horizontal axis and with two columns on the vertical axis, 'Term 1' and 'Term 2'. The first column concerns the field theoretically, and the second deals with the field in practice.

Field	Term 1	Term 2
science	Theory (contemplation)	Practice (things)
metaphysics	principle	manifestation
religion	myth	ritual
philosophy	mentality	activity
technology	Idea (project)	realisation (implementation)
common use	thinking	action

Of course, the consideration of these columns in itself can bring us to some very interesting conclusions; starting with the question of what theory is in terms of science (i.e., contemplation, vision) and what is praxis (the term, formed from the Greek *pragma*, i.e., object, objectification, acting). When the problem of defining what a 'thing' is (*res*, hereafter 'reality') arose a few years ago, the attempts to come across a counterpart of this basic term in contemporary philosophy led to the revelation that there is no acceptable equivalent for this Latin word in Greek at all. There is *pragma* as an 'action' and the 'act' at the same time. It is an active object, but not as an accomplishment. And there is an 'existent' from Aristotle, which is expounded as *res* in further Latin translations.

Therefore, there is no such word as 'thing' in Greek, and this is very important, because it means that the concept of reality is also absent. Reality is formed on the basis of *res*, reality is a property of *res*, reality *is* (whose? what?) — something referring to the 'thing', or 'thingness'. Therefore, there are the Greek words *pragma*, 'existent' and 'practice' for the Latin *res*. *Pragma* is the action and the object at the same time.

It is very interesting: the entirety of Greek metaphysics evolves between 'theory' as contemplation and 'action' (*praxis*), keeping short of severe Latin subjectivity, the 'thingness' hidden in the term *res*.

If we amplify the aforementioned duality of this table, we would come across Guénon's[1] model of the 'principle of the manifested';[2] notably, that the manifestation here is closer to the practice, but not to that which is manifested; we can see the activity in the second column, concerning practice. If we make some further assertions in the history and sociology of religion, we would come across functionalism and the human sociology of Malinowski,[3] which examines this division between myth and ritual.

The original Greek definition of myth must be remembered: myth is a story being told during a ritual. The duality of myth and ritual is one of the basic items extensively discussed in both the history of religion and of social anthropology. In philosophy can be seen the 'mentality-activity', or 'mental-activity' (this pairing and duality of terms is similar to that of

1   René Guénon (1886-1951) was a French writer who founded what has come to be known as the traditionalist school of religious thought. Traditionalism calls for a rejection of the modern world and its philosophies in favour of a return to the spirituality and ways of living of the past (Guénon himself ended up living as a Sufi Muslim in Cairo).

2   Guénon discusses this in his *Man and His Becoming According to the Vedanta* (Hillsdale, New York: Sophia Perennis, 2001).-Ed.

3   Bronisław Malinowski (1884-1942) was a Polish anthropologist. His ethnographic studies, based upon extensive field work among tribal populations, were pioneering in their approach.-Ed.

'theory-practice'). And finally, technology is rather simple — it is the duality of a project and its realisation.

So, we have two columns. If the Fourth Political Theory is added to the first column, Term 1, then we can probably find some specific concept in the Fourth Political Practice to place in the column Term 2 in accordance with it. If the Fourth Political Theory was an ideological variation, or some combination of the elements of the political theories of modernity, we would follow this strictly. That is to say, if we create an additional concept, constructed of the same elements and based on the same topography as the political ideologies of modernity are, we should talk about the field not only theoretically, but also in practice, in the column Term 2.

And generally, it would be interesting to do this, because talking about semantic fields associated with the Fourth Political Theory in connection with the column Term 2 could be very useful. But I leave this problem for someone else, and propose another way.

The point is that if we talk about the very core of the Fourth Political Theory and its fundamental problems, we understand that the main idea of the Fourth Political Theory is to walk away from the dualism between the subject and the object, between intention and realisation, and from the dual topography which the philosophy of modernity, the science of modernity, and the *politology* of modernity are based on.

It is not mere chance that we talk about *Dasein* as the subject of political theory. *Dasein*, as proposed by Heidegger, is a way to overcome the subject-object duality, that is, an aspiration to find the root of ontology.

Heidegger mentioned the *inzwischen*, or the 'between', while talking about the existence of *Dasein*. The principal nature of *Dasein* is being 'between'. *Dasein* is *inzwischen*. We should not use the system of classical political dualism, the scientific topography of both modernity and Aristotle's time while talking about the Fourth Political Theory, and presume the fact that the subject and its core, the basis of the Fourth Political Theory pole, is *Dasein*.

It is necessary, instead, to examine Fourth Political Practice in another way, taking into account Heidegger's criticisms of constructing non-fundamental ontology, i.e., ontology as it is. Heidegger said that if we want to understand *Dasein*, we should realise and construct a fundamental ontology which would not lose contact with the *ontic* (that which exists; reality) roots of *Dasein*, and would not ascend or sublimate, sooner or later, to anything correlated with the 2000-year-old (from Plato, or even the last of the Pre-Socratic philosophers, up to Nietzsche) general philosophical constructions on which modernity is based.

We should put *Dasein* as the centre and the pole of the Fourth Political Theory. What does this mean in the context of practice? It means that *Dasein* should not be qualified either as a theoretical construction, or as a principle. Should it be used as a myth, like a narrative? This comes much closer, but it should be carefully considered. It should not exactly be used as a mentality, at least not as an ontological mentality. Likewise, it should not be used as an idea or anything concerning the subject.

Keeping this universal and pre-dualistic status of *Dasein* in Heidegger's philosophy in mind, I want to suggest a reference to some root, to something that predates this dualism, to define Fourth Political Practice. In other words, what is the centre of Fourth Political Practice? This centre is something that lies between the columns, between Term 1 and Term 2, between theory and practice. But this does not at all mean their combination or a happy medium. A 'happy medium' is nonsense that we should distance ourselves from. We should not look for a happy medium or a compromise of column 1 and column 2, the polarity of theory and practice, but we should find the root that these pairs grow from, their common root. From the perspective of *Dasein* analytics, both the subject and object are ontological constructions, grown from the 'between', i.e. the *inzwischen*.

We are interested in the instance that both theory and practice appeared from, the instance where theory and practice are not yet divided and, *a fortiori*,[4] are not opposites. We are interested in that kind of instance where both principle and manifestation have a common root (they can never have a common root, not for a moment, and that is most interesting for us), that kind of instance where myth and ritual are not yet separated, at that instance where mentality and activity are in common, where idea means realisation and realisation is idea, and where thinking and acting have one source.

We are interested in this very intermediate level not achieved by a horizontal consideration of these pairs, but only by a new, non-horizontal dimension. Unlike Hegelianism, Marxism, communication theory, and in principle, the entire structure of modernity, we are not interested in anything that sits upon the line between theory and practice. We are looking for something that does not belong to horizontal subspace, or to some ratio-based configuration of the columns, or to the line between theory and practice. We are interested in something hidden under the theory and practice, somewhere in the common root they both grow from. From this point of view, the question of the prioritisation of either conscience or

---

4   Latin: 'an argument from a stronger position'.-Ed.

matter during the Soviet period is absolutely wrong. The priority for us is the problem of the common root, and we should grow the Fourth Political Theory and its Practice from this root.

Having acknowledged this notion as being basic, we can say that Fourth Political Theory is Theory to the same degree as it is Practice, and it is Practice to the same degree as it is Theory.

In other words, if we can feel the 'between' related in depth over these two columns, if we can seize the geometry of this political vector (that is, of course, its real philosophical and metaphysical vector), we will see that these two trees grow from the same root.

If we focus on the subject of the Fourth Political Theory, meaning *Dasein* or *inzwischen*, we will understand that it does not belong to the horizontal disposition between these two columns. Why do we talk about roots but not the head? This is a very serious and deep moment, because we should realise the reduction that is being made. If we realise the horizontal reduction first, and we get an unsatisfactory result, we will conclude that we should instead realise the vertical reduction, to move towards *ontic* roots but not ontological heights. Therefore, we should postpone such notions as the dimension of spirit and the divine, and move towards chaos and other vertical and depth-oriented concepts.

Nietzsche said, 'Not when truth is dirty, but when it is shallow the seeker of knowledge steps reluctantly into its water.'[5] According to this, how can we try to form a clear conception of what Fourth Political Practice is? By reversing the order of these two columns as a first step. We should obtain practice as theory, take principle as manifestation, mentality as activity and thinking as action. What is Fourth Political Practice? It is contemplation. What is the manifestation of the Fourth Political Practice? It is a principle to be revealed. In what aspect is the myth realised as ritual? It becomes theurgic fact (let us recognise that Neoplatonic theurgy is the reanimation of statues). What is activity as mentality? It is the idea that thoughts are magic, that thoughts can change reality; it is a suggestion that thoughts replace reality as fact. Fourth Political Practice brings us to the nature of the supranatural world, to the antithesis of Weber's[6] metaphor in the realisation of the technological aspect of the project. What is the supranatural world? It is a world where there is no barrier between idea and realisation. It is the principle of adopting a magical view of the

---

5   Friedrich Nietzsche, *Thus Spoke Zarathustra* (Cambridge: Cambridge University Press, 2007), p. 161.-Ed.

6   Max Weber believed that science and technology had made it impossible for modern man to believe in the supranatural, which he termed the 'disenchantment of the world'.-Ed.

world based on the idea that thought is the only thing that crosses worlds, and everything we cross with is nothing more than a thought. What kind of thought is it? Pure thought. The vehicle of Fourth Political Theory and Practice lives in a supranatural world. What is 'menactivity'? It is a trans-substance, a transformation of spirit into body and body into spirit, and it is the main problem of hermeticism.

We have come to the realisation that Fourth Political Practice is not a rough realisation of Fourth Political Theory in some space where the theory is suggested to be different from its practice. There is no more space, no more *topos*,[7] and no more topology in Fourth Political Practice aside from theory; we have annihilated any other spaces before we started, not in the consummation, but in the very beginning, before we started in a pre-ontological context. In other words, we should not look forward (it will never be changed) or backward if we really want to change the squalor we live in, because all the remnants that have made this ultimate form of degeneration possible and real have appeared and been stored there. These roots are not mere chance. The scrap-heap we exist in is not accidental and has a profound logic. Here, primordial metaphysics is expressed in techniques both modern and postmodern. Accordingly, the only path for real political struggle is appealing to the Fourth Political Practice as to the roots, free from the evolutionary process, from the very conception to the final point where we are now, because either our political struggle is soteriological and eschatological, or it has no meaning.

And here we come to the last point. What does a world avoiding any duality look like? It looks like postmodernity, like virtuality. The wired and virtual contemporary world just says: this is not theory and not prac-tice, not principle and not manifestation, not myth and not ritual, not thought and not action. Virtuality is just a mockery of Fourth Political Theory and Practice. It is counterintuitive enough, but this postmodern reality is closer than all previous topologies, including the theological and proto-theological. Virtuality is closer to the very unique model of Fourth Political Theory and Practice than any other element.

Thus we can raise the question, how does our traditionalism or new metaphysics relate to postmodernity? I consider them to be very close. Virtuality tries to mix the semantic fields of the columns on the horizontal level so as to become indistinguishable. We can say that Deleuze's rhizome is a postmodern and post-structural mockery of Heidegger's *Dasein*. They are alike and they are often described in the same terms. But pay attention to the fact of how postmodernism solves the problem of the reversal of

---

7   Classical Greek: 'place'.-Ed.

the column's order. It solves the problem by appealing to the surface, and this is the main idea we see with Deleuze. Remember his interpretation of Artaud's[8] 'body without organs',[9] his interpretation of the necessity of destruction, of the leveling of structure, and his interpretation of man's epidermis, his outer layer, as the basis for the screen onto which his image is projected. It is a point of mockery where Fourth Political Theory and postmodernism meet each other. If the columns mix horizontally, some madness appears. We can use the thesis that *Homo integros*, the complete integral man, consists of *Homo sapiens* and *Homo demens*.[10] Deleuze says, 'Free *Homo demens!*' He says that madness should escape from under *Homo sapiens* and realise the transgression between these two columns in the political sphere. Here comes the rhizomatic process, Ionic and chronological ideas of temporality. This postmodern dementia is much like the Fourth Political Theory, and differs from it only in its horizontality and flatness. The main problem of postmodernity is its elimination of any vertical orientation in terms of both height and depth.

The end times and the eschatological meaning of politics will not realise themselves on their own. We will wait for the end in vain. The end will never come if we wait for it, and it will never come if we do not. This is essential because history, time, and reality have special strategies to avoid Judgment Day, or rather, they have a special strategy of a reversionary manoeuvre that will create the impression that everyone has come to a realisation and an understanding. This is the huge arsenal of Heidegger's *noch nicht*, or eternal 'not yet…' If the Fourth Political Practice is not able to realise the end of times, then it would be invalid. The end of days should come; but it will not come by itself. This is a task, it is not a certainty. It is active metaphysics. It is a practice. And it can be a potential and rational solution of the enigmatic layers that are discovered while talking about Fourth Political Practice.

---

8   Anton Artaud (1896-1948) was a French artist and dramatist who developed the concept of the 'theater of cruelty', by which he did not mean sadism but a method for destroying falsehoods for the audience and unveiling the truth beneath.-Ed.

9   In Artaud's play 'To Have Done with the Judgment of God' (1947), he wrote, 'When you will have made him a body without organs, then you will have delivered him from all his automatic reactions and restored him to his true freedom.' In Antonin Artaud, *Selected Writings* (Berkeley, California: University of California Press, 1976), p. 571.

10   Latin: 'madman'.-Ed.

13

GENDER IN THE FOURTH POLITICAL THEORY

To begin with, let us analyse what tenets about gender are characteristic of the political theories of modernity. If we attentively examine the perspective from which socialism, liberalism, nationalism, fascism, and National Socialism all operate, we will notice that some features are common to the classical understanding of gender in all the political theories of modernity. On the one hand, it is not original to modernity, because modernity here follows traditional European society (even pre-modern Christianity), which was mostly patriarchal. Even before Christianity, it was patriarchal, back until those immemorial times in the Mediterranean which were discussed by Bachofen in his book, *Mother Right*.[1] In other words, behind modernity, and behind modernity's conception of gender, is Western or global patriarchy. This patriarchy has heavily influenced the structure and political understanding of gender in modernity. However, this patriarchy has undergone certain modifications in the final formulation of gender norms in the political theories of modernity.

It is acceptable to consider 'a gender' in sociological terms, in other words, gender as a socially-constructed phenomenon. This is in contrast to the anatomical 'sex' inherent in biological terms. Gender is a social convention which can change from society to society. At the same time, the political formulation of gender is the social norm, which is approved as an imperative on the basis of political power. Thus, archaic societies practise rites of passage or initiations after which a boy can be regarded as a 'man', otherwise he has no social sex, no 'gender', and is deprived of a man's social functions (marriage, participation in hunting, and ritual). Depending on a society's requirements, gender tenets can change. For

---

1   Johann Jakob Bachofen (1815-1887) was a Swiss anthropologist who asserted in his book, *Mutterrecht* (translated into English in the volume *Myth, Religion, and Mother Right* [Princeton: Princeton University Press, 1992]), that lunar matriarchy was the primordial condition of human society, and that solar patriarchy emerged later in opposition to it.-Ed.

example, in some slaveholding societies, male slaves were not thought of as men, and were made to wear women's clothing. Slaves were used as women because they did not have the social status of men. Hence the phenomenon of castration — the deprivation of the physical attributes of men on a par with their social status. Therefore, gender is both a social phenomenon and a political one. Political, because we are dealing with the management of social norms regulated by a society: community, police, and so on, the retreat from which leads to a variety of sanctions.

The three political theories of modernity all ask the same questions: 'Who is the political person? And what is the political gender?' At first, 'the person' is the man. From the sociological point of view, women became 'persons' only recently, and this raises the question of women's political rights. From the viewpoint of modernity, a woman is not a person. A person can only be a man; however, not every man, only a special type of man. The characteristics of a real man include wealth (until the end of the Nineteenth century in Europe, property was a necessary attribute of *citizenship*, i.e., political gender), rationality, thrift, and living in a city (the peasant was not considered an equal in sociopolitical significance). Thus, in the elections of the first state Duma in Russia in 1905,[2] the voice of one townsman was equal to 100 peasants' voices. In modernity, a peasant is not quite a 'person'. Other characteristics of being a 'man' include maturity and age. These socio-professional and age categories are included in the concepts of gender and gender functions. The last characteristic is that a 'man' must belong to European civilisation and have white skin. When considerations of cultural superiority and racism are taken together, this is the 'political man', or *l'home politique*, from an anthropological point of view.

Such gender tenets are an axis for all three major political ideologies of modernity and their derivations. However, within these ideologies there are differences in relation to this figure of the 'man'. The most 'male-affirming' is the theory of liberalism, as it considers this figure of the rational, rich, adult White male as the norm and as a natural phenomenon. Liberalism canonises this conception of gender and standardises it, trying to eternalise this bourgeois social system, typical of Eighteenth- and Nineteenth-century Europe. Liberalism asserts the factuality of this gender and projects it onto the future: 'The modern world is constructed

---

2   Following the Russian Revolution of 1905, the State Duma was convened, supposedly with the intention of acting in an advisory role to the monarchy as a lower house of parliament. However, laws enacted in 1906 ensured that the Duma would have little in the way of influence over the Czar and his ministers, and supreme power continued to rest with him.-Ed.

by men, conceived and anticipated by men, and will belong to men, *Homo oeconomicus* and *Homo faber*.[3] Such an understanding of gender is undergoing changes with time: the area of gender that is 'men' increases; the standard archetype begins to include the peasants, the poor, women, and then the non-White 'races'. How does this mechanism apply to the case of women? For women, 'manly' characteristics start to be attributed to them: a businesswoman is one who manifests male qualities; White females become 'citizens'. Thus, 'the woman' starts to be thought of as 'the man'. So, liberal feminism, or the aspiration to give women freedom, means to identify a woman as a man and thus equalise them socio-politically, that is, represent a woman as a man socially. The same procedure is applied to represent the rural peasant as an urban city-dweller, the non-White 'races' as White, the poor as rich, the 'stupid' as reasoning. A woman who sits behind the wheel of a car is a man or a caricature of a man. However, under liberalism, the divisions of the social conceptions of gender remain. Woman may acquire the same technical rights as men, and thus, in performing the functions of 'a man', may be considered as equal to men, but the social construction of 'the man' and 'the woman' is unchanged.

The second political theory, Marxism, starts from the same position; that gender is a bourgeois political construction. But this situation is criticised, and the need to change this situation is expressed. From here develops an idea of total equality, including in terms of gender. The concept of gender equality in the second political theory qualitatively differs from the understanding of equality in the first political theory. The feminism or gender egalitarianism of Marxism contends that both men and women who exist in the context of Marxist ideology cease to be men and women who constitute the standard and imperative gender division of liberalism. That is, we see a desire to move beyond gender in the bourgeois interpretation. In fact, 'the man' here loses the sole possession of rationality. The Hungarian neo-Marxist philosopher Georg Lukács[4] said that 'the dialectical method as the true historical method was reserved for the class which was able to discover within itself on the basis of its life-experience the identical subject-object, the subject of action; the 'we' of the genesis: namely

---

3   Latin: 'economic man' and 'man the creator', respectively.-Ed.

4   Georg Lukács (1885-1971) was a Hungarian Marxist philosopher and critic who sought an alternative mode of Marxism to the orthodoxy promoted by the Soviet Union. His writings remain influential today, particularly in the field of literary theory. He also briefly held the post of Minister of Culture in the brief Hungarian Soviet Republic of 1919.-Ed.

the proletariat'.[5] Proceeding from such a formulation, classical Marxists consistently call for insanity, to schizophrenia, to the schizo-revolutionary (Deleuze). They rely on the urban poor and the proletarians, who could never become full-fledged bourgeois; they turn to the non-White urban populations; however, they ignore those who live in rural areas or peasants, seeing them through the prism of bourgeois perception. But on the whole, in the gender policy of the Communists, we see a new tendency: they recognise the status quo of gender and offer to change it under the banner of historical materialism. This means the transgression of bourgeois man in the downward direction, and the appeal to the material substance (literally 'what stands below' — the sub-state), to the undifferentiated realm of work, where there is no qualitative difference between the 'good cooking woman',[6] the sailor, or the masculine hero. Marxists venture even lower down, where nothing is left of gender hierarchies and strategies. Thus, the most extreme Marxist ideas have a desire to destroy the bourgeois archetype. The reality of practise, however, was different from the theory: in Stalin's Russia, the male archetype, the 'rational, domineering man' prevailed, despite attempts to recreate Marxist gender equality immediately commensurate with the revolution of 1917. But the idea of overcoming the social construction of 'the man' through the reference to anatomy, to the 'desiring-machine',[7] is characteristic of Marxism.

Fascism, the third political theory, accepts the model of the urban, White, European, rational, wealthy 'man', and exalts in it. If liberalism accepts this model as the norm, then fascism begins to gift 'the man' with additional properties. In National Socialism, he should be not simply be White, but Nordic White; not just rational, but in possession of the unique form of reason that only the Germanic Aryan race possesses. This is similar to the position of Lévy-Brühl, who postulated that only the Europeans have a *logos*, and that other peoples are guided by pre-logical, non-civilised social structures. Masculinity was further exalted, and women were urged to be engaged only in *kinder, kirchen, und küchen* (children, church, and kitchen). Other tenets of gender were offered peripherally: for example, by

---

5   Georg Lukács, *History and Class Consciousness: Studies in Marxist Dialectics* (London: Routledge & Kegan Paul, 1971), pp. 148-149.-Ed.

6   Vladimir Lenin once said, 'Under socialism any good cooking woman could, with the same ease, rule a state.'-Ed.

7   Deleuze and Guattari use the term desiring-machine to describe what they see as the essentially mechanistic nature of desire, viewed as a type of machine embedded in a network of other biological machines.-Ed.

Julius Evola in his *The Metaphysics of Sex*,[8] in which the superiority of the masculine over the feminine is asserted, it is argued that men are dormant potential gods, and women are dormant potential goddesses, but standing a little lower in the hierarchy of the sexes. While considering the third political theory, the fringe conception of 'Nordic matriarchy' should also be mentioned: there was an ontology of the feminine. Herman Wirth,[9] a disciple of Bachofen, argued that the Supreme Being is a woman, but that women are completely different from men, a woman in her ontology, *weisse Frau*. However, in the third political theory, the image created by liberalism and then exaggerated remained the norm.

The Fourth Political Theory represents an aspiration to overcome the gender construction of the three political theories of modernity. In this case, what is its gender strategy, its imperative? First of all, the Fourth Political Theory puts outside the brackets 'the man', in other words, that 'man' as a gender with social constructions that are characteristic of modernity. The Fourth Political Theory does not address such a 'last man', as he represents the closed archetype of Modernity. Outside of the sphere of gender, the Fourth Political Theory gropes with the contours of its 'man'. In the face of this construction of 'man' as he who possesses reason, wealth, responsibility, city, white skin color, and so on, we revolt. This image of man must die; he doesn't have a chance to survive, as he is closed inside modernity's historical deadlock. He reproduces the small hierarchies and cannot go beyond his own borders. Such a man believes himself to be immortal. In self-reflection he creates permanent realities, mirrors looking in mirrors. The same goes for all those images to which the man of modernity has been extended: the businesswoman, non-Whites in 'respectable' roles, and so on.

The positive attribute of man, beyond the paradigm of modernity, is the non-adult. The subject of the Fourth Political Theory is a non-adult male. For example, *Le Grand Jeu* of Gilbert-Lecomte and René Daumal,[10] who offered to live their lives without maturing to remain playing at

---

8   Julius Evola, *Eros and the Mysteries of Love: The Metaphysics of Sex* (Rochester, Vermont: Inner Traditions, 1991).-Ed.

9   Herman Wirth (1885-1981) was a Dutch German who believed that there was an ancient, worldwide Nordic culture which has been forgotten apart from some traces which remain encoded in ancient myths and symbols. He devoted his life's work to proving this thesis. He was briefly involved with the SS Ahnenerbe in the 1930s, although when he refused to make his theories conform to those of the National Socialists, he was rejected by them and forced into exile.-Ed.

10 *Le Grand Jeu* (The Great Game) was the journal of a small group around Daumal in Paris between 1928 and 1932, known collectively as the Simplists. They attempted to synthesise avant-garde art with their knowledge of Eastern traditions.-Ed.

being children. This can be considered as an invitation to develop gender tenets for the Fourth Political Theory, a system of aesthetic and political philosophy. Under the concept of the non-White 'man' lies the pre-logical world system of Lévy-Brühl, where the *logos* is not the only means of social organisation. Here we draw from Lévi-Strauss a theory of social anthropology and ethno-sociology drawn from the analysis of the experience of many non-White societies. Further, from madness: all forms of intellectual transgression, the practise of voluntary insanity from Friedrich Hölderlin and Nietzsche to Bataille and Artaud. Madness is part of the gender arsenal of the Fourth Political Theory. In general: non-White/European, insane, non-urban or defined by a constructed landscape. For example, the ecologist or aboriginal: that is, the person who did not break with nature, as discussed by Redfield in his *The Folk Society*.[11] Thus, we create a search algorithm woven of all those elements that are ignored or rejected by modernity. These elements make up a huge field of existence and metaphysics, a field of the intensive being of the Fourth Political Theory. Supplementing the Fourth Political Theory, we should refuse all those tenets about gender which liberalism carries within itself. From the second political theory's gender conception, it would be permissible to borrow the idea of 'the desiring-machine', the idea of overcoming 'the man' through global egalitarianism within the limits of the material. From the classical fascist gender model of the third political theory, as well as liberalism, there is nothing to learn, while the conceptions developed on their fringes may be of great interest, namely sex ontologisation (from Evola) and the idea of Nordic matriarchy.

What is the subject of the Fourth Political Theory? The subject of the Fourth Political Theory is *Dasein* or *Zwischen*, the 'between' in the space between the subject and the object which it is possible to identify with the anthropological trajectory of Gilbert Durand. Within *Dasein*, trajectory,[12] *l'imaginaire*,[13] is there a social conception of sex? And what is the gender of *Dasein*? It is necessary to formulate the normative and imperative gender of the Fourth Political Theory. Gender in the Fourth Political Theory is the same as sex in *Dasein*, that is, we have explained one unknown through another. *Dasein* can somehow be sexualized, but that sex which it has cannot be either male or female. It may make

---

11 Robert Redfield, *The Folk Society* (Indianapolis: Bobbs-Merrill, 1947).-Ed.

12 Anthropological trajectory was the term coined by Durand to describe the relationship between physiology and society.-Ed.

13 In this sense, *l'imaginaire*, or the imagination, is used in the sense that it is a tool which allows humans to rediscover the relationship between the material world and the world of ideal forms, or the spiritual world.-Ed.

sense to speak about it in terms of the androgyne. Should we say that the Fourth Political Theory may be addressed to the androgynous being, and its gender is the androgyne? Perhaps, but only if it is possible not to project onto the androgynous the obviously split models of sex as halves of a whole. Sex, according to Plato, is a unity that has been divided. So *trajectory* is that which, according to Durand, is between the subject and the object, and is defined in relation to them, as in *Dasein* which, according to Heidegger, is in *Zwischen*, on the border between the internal and external, constituting itself on the existential border between the division of unity. And the concept of *l'imaginaire* contains division within itself (in Greek, διαίρεσις) as one of its possible regimes. So, if we understand the androgyne in this way, not as something that is composite, but as something rooted or radical, then we can talk about a radical notion, which is not sex in the sense that it is half of something else. That is, the gender of the Fourth Political Theory is that half, that sex which is simultaneously the whole and does not need its antithesis, and is therefore self-sufficient within itself. We can theorise about this gender that it does not so much come about from an analysis of sexual or gender archetypes, but because of thinking philosophically and politically upon the subject of the Fourth Political Theory. Thus, we change the formulation of the question. We do not ask which sex is *Dasein*, we answer that the gender of the subject of the Fourth Political Theory is the same as that of *Dasein*. In this case, we can also talk about the radical ('root': from the Latin, *radicula*) androgyne, which exists not as a result of a combination of the man and the woman, but that represents instead the primordial, untouched unity.

How does gender change under the conditions of postmodernity? The postmodern represents a combination of all three political theories. On the one hand, this is an accomplished modernity which has reached its logical end as *hypermodern* (or 'ultramodern'). Thus, all three political theories project onto postmodernity their own gender archetypes, which represented the limits of their own structures. These limits are expressed through an institutionalisation of gender in postmodernity. What is the postmodern gender? It is a maximisation of 'the liberal man', the archetype of which applies to all of its antitheses: the stupid, the poor, the non-White, the little, and so forth. It is also the gender of globalisation, when the properties of a certain type are extended as social standards onto all other types as universalism. Hence the idea that the proletarians are only the bourgeoisie who have not grown rich yet, Blacks are unmodernised whites, and women are not yet fully liberated men. That is, we see that this all-consuming archetype becomes meaningless. The re-extension of existing gender models can lead to the explosion of the hypermodern like a rotting fungus, and its gender archetypes will fail. Now we are in this moment of a postmodern re-extension, and the final breaking of gender. The stages of this break are feminism, homosexuality, sex-change operations, and transhumanity.

In the West, the second political theory had a great influence on the elites, particularly the creative professions (actors, writers, philosophers, etc.). This is 'the desiring-machine', incorporating Leftist feminism with its ideas of freedom from sex. Donna Haraway[14] is such a feminist, or rather loosely a neo-Marxist and a postmodernist. She argued that while the mature woman may feel an urge to be 'liberated', liberation in our culture involves definition of the opposite. Therefore it is necessary to overcome both the man and the woman through becoming a cyborg. According to her, sex can be overcome only by having overcome being human. In a similar vein is Foucault's[15] conception of sexuality, that is, sexuality prior to sex, as a neutral dispositive: sexuality, spreading along the surface of the screen, the 'body without organs'. This pan-sexuality, which is a smooth surface of sexual arousals, remains unclear in terms of from whom it is derived, for what reason, and most importantly, no matter in what orientation or direction. As a whole, in terms of the erosion and destruction of the gender constructions of modernity, Marxist thought introduces the most significant contribution. Elements of fascism in postmodernity are represented by the practise of BDSM.[16] Contemporary fascism contains strong elements of sadomasochism, and perverted fascism is an essential attribute of postmodernism, along with feminism, cyborgs, a 'body without organs', and so on.

Eventually we find ourselves in an interesting situation: the predominant gender of modernity is exposed as a re-extension of its original conception, is fast eroding and, in some instances, is about to explode, or perhaps has already exploded. We stand on a transition between the hypermodern and the postmodern, and we do not know where the truth and where the reality lies. So, in a postmodern construction of gender,

---

14 Donna Haraway (b. 1944), a Professor at the University of California at Santa Cruz, has developed what she terms 'cyborg feminism'. The theory is complex, but basically suggests that concepts of gender roles are artificially constructed rather than having any root in biological reality.-Ed.

15 Michel Foucault (1926-1984) was an erudite French philosopher, historian and sociologist who has been associated with both structuralism and postmodernism, although he rejected both labels. He wrote not only on philosophical themes, but also on the subjects of insanity and its treatment, prisons, medicine, and the history of sexuality.-Ed.

16 Bondage and discipline, dominance and submission, sadism and masochism. –Ed.

there will not be any men. Let us imagine this situation: the archetype of 'the man' falls into pieces, which do not constitute parts of the whole any-more, but symbolise only themselves. Conservative forces can stand up for this archetype, demand the return of masculinity — this reasonable, wealthy white person — but thereby, they only try to continue modernity through gender reconstructions. This position seems hopeless, and here again the Fourth Political Theory, in our opinion, goes forward. We sug-gest taking a step towards gender as *Dasein*, despite the notorious repre-sentations and opprobrium that we will cause. By going beyond the limits of gender which we know, we get to the domain of uncertainty, androgyny, and sex as practised by the angels. In the same sphere, it is necessary to search for a gender of the Fourth Political Theory, namely by taking risks in looking behind the limits of the collapsed chimera of modernity. We can as yet provide only outlines: we know that it is the gender of *Dasein* and trajectory, that this gender represents a root reality, that it belongs to *l'imaginaire*. By extending our investigation, we can raise the question about the gender of the Radical Self, which is beyond the basic paradigms.

14

AGAINST THE POSTMODERN WORLD

The Evil of Unipolarity

The current world is unipolar, with the global West as its centre and with the United States as its core.

This kind of unipolarity has geopolitical and ideological characteristics. Geopolitically, it is the strategic dominance of the Earth by the North American hyperpower and the effort of Washington to organise the balance of forces on the planet in such a manner as to be able to rule the whole world in accordance with its own national, imperialistic interests. It is bad because it deprives other states and nations of their real sovereignty.

When there is only one power which decides who is right and who is wrong, and who should be punished and who not, we have a form of global dictatorship. This is not acceptable. Therefore, we should fight against it. If someone deprives us of our freedom, we have to react. And we will react. The American Empire should be destroyed. And at one point, it will be.

Ideologically, unipolarity is based on modernist and postmodernist values that are openly anti-traditional ones. I share the vision of René Guénon and Julius Evola, who considered modernity and its ideological basis (individualism, liberal democracy, capitalism, consumerism, and so on) to be the cause of the future catastrophe of humanity, and the global domination of the Western lifestyle as the reason for the final degradation of the Earth. The West is approaching its terminus, and we should not let it drag all the rest of us down into the abyss with it.

Spiritually, globalisation is the creation of a grand parody, the kingdom of the Antichrist. And the United States is the centre of its expansion. American values pretend to be 'universal' ones. In reality, it is a new form of ideological aggression against the multiplicity of cultures and traditions still existing in the rest of the world. I am resolutely against Western values which are essentially modernist and postmodernist, and which are promulgated by the United States by force of arms or by obtrusion (Afghanistan, Iraq, Libya, and perhaps soon, Syria and Iran) .

Therefore, all traditionalists should be against the West and globalisation, as well as against the imperialist politics of the United States. It is the only logical and consequent position. So traditionalists and partisans of traditional principles and values should oppose the West and defend the Rest, if the Rest show signs of the conservation of Tradition, whether in part or in its entirety.

There can be and there really exist people, in the West and even in the United States of America itself, who do not agree with the present state of affairs and do not approve of modernity and postmodernity. They are the defenders of the spiritual traditions of the pre-modern West. They should be with us in our common struggle. They should take part in our revolt against the modern and postmodern worlds. We would fight together against the common enemy.

Another question is the structure of a possible anti-globalist and anti-imperialist front and its participants. I think that we should include in it all forces that struggle against the West, the United States, against liberal democracy, and against modernity and postmodernity. The common enemy is the necessary instance for all kinds of political alliances. This means Muslims and Christians, Russians and Chinese, both Leftists and Rightists, the Hindus and the Jews who challenge the present state of affairs, globalisation and American imperialism. They are thus all virtually friends and allies. Let our ideals be different, but we have in common one very strong feature: hatred of the present social reality. Our ideals that differ are potential ones (*in potentia*). But the challenge we are dealing with is actual (*in actu*). That is the basis for a new alliance. All who share a negative analysis of globalisation, Westernisation and postmodernisation should coordinate their effort in the creation of a new strategy of resistance to the omnipresent evil. And we can find common allies even within the United States as well, among those who choose the path of Tradition over the present decadence.

Towards the Fourth Political Theory

At this point, we should raise a very important question: what kind of ideology should we use in our opposition to globalisation and its liberal democratic, capitalist, and modernist (postmodernist) principles? I believe that all previous anti-liberal ideologies (Communism, socialism, and fascism) are no longer relevant. They tried to fight liberal capitalism and they failed. This is partly because, at the end of time, it is evil that prevails; and partly because of their inner contradictions and limitations. So it is time to begin a deep revision of the illiberal ideologies of the past. What are their positive sides? Their positive side is the very fact that they were anti-capitalist and anti-liberal, as well as anti-cosmopolitan and anti-individualist. These features should be accepted and integrated into a future ideology. But Communist doctrine itself is modern, atheist, materialist and cosmopolitan. That should be thrown out. On the other hand, Communism's social solidarity, social justice, socialism and general holistic attitude to society are good, in and of themselves. So we need to separate out the materialist and modernist aspects of Communism and reject them, while preserving and embracing its social and holistic aspects.

As for the theories of the Third Way — which were dear, up to a certain point, to some traditionalists such as Julius Evola — there were many unacceptable elements, foremost among these being racism, xenophobia and chauvinism. These are not only moral failures, but also theoretically and anthropologically inconsistent attitudes. Differences between ethnicities do not equate to superiority or inferiority. The differences should be accepted and affirmed without any racist sentiments or consideration. There is no common or universal measure to judge different ethnic groups. When one society tries to judge another, it applies its own criteria, and so commits intellectual violence. This ethnocentric attitude is precisely the crime of globalisation and Westernisation, as well as of American imperialism.

If we free socialism from its materialist, atheistic and modernist features, and if we reject the racist and narrow nationalist aspects of the Third Way doctrines, we arrive at a completely new kind of political ideology. We call it the Fourth Political Theory, or 4PT, the first being liberalism, that we essentially challenge; the second being the classical form of Communism; and the third being National Socialism and fascism. Its elaboration starts from the point of intersection between different anti-liberal political theories of the past (namely Communism and the Third Way theories). So we arrive at National Bolshevism, which represents socialism without materialism, atheism, progressivism, and modernism, as well as the modified Third Way theories.

But that is only the first step. The mechanical addition of deeply revised versions of the anti-liberal ideologies of the past will not give us a final result. It is only a first approximation and preliminary approach. We must go further and make an appeal to Tradition and to pre-modern sources of inspiration. There we have the Platonic ideal state, Medieval hierarchical society, and theological visions of the normative social and political system (Christian, Islamic, Buddhist, Jewish or Hindu). These pre-modern sources are a very important development for the National Bolshevism synthesis. Therefore, we need to find a new name for this kind of ideology, and Fourth Political Theory is quite appropriate. It does not tell us what this theory is, but rather what it is not. So it is a kind of invitation and appeal, rather than dogma.

Politically, we have here an interesting basis for the conscious cooperation of the radical Left-wingers and the New Right, as well as with religious and other anti-modern movements, such as the ecologists and Green theorists, for example. The only thing that we insist on in creating such a pact of cooperation is to put aside anti-Communist, as well as anti-fascist, prejudices. These prejudices are the instruments in the hands of liberals and globalists with which they keep their enemies divided. So we should strongly reject anti-Communism as well as anti-fascism. Both of them are counter-revolutionary tools in the hands of the global liberal elite. At the same time, we should strongly oppose any kind of confrontation between the various religious beliefs — Muslims against Christians, the Jews against Muslims, the Muslims against the Hindus and so on. The inter-confessional wars and tensions work for the cause of the kingdom of the Antichrist who tries to divide all the traditional religions in order to impose its own pseudo-religion, the eschatological parody.

So we need to unite the Right, the Left and the world's traditional religions in a common struggle against the common enemy. Social justice, national sovereignty and traditional values are the three main principles of the Fourth Political Theory. It is not easy to put together such a varied alliance. But we must try if we want to overcome the foe.

In France, there is a saying coined by Alain Soral: *la droite des valeurs et la gauche du travail*. In italian it goes: *La Destra sociale e la Sinistra identitaria*. How exactly it should sound in English we will see later.

We could go further and try to define the subject, the actor of the Fourth Political Theory. In the case of Communism, the central subject was class. In the case of the Third Way movements, the central subject was either the race or the nation. In the case of religions, it is the community of the faithful. How could the Fourth Political Theory deal with this diversity and the divergence of subjects? We propose, as a suggestion, that the main subject of the Fourth Political Theory can be found in the Heideggerian concept of *Dasein*. It is a concrete, but extremely profound instance that could be the common denominator for the further ontological development of the Fourth Political Theory. What is crucial for consideration is the authenticity or non-authenticity of the existence of *Dasein*. The Fourth Political Theory insists on the authenticity of existence. So it is the antithesis to any kind of alienation — social, economic, national, religious or metaphysical.

But *Dasein* is a concrete instance. Every individual and every culture possesses their own *Dasein*. They differ between each other, but they are always present.

Accepting *Dasein* as the subject of the Fourth Political Theory, we should progress toward the elaboration of a common strategy in the process of the creation of a future that fits to our demands and our visions. Such values as social justice, national sovereignty and traditional spirituality can serve us as the foundation.

I sincerely believe that the Fourth Political Theory, and its secondary variations, National Bolshevism and Eurasianism, can be of great use for our peoples, our countries, and our civilisations. The key manager of differences is multipolarity in all senses — geopolitical, cultural, axiological, economic, and so on.

The important concept of *nous* (intellect) developed by the Greek philosopher Plotinus[1] corresponds to our ideal. The intellect is one and multiple at the same time, because it has multiple differences in itself — it is not uniform or an amalgam, but taken as such with many parts, and with all their distinct particularities. The future world should be *noetic in* some way — characterised by multiplicity; diversity should be taken as its richness and its treasure, and not as a reason for inevitable conflict: many civilisations, many poles, many centres, many sets of values on one planet and in one humanity. Many worlds.

But there are some who think otherwise. Who are aligned against such a project? Those who want to impose uniformity, the one (American) way of life, One World. And their methods are force, temptation, and persuasion. They are against multipolarity. So they are against us.

---

1   Plotinus (ca. 204 -270) was a Greek philosopher who was the founder of the mystical school of thought now known as Neoplatonism.-Ed.

Appendix I

I. Political Post-Anthropology

1. Each type of political system and each stage of political history operates in accordance with the normative, political type of the human. We say 'a man of the Middle Ages', 'a man of modernity', and so on, describing the specific historical and political constructs. These constructs are directly dependent on the organisation and formalisation of *power relations* in a society and relate to the axis of power, which is the essence of the political, and with the designation of one's friend and enemy (C. Schmitt), which is also the essence of the political. The political is power and political identification (the Self/ the Other). Each political form provides a different model of power and such identification. However, many political systems exist, and each has its own political anthropology. Political theology (C. Schmitt)[1] suggests that the policy and political system reflects, and in certain cases constitutes, a standard of political anthropology.

2. The political human is transformed from one form of the political to another. This is sufficiently traced in the 'philosophy of politics' and 'post-philosophy'. Now we will focus on which form of political anthropology meets postmodernity.

3. Postmodernity is something that sets in and *steps on* — steps on us. But it has not stepped yet. Therefore, the study of postmodernity suffers from an absurd creative gap. Although it can step on us, it may also not step on us, and we can (or cannot, it is not yet clear) wriggle out from under it. So, talking about postmodernity is interesting, exciting and at the same time risky. It is a process with an unknown end and uncertain meaning. It is still possible to influence this end and this meaning. History, apparently, has ended, and post-history is only beginning, and one has to search in it for a space of struggle, to win back this space and expand it.

---

1   Carl Schmitt, *Political Theology* (Chicago: University of Chicago Press, 2005).

4. Political post-anthropology is about forecasting and constructing the political human in postmodernity. It is normative. We do not just study what exists; we follow the process and try to affect it. Wishful thinking and self-fulfilling prophecy is quite legitimate and welcome here. By exploring political post-anthropology, we bring the political back to life.

II. Political Post-humanity and the Post-State

1. The absolute features of the post-humanity of postmodernity are:
   - depoliticisation;
   - autonomisation;
   - microscopisation;
   - sub- and transhumanisation (as a special form of dehumanisation);
   - *Dividualisation* (fragmentation).

   That is, the rejection and denial of something that was political in the previous phases of history becomes the dominant form of politics. Politicisation meets with depoliticisation. The politics of the post-human of postmodernity lies in the attempt to escape from it, and in the projection of the political into the new sphere. The post-human of postmodernity declares war on the political: first, based on the economy (*homo oeconomicus* vs. *homo politicus*), then against the classical subject-object economy in the name of the network dynamics of the free, creative game of disengaged 'sets' (Negri and Hardt). The industry of fashion, celebrity, glamour and show business inculcates the idea that, to attain material prosperity, one does not need to earn money through work; one must instead enter and be recognised by the relevant social set and become a member of the ever-changing glamour network. Glossy pages, on which a body without organs is sliding right and left, are like a concrete embodiment of Deleuze's *l'espace lisse*[2] — an image of post-economics. Actual work is not necessary, it is optional.

2. The post-political post-human overthrows power and the collective, and then his or her own dividualised identity. He does not recognise the power relations over or under him, does not know Self and Other, and does not accept or understand anything that

---

2 French: 'the smooth space'. In *A Thousand Plateaus*, Deleuze and Guattari distinguish between smooth space and striated space. They claimed that smooth space was synonymous with the ocean and the desert, areas inhabited by nomads, and that smooth space was a place of constant change.-Ed.

200 THE FOURTH POLITICAL THEORY

lies beyond the scope of his microcosm. His policy is expressed in the form of desires and vegetative impulses of unknown ownership and aims. Maybe it is 'desire', but this 'desire' is no one's and is not specifically addressed anywhere.

3. It is from a random game of sub-individuality and trans-individuality that the post-human creates a model of the post-state. The post-state is an ironic parody of the State. It is the State vice-versa, the State-as-phantom, the State-as-mockery. In the post-state, institutions are mobile and ephemeral. Policies and legal principles are continuously and rapidly changing. It has neither vertical, nor horizontal symmetry, aiming instead to merge with the network. It is sort of a pirate republic placed in cyberspace, or a Brazilian carnival, which replaces the routine with a routine of spectacle. In the post-state, the serious and frivolous swap, and it is a kind of Saturnalia[3] rendered permanent. In post-politics, post-humanity constitutes this post-state through being amused by its own deadly, hallucinatory game.

4. In political post-anthropology, all is reversed: leisure and work (the most serious occupation, actual *work*, is watching television shows), knowledge and ignorance (complete idiots are given jobs as academics), public and private .The tiniest, most inane details of one's life are the centre of attention in this reality show, even in political debate. Traditional male and female roles are reversed. Rather than being esteemed and experienced elders, politicians are chosen for their youth, glamour, appearance and inexperience. Victims become the criminals and vice versa...

5. Why are we talking about post-politics when it is obviously about something directly opposite to the political? Because such an anthropological type of postmodernity, in theory and social practice, *steps on*, i.e. it attacks, persistently imposes itself, introduces itself, and gradually becomes the norm. It acts as a basic personality (A. Kardiner).[4] And for such an attack and such an advance, *dispositif*[5] of power and collective identification, the political, again, is

---

3 Saturnalia was a Roman festival for the god Saturn. A week-long carnival was held, which included the masters serving their slaves throughout the period.-Ed.

4 Abram Kardiner (1891-1981) was an American anthropologist and psychologist. Kardiner maintained that culture was a product of the personalities of the individuals who comprised it, which was in turn a product of social conditionings resulting from social institutions.-Ed.

5 *Dispositif*, sometimes translated as 'apparatus', is a term used by Foucault to refer to the methods — physical, ideological and bureaucratic — that are used by a society to enforce its will upon its members.-Ed.

required. But, in this case, models of counter-power tend to affirm their own power, and those models that deny all forms of a *type* as such insist on universalisation of *their* type (type, in this case, is a synonym for *eidos* or universality). Apolitical singulars and divides compose a sort of a ruling party of postmodernity. The Influential and those close to them seize power or are already in power.

6. This 'party' has a stylistic and strategic arsenal. This is fashion and interactive information technologies (Twitter, mobile phones, social networks, blogs). In French, 'fashionable' is often referred to by a slang word, *branche*, literally 'connected'. Fashion and technology are changing rapidly, and the one who is 'connected' is the one who is changing along with it, here and now, rapidly and dynamically. There is no yesterday and tomorrow, not even today. There is only *now*. Now it is Google and Twitter, but in a moment they will be prehistoric events, such as typewriters or Atari. Herein is a *dromocratic*[6] aspect (Paul Virilio).[7]

7. Twitter revolutions in the Arab world or iPad presidents, such as Dmitri Medvedev, are clear signs of political post-anthropology and the phenomenon of the post-state. The revolt of the elites and the oscillation of the intensity level of consciousness of the ruling groups are near zero. A classic example is a drug addict as political strategist.

III. The Political Soldier and His Simulacrum

1. Like any political model, the political post-anthropology can be accepted and may be rejected. It does not matter how much it would insist on its own 'naturalness'. A person can choose both the structure of power and his identity. The post-state, Twitter revolutions, and iPad Presidents are all part of a single trend, stepping on and intruding. They may be mainstream, but are not unique. There may also be alternatives.

2. The first alternative is the political anthropology of previous forms. In the face of political post-anthropology, it can be generalised by

---

6 Virilio coined the term 'dromocratic' to describe what he saw as the most salient feature of modernity, which is the pursuit of ever-increasing speed through technical and scientific advancement. Virilio believed that we are approaching the limit of such speed, and that the reaching of this limit would mean the end of modernity.-Ed.

7 Paul Virilio (b. 1932) is a French philosopher who writes primarily about technology, as well as what the use of physical space tells us about the institutions that utilize it.-Ed.

the figure of a 'political soldier'. This is an anthropological concept. It gives no idea of what political ideology the 'political soldier' follows. But this concept implicitly contains a belief in the existence of political ontology: the political soldier fights for a model of power relationships, and directly and openly identifies himself with a particular group ('ours'). A fundamental distinction of the political soldier is that he is ready and able to die for his political idea. This differentiates him from an ordinary soldier and an ordinary politician. A soldier dies, but not for a political idea. A politician fights for a political idea, but is not ready to die for it.

3. The political soldier may be a Communist, a nationalist, or even a liberal. But in any case, he personalises modernity, modernity in its specific political forms. The political soldier is a *mediastinum*[8] of the political anthropology of modernity. And as such, in theory, it can fight political post-anthropology. This will be a conservative answer. An individual fights an individual. A present 'ending' rejects the atemporal, post-historical 'future'. The drama of the 'last' humans clashing with post-humans in a political conflict is at once very heroic, tragic, poetic and...hopeless.

4. But: political post-anthropology makes such a position almost impossible. The political soldier in the unique conditions of the corrosive waters of postmodernity is immediately converted into a simulacrum. This is the main delicacy of postmodernity: it carries an ironic mutation in regard to all aspects of modernity, in regard to anthropology — in the first place. Today it is already no longer possible to meet with the political soldier; we can only meet with his *double*, his simulacrum, his fake.

5. In an anthropological series of political and anthropological forms, postmodernity installs *a* vicious link. All the threads that connect the political arena of postmodernity with modernity and deeper into political history are broken at the moment of postmodernity, and there is found a knot. After that knot, with all the visible continuity, a fake segment is situated.

6. Today there are no political soldiers. All that remains is their shells.

---

8   The organs that lie within the thorax, including the heart, the esophagus, and the lymph nodes.-Ed.

IV. Alternative in Political Post-anthropology: Pre-human and PC

1. My thesis is reduced to the following affirmation: in the context of political post-anthropology, postmodernity and the post-human (dividual) cannot be opposed to modernity and human (individual). Opposing dualities will not be like the dividual vs. individual and post-human vs. human, but like dividual vs. pseudo-individual and post-human vs. pseudo-human. The anthropological fold (Deleuze) of postmodern anthropology is this: a simulacrum meets with a simulacrum.

2. In postmodernity, a political soldier is impossible. It can only be a simulacrum.

3. Consequently, the opposition must be different. It is not a previous anthropological link that is designed to collide with a post-anthropological segment of an anthropological series, which is located *after* the substituted element (knot), but an entirely different figure. That is, one should speak of the political expression of the Radical Subject.

4. This topic should be integrated into the Fourth Political Theory. It is beyond the scope of this book to develop it. But in general we can say: an alternative to political post-anthropology is also post-anthropology, but different.

5. The routes of the transgression of humanity's boundaries or limitations may not be as such as in the case of the dividual. It is not really the human that meets with the post-human in the political post-anthropology, but a pre-human, the pre-concept of the human. The point of origin that came before the human is parallel to him and will remain after him.

6. Here we can also touch on the delicate theme of angelomorphosis. It is no accident that in the eschatology of most religions and traditions we are dealing with the *Endkampf*[9] panoramic view, which necessarily involves angels. In Hollywood blockbusters, indeed, this also suffers from simulation. But it is inevitable.

The political expression of the Radical Subject can be defined, not as the area of political theology (Carl Schmitt), but as the area of political *angelology*. This topic requires further development.

---

9 German: 'final battle'.-Ed.

APPENDIX II

The Metaphysics of Chaos

Modern European philosophy began with the concept of *logos* and the logical order of being. For over two thousand years, this concept became fully exhausted. All the potentialities and the principles laid in this *logocentric* way of thinking have by now been thoroughly explored, exposed and abandoned by philosophers.

However, the problem of chaos and the nature of chaos was neglected and put aside from the very beginning of this philosophy. The only philosophy we know at present is the philosophy of *logos*. But chaos is something opposite to *logos*, its absolute alternative.

From the Nineteenth century and continuing until the present day, the most important and brilliant European philosophers (such as Friedrich Nietzsche and Martin Heidegger) began to suspect that *logos* was fast approaching its end. Some of them dared to suggest that, from now on, we are living in the time of the end of *logocentric* philosophy, and approaching... something else.

European philosophy was based on the *logocentric* principle corresponding to the principle of exclusion, the differentiating, Greek *diaeresis*.[1] All this corresponds strictly to the masculine attitude and reflects a patriarchal, authoritative, vertical, and hierarchical order of being and knowledge.

This masculine approach to reality imposes order and the principle of exclusivity everywhere. That is perfectly manifested in Aristotle's logic, where the principles of identity and exclusion are put in the central position in the normative manner of thinking. A is equal to A, not equal to not-A. This identity excludes non-identity (alterity)[2] and vice-versa. Here it is the male who speaks, thinks, acts, fights, divides, orders, and so on.

---

1   A term originally used by Plato in his dialogues, which refers to a group of concepts or objects which are divided and subdivided until a definition of the item in question has been found.-Ed.

2   A term, first defined in its modern usage by Emmanuel Lévinas, which refers to 'otherness', meaning the act of exchanging one's perspective for that of the theoretical Other.-Ed.

Nowadays all this *logocentric* philosophy has come to an end, and we must consider another road for thought, not in the *logocentric*, phallocentric, hierarchical and exclusivist way.

If *logos* no longer satisfies us, fascinates us, or mobilises us, then we are inclined to try something else and at last to address the problem of chaos.

To begin with: there are two different concepts of chaos. Modern physics and philosophy refers to complex systems, bifurcation or non-integrating equations and processes, using the concept 'chaos' to designate such phenomena. They understand by that not the absence of order, but a more complicated form of order that is difficult to perceive as such, and is, in fact, its essence. Such chaos or turbulence is calculable in nature, but with more sophisticated theoretical and mathematical means and procedures than the instruments that classical natural science is dealing with.

The term 'chaos' is used here in a metaphorical manner. In modern science we are continuing to deal with an essentially *logocentric* manner of exploring reality. So the 'chaos' here is no more than a dissipative structure of *logos*, the last result of its decay, fall, and decomposition. Modern science is dealing, not with something other than *logos*, but with a kind of post-*logos*, or ex-*Logos*: *logos* in the state of ultimate dissolution and regression. The process of the final destruction and dissipation of *logos* is taken here for 'chaos'.

In reality, though, it has nothing to do with chaos as such, with chaos in the original Greek sense of the term. It is rather a kind of utmost confusion. René Guénon has called the era we are living through now an era of confusion. 'Confusion' means the state of being that both runs parallel to order and precedes it. Thus, we should make a clear distinction between two different concepts. On one hand we have the modern concept of chaos that represents post-order, or a mixture of contradictory fragments of being without any unity and order, linked amongst themselves by highly sophisticated post-logical correspondences and conflicts. Gilles Deleuze has called this phenomena a 'non-co-possible system composed by the multitude of the monads' (using the concept of monads and co-possibility introduced by Leibniz),[3] becoming for Deleuze the 'nomads'.[4] Deleuze describes postmodernity as a sum of non-co-possible fragments which

---

3   Gottfried Wilhelm Leibniz (1646-1716) was a German philosopher and mathematician. In his text, *The Monadology*, he claimed that substances could be divided into monads (a concept which pre-dated him), and that each monad was pre-set to act in a specific way in interaction with the other types of monads.-Ed.

4   To Deleuze, a nomad represents a state of being that exists between fixed points, just as a desert nomad is perpetually moving from place to place along pre-set patterns.-Ed.

can coexist. It was not possible in Leibnitz's vision of reality, based on the principle of co-possibility. But within postmodernity we can see excluding elements coexisting. The non-ordered non-co-possible monads, or nomads, swarming around could seem to be chaotic, and in this sense we usually use the word chaos in everyday speech. But strictly speaking, we should make a distinction.

We need to distinguish between two kinds of chaos, the postmodernist 'chaos' as an equivalent to confusion, a kind of post-order, and the Greek chaos as pre-order, as something that exists before ordered reality has come into being. Only the latter can be considered as chaos in the proper sense of the word. This second, but actually the original, conception of chaos should be examined carefully and metaphysically.

The epic vision of the rise and fall of *logos* in the course of the development of Western philosophy and Western history was first espoused by Martin Heidegger, who argued that in the context of European or Western culture, *logos* is not only a primary philosophical principle, but also the basis of the religious attitude forming the core of Christianity. We can also notice that the concept of *kalam*, or intellect, is at the centre of Islamic philosophy and theology. The same is true for Judaism (at least in the vision of Philo of Alexandria,[5] and above all in Medieval Judaism and the *Kaballah*). Thus in high modernity, where we are living, we assist the fall of *logos* accompanied by the corresponding decline of classical Greco-Roman culture and monotheistic religion as well. These processes of decadence are completely parallel to what Martin Heidegger considers the present condition of Western culture as a whole. He identifies the origin of this condition of decline in some of the hidden and hardly recognisable errors committed during the early stages of Greek thought. Something went wrong at the very beginning of Western history, and Martin Heidegger sees this wrong turn precisely in the affirmation of the exclusivist position of an exclusivist *logos*. This shift was made by Heraclitus[6] and Parmenides,[7] but above all by Plato with the development of philosophic thought that envisaged two worlds or layers of reality where existence was perceived as the manifestation of the hidden. Later, this hidden element was recognized as *logos*, as the idea, the paradigm, the example. From that point on, the referential theory of truth proceeds. Truth lies in

---

5   Philo of Alexandria (20 BCE-50 CE) was a Jewish philosopher. He believed that the *logos* was God's method for influencing the material world.-Ed.

6   Heraclitus (ca. 535-475 BCE) was a pre-Socratic Greek philosopher. Only fragments of his work survive.-Ed.

7   Parmenides was a Greek philosopher of the Fifth century BCE. Only fragments of one of his poems survive.-Ed.

the fact of the immediate correspondence of the given to the presumed invisible essence, or 'the nature that likes to hide'[8] according to Heraclitus. The Pre-Socratics were at the forefront of this philosophy. The unfettered explosion of the modern technique is its logical result. Heidegger calls it *Ge-stell* and thinks it is the reason for the catastrophe and annihilation of mankind that inevitably approaches. According to him, the very concept of *logos* was wrong, so he proposed to radically revise our attitude to the very essence of philosophy and the process of thought, and to find another way which he called 'the other beginning'.

Logos first appeared with the birth of Western philosophy. The earliest Greek philosophy arose as something that already excluded chaos. Precisely at the same time, *logos* began to flourish, revealing a kind of mighty will to power and the absolutisation of the masculine attitude to reality. The becoming of *logocentric* culture ontologically annihilated the polar opposite to *logos* itself — the feminine chaos. So chaos as something that preceded *logos*, was abolished by it, and its exclusivity were both manifested and dismissed at the same time. Masculine *logos* ousted feminine chaos. Exclusivity and exclusion subdued inclusivity and the inclusion. So the Classical world was born, stretching its limits for 2500 years — up until modernity and the rationalist scientific era. This world has come to its end. But nevertheless, we are still living in its outskirts. At the same time, in the dissipating postmodern world, all the structures of order are degrading, dispersing, and becoming more and more confused. It is the dusk of *logos*, the end of order, the last chord of masculine, exclusivist domination. But still we are inside the logical structure rather than outside it.

By stating this, we have conjured some basic solutions concerning the future. The first possible solution is the return to the kingdom of *logos*, the Conservative Revolution, the restoration of male full-scale domination in all spheres of the life — in philosophy, religion, and in everyday life. This could be done spiritually, socially or technically. This way where technique meets spiritual order was fundamentally explored and studied by Heidegger's friend, Ernst Jünger. It is a return to classicism accompanied by an appeal to technological progress. It is an effort to save the falling *logos*, the restoration of traditional society, and the eternally new Order.

The second possible solution is to accept the current trends and to follow the direction of confusion, becoming more and more involved in the

---

8   One of Heraclitus' fragments reads, 'Nature loves to hide itself.' It is Fragment B17 in *Heraclitus: The Complete Fragments*, available at community.middlebury.edu/~harris/ Philosophy/heraclitus.pdf.

dissipation of structure, in post-structuralism, and trying to get pleasure out of the comfortable glide into nothingness. That is the option chosen by the Left and the liberal representatives of postmodernity. It is modern nihilism at its best — originally identified by Nietzsche and explored thoroughly by Heidegger. The concept of nothing being the potential present in the principle of identity proper to *logos* itself is not the limit of the process of the fall of the logical order, but rather the construction of a rational realm of the unlimited expansion of horizontal decay, the incalculable multitudes of the flowers of putrefaction.

However, we could choose a third path and try to transcend the borders of *logos* and step out beyond the crisis of the postmodern world, that is literally postmodern, i.e., lying beyond modernity, where the dissipation of *logos* reaches its limit. So the question of this very limit is crucial. Seen from the standpoint of *logos* in general, including its most decayed aspects, beyond the domain of order lies nothing. So crossing the border of being is ontologically impossible. Nothing *is not*: so speaks all *logocentric* Western ontology after Parmenides. This impossibility asserts the infiniteness of the outskirts of *logos* and grants to the decay, inside the realm of order, eternal continuity. Beyond the border of being lies nothing, and to move toward this limit is analytically infinite and unending (the *aporiae*[9] of Zeno of Elea[10] are here fully valid). So, no one can cross that frontier into the non-existent *not-being* that simply is *not*.

If we insist, nevertheless, in doing this, then we should appeal to chaos in its original Greek sense, as to something that proceeds being and order, something pre-ontological.

We stand in front of a really important and crucial problem. A great number of people today are unsatisfied with what is going on around us, with the absolute crisis of values, religions, philosophy, political and social order, with postmodern conditions, with the confusion and perversion, and with this age of the utmost decay in general.

But considering the essence of the decline of our civilisation to the present state, we cannot look to the preceding phases of the *logocentric* order and its implicit structures, because it was precisely *logos* itself that has brought things to the state where they are now, bearing within itself the germs of the present decay. Heidegger identified, with extreme credibility, the roots of the technique in the Pre-Socratic solution to the problem of

---

9 In philosophy, an *aporia* is a problem that has no clear solution, such as a paradox.-Ed.

10 Zeno was a student of Parmenides and a pre-Socratic Greek philosopher. He is best-known for his *aporiae*, or paradoxes.-Ed.

being by means of *logos*. *Logos* cannot save us from the situation that it is the cause of. *Logos* is of no use to us here anymore.

Only the pre-ontological chaos can give as a hint about how to go beyond the trap of postmodernity. It was put aside on the eve of the creation of the logical structure of being as a cornerstone. Now it is its turn to come into play. Otherwise, we will be doomed to accept the post-logical dissipated postmodernity that pretends to be eternal in some way because it annihilates time. Modernity has killed eternity and postmodernity is killing time. The architecture of the postmodern world is completely fragmented, perverse and confused. It is a labyrinth without an exit, as folded and twisted as a Moebius strip.[11] *Logos,* which was the guarantor of strictness and order, serves here instead to grant curvature and crookedness, being used to preserve the impassability of the ontological border with nothing from the eventual and inevitable trespassers seeking to escape into the beyond.

So the only way to save ourselves, to save humanity and culture from this snare, is to take the step beyond the *logocentric* culture, towards chaos.

We cannot restore *logos* and order, because they bear in themselves the reason for their own eternal destruction. In other words, to save the exclusive *logos,* we should make an appeal to the alternative inclusive instance that is chaos.

But how could we use the concept of chaos and base our philosophy on it if, up to now, philosophy has always been for us something logical by definition?

In order to resolve this difficulty, we should approach chaos not from the position of *logos* but from that of chaos itself. It can be compared to the feminine vision, the feminine understanding of the Other that is not excluded but, on the contrary, included in the sameness.

Logos regards itself as what is and as what is equal to itself. It can accept the differences inside itself because it excludes the Other that lies without. So the will to power is working, the law of sovereignty. Beyond *logos,* *logos* asserts, lies nothing, not something. So *logos,* excluding all other than itself, excludes chaos. Chaos uses a different strategy. It includes in itself all that it is, but at the same all that it is not. So all-inclusive chaos includes also what is not inclusive, namely that which excludes chaos. So chaos does not perceive *logos* as the Other, but as itself, or as something non-existent. *Logos* as the first principle of exclusion is included in chaos, present in it, enveloped by it, and has a place granted inside of it, as the mother bearing the baby bears in herself what is a part of herself and what

---

11 A Moebius strip is a structure that has only one side and only one edge.-Ed.

is not a part of her at the same time. Man conceives woman as an external being and seeks to penetrate her. Woman considers man as something internal and seeks to give him a birth, and to give birth to him.

Chaos is the eternal nascence of the Other, that is, of *logos*.

To sum up, chaotic philosophy is possible because chaos itself includes *logos* as some inner possibility. It can freely identify it, cherish it and recognise its exclusivity included in its everlasting life. So we come to the figure of the very special, chaotic *logos*, that is, a completely and absolutely fresh *logos* being eternally revived by the waters of chaos. This chaotic *logos* is at the same time exclusive (this is why it is properly *logos*) and inclusive (being chaotic). It deals with sameness and otherness differently.

Chaos can think. We should ask her how she does this. We have asked *logos*. Now it is the turn of chaos. We must learn to think with chaos and within the chaos.

I could suggest, as an example, the philosophy of the Japanese thinker Kitaro Nishida,[12] who has constructed the 'logic of *basho*' or the 'logic of places', in place of Aristotle's logic.

We should explore other cultures, rather than Western, to try to find different examples of inclusive philosophy, inclusive religions, and so on. Chaotic *logos* is not only an abstract construction. If we seek well, we can find the real forms of such intellectual traditions in archaic societies, as well as in Eastern theology and mystical currents.

To make an appeal to chaos is the only way to save *logos*. *Logos* needs a savior, it cannot save itself. It needs something opposite to itself to be restored in the critical situation of postmodernity. We could not transcend postmodernity. The latter cannot be overcome without appeal to something that has been prior to the reason of its decay. So we should resort to philosophies other than Western.

In conclusion, it is not correct to conceive chaos as something belonging to the past. Chaos is eternal, but eternally coexisting with time. Therefore, chaos is always absolutely new, fresh, and spontaneous. It could be regarded as a source of any kind of invention and freshness because its eternity has, in itself, always something more than was, is, or will be in time. *Logos* itself cannot exist without chaos, like fish cannot live without water. When we take a fish out of water, it dies. When the fish begins to insist excessively that there is something other than water around it, even if it is true, it come to the shore and dies there. It is a kind of mad fish.

---

12 Kitaro Nishida (1870-1945) was a Japanese philosopher who was the founder of the Kyoto school of philosophy. He conceived *basho* logic as a way of overcoming the subject-object duality.-Ed.

When we put it back in the water, it only jumps out again. So, let it die this way if it wants. There are other fishes deep in the water. Let us follow them.

The astronomical era that is coming to an end is the era of the fish constellation, of Pisces. The fish on the shore. The dying one. So we need water now very badly.

Only a completely new attitude to thought, a new ontology, and a new gnoseology can save *logos* out of the water, on the shore, in the desert that grows and grows, as Nietzsche foresaw.

Only chaos and the alternative philosophy based on inclusivity can save modern humanity and the world from the consequences of the degradation and decay of the exclusivist principle called *logos*. *Logos* has expired and we all will be buried under its ruins unless we make an appeal to chaos and its metaphysical principles, and use them as a basis for something new. Perhaps this is 'the other beginning' Heidegger spoke of.

OTHER BOOKS PUBLISHED BY ARKTOS

OTHER BOOKS PUBLISHED BY ARKTOS

OTHER BOOKS PUBLISHED BY ARKTOS

OTHER BOOKS PUBLISHED BY ARKTOS

P R Reddall	*Towards Awakening*
Claire Rae Randall	*The War on Gender*
Steven J. Rosen	*The Agni and the Ecstasy*
	The Jedi in the Lotus
Nicholas Rooney	*Talking to the Wolf*
Richard Rudgley	*Barbarians*
	Essential Substances
	Wildest Dreams
Ernst von Salomon	*It Cannot Be Stormed*
	The Outlaws
Werner Sombart	*Traders and Heroes*
Piero San Giorgio	*Giuseppe*
	Survive the Economic Collapse
	Surviving the Next Catastrophe
Sri Sri Ravi Shankar	*Celebrating Silence*
	Know Your Child
	Management Mantras
	Patanjali Yoga Sutras
	Secrets of Relationships
George T. Shaw (ed.)	*A Fair Hearing*
Fenek Solère	*Kraal*
	Reconquista
Oswald Spengler	*The Decline of the West*
	Man and Technics
Richard Storey	*The Uniqueness of Western Law*
Tomislav Sunic	*Against Democracy and Equality*
	Homo Americanus
	Postmortem Report
	Titans are in Town
Askr Svarte	*Gods in the Abyss*
Hans-Jürgen Syberberg	*On the Fortunes and Misfortunes of Art in Post-War Germany*
Abir Taha	*Defining Terrorism*
	The Epic of Arya (2nd ed.)
	Nietzsche is Coming God, or the Redemption of the Divine
	Verses of Light
Jean Thiriart	*Europe: An Empire of 400 Million*
Bal Gangadhar Tilak	*The Arctic Home in the Vedas*
Dominique Venner	*For a Positive Critique*
	The Shock of History
Hans Vogel	*How Europe Became American*
Markus Willinger	*A Europe of Nations*
	Generation Identity
Alexander Wolfheze	*Alba Rosa*
	Globus Horribilis
	Rupes Nigra

www.ingramcontent.com/pod-product-compliance
Lightning Source LLC
Chambersburg PA
CBHW030837300326
41935CB00037B/514